Mary Allan

Conceptualising Social Space in Cyberspace

Mary Allan

Conceptualising Social Space in Cyberspace

A Study of the Interactions in Online Discussion Forums

VDM Verlag Dr. Müller

Imprint

Bibliographic information by the German National Library: The German National Library lists this publication at the German National Bibliography; detailed bibliographic information is available on the Internet at http://dnb.d-nb.de.

Any brand names and product names mentioned in this book are subject to trademark, brand or patent protection and are trademarks or registered trademarks of their respective holders. The use of brand names, product names, common names, trade names, product descriptions etc. even without a particular marking in this works is in no way to be construed to mean that such names may be regarded as unrestricted in respect of trademark and brand protection legislation and could thus be used by anyone.

Cover image: www.purestockx.com

Publisher:
VDM Verlag Dr. Müller Aktiengesellschaft & Co. KG , Dudweiler Landstr. 125 a, 66123 Saarbrücken, Germany,
Phone +49 681 9100-698, Fax +49 681 9100-988,
Email: info@vdm-verlag.de

Zugl.: Christchurch, University of Canterbury, Diss., 2005

Produced in USA and UK by:
Lightning Source Inc., La Vergne, Tennessee, USA
Lightning Source UK Ltd., Milton Keynes, UK
BookSurge LLC, 5341 Dorchester Road, Suite 16, North Charleston, SC 29418, USA

ISBN: 978-3-639-02344-2

CONTENTS

DETAILED TABLE OF CONTENTS

List of Tables

List of Figures

1. INTRODUCTION

Preamble

Scenario:

> *Imagine an extra terrestrial spaceship orbiting around our planet, and taking pictures of the inside of classrooms in schools all around the world, collecting data for studying the teaching approaches being implemented on earth.*
>
> *What would these pictures taken from space tell about the teaching in classrooms? Well, some pictures will show rooms full of learners all facing in the direction of one person who seems to be speaking to them. Other pictures will show rooms in which learners are sitting in small groups, facings each other and seem to be conversing.*
>
> *In a report to their leader, the space people concluded their observation stating that in some classrooms on planet earth, learners follow the words of a leader, and in others they seem to engage with the words of each other.*

Of all the things observable in our classrooms, the extra terrestrial observers chose to report to their leader on the different ways in which people related to each other through words.

The uniqueness of the observation made by the extra terrestrial visitors lies not in their choice of focal point, as verbal interactions are no doubt one of the more important issues in classrooms' activities. However, their uniqueness lies in the point of entry they chose for studying classrooms focusing on the visual observation of seating arrangement, and using these as trajectory points for studying the dynamics of verbal interactions.

Mundane as they may seem, seating arrangements in classrooms are important in supporting working arrangements, and need to be consistent with learning aims. For example, learners seated in rows facing the teacher may be more suitable for a teacher centred approach, whereas group seating would suggest collaborative work (Blatchford, Kutnick, Baines, & Galton, 2003). Furthermore, a classroom seated in a teacher centred

1

model denotes that the control is in the hands of the teacher, while group seating arrangement implies a balance of ownership in which the control is shifted towards the learners themselves(Zajac & Hartup, 1997).

McGregor(2004) argues that the nature of space is critical to our understanding of what goes on in classrooms. The author contests the common conceptions of space as a fixed, physical, container for social interactions, arguing that we should perceive space as *socially produced*. This concept of *'space'* allows us to detect *social* arrangements and power relations, perceiving the notion of *'space'* as more than merely a backdrop to social interactions, but as created through interaction with the social. Conceptualising 'space' as a socially constructed entity prompts an investigation of our concepts of social structures not as fixed entities but rather as socially constructed.

In this study I chose to address these notions by first attempting to conceptualise, and demarcate socially produced spaces in cyber space. Then proceed to investigate the nature of these socially constructed structures, and their social arrangements of power, as emerging from the social interactions observed in Online Discussion forums (ODF) used in learning contexts. This decision entails two methodological implications. First, it would entail visual conceptualisation, observation, and analysis of the socially produced spaces. Second it implies a focus on the study of the social interactions, or more specifically 'what people do' in ODF.

Where Do I Begin

Observing 'space' in cyberspace is not as straightforward as it is for observing planet earth's classrooms. To be able to study the dynamics of verbal interactions through looking at "seating arrangements" in cyberspaces such as online discussion forums I first needed to find a way of conceptualising , and making detectable observable and describable the socially constructed spaces. Choosing this route of study may seem awkward, and some may ask 'why begin with something that is not there in the first place'? One of the most pressing issues in the study of online discussion forums

2

in the context of learning is the lack of empirical studies. This view was expressed by researchers such as Wellman(2003), Cox, Hall, Loopuyt, and Carr (2002), Dillenbourg (1999),and Edwards,(2002), all arguing that the increasing use of online discussion forums in online learning contexts is creating a growing need for empirical evidence of the learning related benefits supposedly supported by these environments.

I hope that by conceptualising and making visible spaces in the cyber learning environments of the online discussion forums I would be able to produce some empiric findings about the ways in which interactions contributed to the nature of social spaces and the social structures they have created. I hope that the study of these structures would provide us with further understandings of how online discussion forums operate as learning environments.

The Role of Online Discussion Forums in Learning Environments

Andrew (1996) argues that the turn of the millennium introduced a shift in our understanding of the meaning of teaching .He describes this shift as changing from the 'efficient' factory model to the 'diverse community.' Tapscott(1998), calls the transformation happening in learning the shift from the "broadcast" learning to "interactive" learning.

For distance learning, particularly in tertiary education, the pedagogical shift was primarily enabled by the arrival of computer networks enabling people to interact with other people for mutually constructing knowledge(Kanuka & Anderson, 1999). The network technology introduced the potential for a paradigm change in the perception of distance teaching and learning to incorporate social theories of mind and learning, and perceive those as processes of learning and knowing(Pulkkinen, 2003).

For learners to benefit from the new opportunities entailed in networked computers, online discussion forums as a computer application provide one form of interface connecting people through their computers to enable the exchange of information and engage with each other's ideas. Online discussion forums as a computer application have the potential to facilitate the creation of interactive learning and the emergence of communities.

Scrutinising the Social Potential of Online Discussion Forums in Learning Contexts

Preece (2000), argues that "Online communities offer new opportunities for students. They can work together, exchange information, comment on each other's work, share resources, meet people from across the world, ..." (,p.54)

Edwards (2002) found that online discussion forums are said to be able to:
1. Create viable communities of learners online.
2. Construct knowledge through dialogue using e.g. e-mail or conferencing software

This may very well be true; the technology of the Internet may well provide a productive meaningful learning environment that would seize and make use of the benefits entailed in constructivist, active and collaborative learning. Online learning groups, or 'communities', as they are loosely referred to are often presumed to be the natural environment for supporting constructivist, collaborative learning. However, I would argue that this assumption has not yet been tested and therefore should not be taken for granted.

In view of the paradigmatic shift, the goals of e- educators have shifted from disseminating information through the websites to creating knowledge- constructing learning communities. There are numerous discussion forums on the Web attempting to reach this goal. There are also numerous studies, papers, and books, that talk about learning communities and their advantages, but the question remaining is 'are we really there yet, have we achieved learning communities where learners construct knowledge collaboratively and achieve quality learning?

I would like to emphasise that throughout this study I am not in any way contesting the advantages of collaborative knowledge construction, neither am I contesting the importance and viability of learning communities for supporting such processes. However, I am arguing that we are assuming things that we cannot yet investigate, or evaluate.

Furthermore, I would argue that we lack not only information about the nature and quality of the processes, but also the tools that would enable supporting and sustaining the aspired goals. I would argue that for achieving these goals we would need formative assessment tools that would inform us of the interventions and moderation strategies needed for supporting collaborative constructivist learning environments.

Further to my own observations, Edwards (2002), argues that the literature of online pedagogy, such as Salmon, (2000), Collison, Elbaum, Haavind, and Tinker, (2000), and Collins and Moonen (2001) takes for granted notions of knowledge construction and community building, defining these as the key competencies of e – educators and moderators. However, Zaiane & Luo (2001) argue that educators using Web-based learning environments are in desperate need for non-intrusive and automatic ways of obtaining objective feedback from learners in order to better follow the learning process and appraise the on-line course structure effectiveness. Furthermore, Edwards(2002) found that research evidence of knowledge construction and community building is still based on speculative and aspirational stances rather than strong theoretical or empirical grounds.

In view of my own observations and the ones exhibited in the literature, I would like to suggest that all we can say at this point in time is that people are participating in discussion groups and exchanging messages. However, we are still unable to ascertain whether these interactions are achieving the pedagogical expectations outlined in the paradigmatic shift.

The illustration below portrays our current state by exhibiting the activities of participants in online discussions as not yet linked to the educational aspirations and the components needed to achieve them.

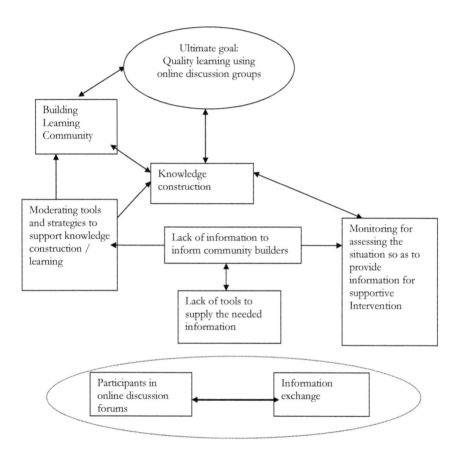

In this study I will focus on the social spaces emerging in the online discussion forums, to identify what the extra terrestrial observers would have referred to as:

"...in some classrooms on planet earth, learners follow the words of a leader, and in others they seem to engage with the words of each other".

To that end, I will study the social dynamics and power relations they imply in an attempt find whether online discussion forums have contributed in any way to the pedagogical shift and the embracing of social learning theories in distance learning contexts.

Online Social Spaces Created by Verbal Interactions

The extra terrestrial observation of classrooms detected social dynamics by looking at seating arrangements. However, detecting these in cyber space would have to focus on the ways in which the verbal interactions are organised so as to be able to follow the 'social space' created and the dynamics and power relations it implies. Following the order in which verbal interactions are generated will enable the reconstruction of the sequences of the messages sent throughout a discussion thread, hence revealing the sequence in which ideas were exchanged. These sequences will be able to chart the dynamics revealing the pattern of interactions to imply forms of distribution of power. Additionally charting the sequences would reveal the meaning making processes occurring throughout the verbal interactions conducted by participants in online discussion forums. To be able to follow these sequences I needed to be able to detect 'who talked to whom'.

Being able to do so is of great importance not only for research but also for e–practitioners facilitating online learning. This notion was raised by two prominent academics whom I have the honour to work with, who on two different occasions mentioned to me that there is no way for us as facilitators of online discussion forums, or the students participating in them to see or know who is talking to whom, which is very important as we need to know who is responding to whom.

The prevalent technological tools supporting discussion forums organise messages posted either chronologically (linear) or bundles together messages bearing the same topic(threaded) (White, 2004). This study will show that neither approach is able to accurately depict the sequence of interactions between participants, nor can they detect the sub topics emerging within 'topic bundled' messages. Being able to detect 'who is talking to whom' is, as I will show, the essence of understanding the emergence of social spaces. Identifying these in discussion forums is important in the unique context in which discussion forums are conceptualised as supporting collaborative environments facilitating the social construction of knowledge, because this will enable us to detect the patterns of distribution of power associated with this nature of learning environments.

Having reviewed the available technological systems, I embarked on the development of an alternative tool that could reconstruct the original sequence of the interactions to recreate meaning making processes emerging.

The Research Problem

My short outline of the field of study indicates that online learning discussion forums are conceptualised as social entities in which social construction of knowledge, and collaborative is expected to be achieved. However, research has not been able to produce empiric evidence demonstrating the achievement of these expectations.

In search of an empiric method for addressing the study of the social aspects of learning in online discussion forums, I chose to adopt the visual point of entry demonstrated in the opening scenario. I hope that by adopting this view I will be able to pave the way for investigations of knowledge construction and collaborative learning in online discussion forums.

To be able to achieve this goal I began the study by finding a way of visualising emerging social spaces in online discussion forums. I then applied these visualisations for two purposes

1. Investigating how the visualisation of spaces contributes to our ability to observe and analyse the learning related dynamics, and social structures emerging in Online Learning Discussion Forums (OLDF)

2. Explore how the visualisation of spaces will begin to illuminate ways in which they operate relative to meaning making and learning processes in OLDF

Engaging with these notions prompted my exploration of conceptual notions such as

1. structures as constructed entities
2. dynamics at play within structures
3. ways of investigating processes involving people's actions in social structures

Addressing Theoretical Notions

The Concept of Structure as Constructed Admitting to socially constructed spaces and structures denotes a theoretical stance which contests the structure> agency divide, and looks for ways of blurring the boundaries between the two. In the study I review theoretical frameworks such as those of Giddens, and Bordieu referred to as '*structurationists*', in search for ways of converging the notion of 'structure' and 'agency and address issues of structures as emerging and constructed rather than structured and stable.

The Concept of Dynamics at Play within Structures Studying the dynamics in online discussion entails studying the interactions between people which can be addressed as studying the relationships between individuals. However, in this study I follow the footsteps of Radcliffe –Brown(1965(1952)) and Nadel(1957) in their abstraction of social structures, perceiving them as comprised of relations between roles or positions rather than particular individuals.

Ways of Investigating Processes Studying processes such as meaning making, and knowledge construction, expected to occur in the online discussion forums, involves people's actions. These can be investigated as resulting from the actors' intentions, or alternatively perceived as enactments of actions, the former taking the 'Action' theories approach and the latter the 'Praxis' approach. For my theoretical framework I chose the praxis route and in particular its ethnomethodological approach, as it enabled me to address two major issues previously identified in this study, (1), the need for an empiric study of online discussion forums, and (2), the notion of studying social structures as emerging entities.

Methodological Implications of the Theoretical Frameworks

Adopting Radcliffe-Brown's(1965(1952)) and Nadel's (1957) notion of structure as being comprised of positions relative to one another, and Bourdieu 's notion of *'field'* as consisting of a set of objective, historical relations between positions anchored in certain forums of power(Bourdieu & Wacquant, 1992), indicates a 'relational ' perception of social structures, and the conceptualisation of structures as networks of social relations among objective positions, rather than relations among individuals.

To translate the relational concepts into an investigating method, I turned to Structural Analysis with its methodology Social Network Analysis (SNA), both of which adopt the 'relational' perception as their core concept(Berkowitz, 1982). SNA draws on its mathematical roots for establishing the nature of relations by measuring their density or frequency and in some cases their ability to exchange or convey information. Each relation or link in a network of relations can be regarded as holding a position which can be mathematically calculated to evaluate the position's influence or ability to convey information in the network, and the role the position may imply. The mathematical roots underpinning SNA also facilitate the visualisation of emerging social spaces constructed by interactions.

In the study I will demonstrate how through the use of SNA I was able to visually and mathematically map the roles and positions of actors through using their contributions to the online discussion threads. This allowed me to demarcate the distribution of power and the route of the participants' meaning making processes as emerging from the structure created by the order in which sequences of messages were posted throughout a discussion thread.

The Scope and Boundaries of the Study

- Online discussion forums are comprised of discussion threads. This study will analyse discussion threads as independent entities within a discussion forum. Focusing on discussion threads rather than the forum as a whole entails strengths as well as limitations. Discussion threads can be said to represent independent conversations within a discussion forum, and hence deserve to be treated independently, providing a focused view of the interactions within them. However, on some occasions, these conversations may indicate some relation to other discussion threads in the forum, or even other forums, particularly in situations like the one observed in which my research participants took part in several forums related to a mutual context such as an online tertiary course.

- Adopting the ethnomethodological stance meant focusing on the 'here and now', which in an online context implied using the data collectable off the discussion forums as encircling the phenomena under investigation. This approach can produce an authentic view of the situation under study; however, it may lead to a decontextualised view of the participants of the study.

- The study attempts to appeals to both e- researchers and online practitioners. It addresses practical as well as theoretical underpinnings surrounding the study of interactions in online discussion forums in learning contexts.

- Although the study is situated in the technologically mediated environment of computer networks, its primary focus is on the social aspects and ways of obtaining clearer views of these in the unique circumstances of the online environment.

The Outline of the Study

In Chapter Two, the study reviews the literature in the field identifying a gap in our ability to observe and analyse the occurrences in online discussion forums. The literature revealed a growing need for substantiating the activities in the online forums in view of the proliferation of the use of these environments in the context of learning in which discussion is perceived as part of the process of learning

Having discovered the gap and the need to fill it, chapter three turned to search for a way of addressing the emerging need by developing an alternative concept of analysis, and introducing an analytic tool facilitating the analysis of online discussion threads as social networks.

In Chapter Four, the analytic tool is applied to a data set comprised of 131 discussion threads each comprised of a minimum of three interactions. The implementation of the tool in this study is a preliminary one and should be considered as a 'test drive' opening the way for further investigations facilitated by its application.

Chapter five discusses the theoretical implications underpinning the study of online discussion forums as constructivist learning environments.

Chapter six summarises the work and outlines its practical implication for both e-researchers and e-practitioners. It also discusses the limitations of this study and suggests routes for further research studies.

About My Writing

This study is a written record of my train of thoughts leading to the realisation of a need for an alternative analytic tool for the study of learning in online discussion forums, and consequently to the development of a tool enabling a pictorial view of the dynamics occurring in online discussion forums in the context of learning.

Although the outline of the work seems to align with the traditional formation of research work, the structure of chapter three and four, which traditionally stand for the methodology and findings, are a little different as the methodology introduces an alternative analytic tool that attempts to address the issues raised in the literature review, and the fourth section – the findings is in fact a 'test drive' and demonstration of the application of the newly developed tool to a real data set.

Summary

In this chapter I have described the 'ground' of the study, identifying the main points it will address and the problems and limitations entailed in the theoretical and methodological choices made. I have also outlined the major sections of the study and their functions. In the next chapter I review the literature.

2. THE PROBLEM WITH STUDYING ONLINE DISCUSSION FORUMS

A review of the literature

Introduction

The Internet and particularly E-learning contexts have become widely acknowledged for their ability to facilitate and create a welcoming environment for collaborative and constructivist learning(Bonk & Cunningham, 1998; Duffy & D.J., 1996; Harasim, 1990a; Sherry, 2000). At the same time, educational leaders need reassurance and guidance that as the formats for electronic collaboration proliferate, computer-mediated communication will enhance student-teacher interaction and positively reorganize the learning process (Bonk & Cunningham, 1998).

As much as I appreciate, and in fact marvel at the inherent features of the Internet to connect people and offer a collaborative learning environment, I feel that the dazzling days of the Internet are over, and technological features and capabilities should now be investigated and analysed, using a wide kaleidoscope of perspectives.

Wellman (2003), argues that about ten years ago, in what he calls the *'first stage'* of Internet studies, the Internet was perceived as a technological marvel, where everyone was supposedly connected, enjoying communication that crossed the boundaries of time and space. Wellman goes on to argue that in that 'euphoria stage', analysis was often informed only by conjecture and anecdotal evidence. However, Wellman argues that around 1998, the world entered the *'second stage'* of Internet studies. By the end of the 1990s, use of the Internet had increased significantly and had become embedded in everyday life prompting policy makers, commercial powers, and academics to the emerging need for systematic accounts of the Internet. Wellman notes that during this 'second stage' Internet studies focused on the documentation of the proliferation of the users and uses of the Internet. The majority of the studies conducted during this stage were based on large-scale surveys. Neither the utopian hopes of the Internet abolishing all boundaries of time and space and facilitating a worldwide spread of global communication and democracy, nor the fears and concerns about high levels of Internet use as resulting in diminishing human contacts have fully materialised.

However, some encouraging phenomena seem to have occurred, and there are encouraging signs of the Internet actually encouraging rather than diminishing human communication (Wellman & Haythornthwaite, 2002). The *'third stage'*, which according to Wellman is the 'stage' we are currently experiencing, is the one where 'real analysis' begins, and for which standard social scientific methods may not suffice (Wellman, 2003). Similar to studies encompassing general uses of the Internet, studies focusing on instructional /educational purposes should by now, the year 2005, have matured to Wellman's *'third stage'* of what he referred to as the 'real analysis'.

In this chapter I will problematise the assumption that a facilitating technological environment that offers people convenient and accessible communication and linkages to other people and information would automatically result in high quality social-constructivist learning where knowledge will be constructed. I would argue that the sheer ability to communicate over time and space with otherwise inaccessible people, creating a cyber communicative reality cannot be assumed to automatically result in the creation of a 'collaborative learning community' simply because for example a group of people enrolled in the same virtual space have a mutual interest.

I will argue that although quality social-constructivist learning and the emergence of collaborative learning communities may possibly exist or could easily evolve in the current technological infrastructure, we would still need to critically investigate the quality and validity of the technology- bewitched assumptions about its existence, by first examining the social dynamics underpinning socio- thematic interactions, and that for this purpose we would need mechanisms, tools and strategies that would enable critical investigation.

Organisation of the Chapter

The chapter begins by outlining the arena of online learning, and the expectations and aspirations surrounding it. The purpose of this outline is to acquaint the reader with the backdrop that fuelled the quest of this study for ways of investigating discussion forums in online learning contexts. In the first section of this chapter, I will also attempt to clarify the terminology associated with online discussion forums.

Section Two, Part One reviews and critiques the available research, and the various methodologies applied in the field of online discussion forums. This section focuses on issues relating to notions of communication in the online environment, and the affects they are perceived to have on learning. Section Two, Part Two focuses on issues addressing collaborative and social constructivist interactions in the online environment. The following section investigates theoretical frameworks for addressing issues raised in the previous section, and the final section investigates the tools available for investigating the issues raised.

Part One – Situating the Study

MEDIATED LEARNING

Using technology for mediating learning has been around since the first 'Distance Learning' (DL) attempts back in 1840 when Isaac Pitman, an Englishman, began teaching shorthand by correspondence in Bath, England. Pitman used the best technology available to him in those days, the postal system. Students were instructed to copy short passages of the Bible and return them for grading via the new penny post system. The notion underpinning Pitman's delivery approach was to open educational opportunities to people who wanted to learn but were not able to attend conventional schools(Porter, n.d.)[1]. Primarily Pitman's notion is still at the centre of distance education.

Historically DL has always relied on technology for reaching the learners. In 1913 Thomas Edison stated that: "*Books will soon be obsolete in the schools. Scholars will soon be instructed through the eye. It is possible to teach every branch of human knowledge with the motion picture. Our school system will be completely changed in ten years.*" (Thomas Edison in the New York Dramatic Mirror, July 9, 1913). When

---

[1] N.D., stands for 'no date' for situations where no date is indicated when referencing an electronic source(APAONLINE, 2003)

television appeared on the stage of technology, educators expected it to become a powerful learning tool. However, television, as a one-way provider of information, failed to fulfil the very essential quality of teaching-the ability to interact with the learner. The necessity to provide interactivity turned the attention to computer-based training, where interactivity took place between machine, (computer) and learner. Computer based training, however, failed to be efficient because no sooner were educational programmes introduced than their content became obsolete(Rosenberg, 2001).

One feature shared by all the learning technologies mentioned so far was their 'traditional' classroom concept primarily advocating the 'sage in the box' model of teaching and learning. The technology- mediated learning was primarily based on signifying some source of authority, a teacher, or an educational computer programme for transmitting a fixed body of information to distant learners. This traditional approach has been contested by constructivist principles, advocating the encouragement of learners to take an active part in the learning process and construct their knowledge by interacting with learning materials, as well as with peers(Sherry, 1996). Furthermore, as early as the late 1980s to early 1990, Garrison (1989) and Garrison and Shale (1990) in their definition of distance education explicitly place sustained real two-way communication at the core of the educational experience, regardless of the separation of teacher and student, suggesting that interactions are a fundamental ingredient for creating effective distance education programs (Gunawardena & Stock McIsaac, 2004). However, adopting these notions required a technological infrastructure that would facilitate interactions from a distance.

THE ADVENT OF NETWORKED COMPUTERS- CONNECTING PEOPLE

The convergence of Information and Communication Technology (ICT) enabled computers to be connected using communication technologies, and introduced Computer Mediated Communication (CMC). The use of CMC became more widely accessible with the arrival of the World Wide Web (WWW) in 1993, which introduced a graphical, user-friendly global communication format for CMC. Computer Mediated

Communication tools connect computers creating computer networks. The ability to connect computers enabled the connecting of people, and the development of network communication tools, using what is referred to under the umbrella term 'Group CMC' (Computer Mediated Communication), or 'Discussion Media'. These discussion media encompassed tools such as Email List forums, chat systems such as Internet Relay Chat (IRC), Multi-User Dungeons(MUD), and Multi-User Domains Object Oriented (MOOs), Computer Conferencing/Bulletin Board systems, Usenet news groups, and Weblogs, enabled people to communicate with other people, and in doing so presumably create social networks(Preece, 2000; Wellman, 2003). Some of these tools enabled *Synchronous* communication– where both parties must be present for interaction to occur, whereas others offered *A-synchronous* that is, in delayed time, where participants are not required to both be present at the same time(Wetherell, Taylor, & Yates, 2001). The environment observed in this study was an a- synchronous online discussion forum, hence I will focus on the study of a-synchronous systems.

A-synchronous systems are *'many-to many'* communication tools that structure information exchange and group interactions (Harasim, 1990a), encompassing a range of formats referred to as electronic discussion groups and computer mediated conferencing such as Usenet and email discussions(Lueg & Fisher, 2003). This variety of tools all share one essential feature, the facilitation of the exchange of written messages among a group of participants by means of networked computers for the purpose of discussing a topic of mutual interest (Gunawardena, Lowe, & Amderson, 1997). According to Preece (2000), online communities consist of People interacting and sharing some purpose or interest, using a computer system supporting and facilitating their interactions (Preece, 2000, pp.,p.10). This rather prevalent, almost generic description of the use people make of 'discussion media' has resulted in a rather premature impulse to label all groups of people interacting online as "communities"(Herring, 2004), creating ambiguity in the use of the terms and making them interchangeable.

ONLINE DISCUSSIONS –ARE THEY ONLINE COMMUNITIES?

Burnett (2000), characterises "virtual communities" broadly as "discussion forums focusing on a set of interests shared by a group of geographically dispersed participants.(pp.1-2)" According to this characterization, almost any Internet discussion group is a virtual community.

The interchangeability of terms is further demonstrated by Rheingold's (1998) definition of online communities as "places where people use words to exchange pleasantries and argue, engage in intellectual discourse, conduct commerce, exchange knowledge, share emotional support, make plans, brainstorm, gossip, feud, fall in love, find friends and lose them, play games, flirt, create a little high art and a lot of idle talk"(Rheingold, 1998p.1). Rheingold's definition, in fact, classifies every group of people utilising discussion media, as an 'online community'. Wellman and Gulia(1999) acknowledge this interchangeability of terms, and question some of the notions attributed to online communities, as is evident in their chapter 'Net Surfers Don't Ride Alone: Virtual Communities as Communities' where they argue that:

> .... members of virtual communities take for granted that computer networks are also social networks spanning large distances (e.g., Rheingold 1993; Jones 1995; Hiltz and Turoff 1993; Stoll 1995). Such computer supported social networks (CSSNs) come in a variety of types such as electronic mail (email), bulletin board systems (BBSs) multi-user dungeons (MUDs), newsgroups and Internet Relay Chat (IRC). All CSSNs provide companionship, social support, information and a sense of belonging. But do they? (Wellman & Gulia, 1999,p. 167).

Whether one can refer to any group of people exchanging messages using *'discussion media'* to connect with other people over computer networks as an online or a virtual community is a debate beyond the scope of this study, and as Fernback, (1997) points out, "the term 'Community' seems readily definable to the general public but is infinitely complex and amorphous in academic discourse"(,p.39). It may well be that this amorphous definition has contributed to the interchanging use of the term *'Virtual'*, or *'Online Community'* when referring to 'Discussion Forum'. In keeping within the scope of this study, I will attempt to neither justify nor reject this terminology exchange; however, I will try to trace the possible origins for this ambiguity. A possible reason could stem from the simple technological reality, where the bulk of the activities in virtual communities, are primarily conducted via discussion media, varying from *listserves* to *e-mail lists* to *discussion forums*, and the ways in which providers of these media use the terminology. For example, MSN.com has a section called 'Communities', where the providers offer a number of discussion forums and chat rooms (Zemliansky, n.d.). EPDigest.com (a source of free online information for email publishing professionals), offers 'community managers' a wide choice of Internet discussion media, ranging from Web-based Discussion Forums, Email Discussion Lists, and Chat rooms, for their communities (Alt, 2000).

Another example for this prevalent terminological ambiguity can be seen in "Link-Up- newsmagazine devoted exclusively to the users of online services, CD-ROM products, & the Internet" (as of October 2002, *Link-Up* magazine was incorporated into ITI's flagship publication, *Information Today),* where Singer Gordon, in her article titled "Online Discussion Forums, Finding Community, Commentary, and (hopefully) answers" writes: "Online discussion group(also referred to as forums, message boards, or virtual communities)....."(Singer Gordon, 2000), suggests that discussion forums are places where one finds 'community'.

As I shall outline further on in this chapter, awareness of the ambiguity of terminology used in the field has helped me realise the confusion surrounding the meanings and features we tend to attribute to online discussion forums,. Furthermore, it helped me uncover research studying people using some form of 'discussion media' in studies said to be engaging in 'online communities', further exhibiting the interchangeability in the use of the terms.

As far as this study is concerned, in view of the ambiguity of the use of terminology, and the inability of theorists to reach a consensus around the definition of 'online communities', , I choose to refer to online environments in which people communicate using networked computers for sending written messages to each other, as Online Discussion Forums (ODF).

COMPUTER NETWORKS FOR SOCIAL AND INFORMATIONAL CONNECTIVITY

Historically, as early as the 1960s, theorists looked for computer networks to facilitate and support collaborative inspirational environments for research and learning(Hauben, n.d.). In the early 1960s, Theodore Nelson designed an experimental self- networking system that permitted users to view hypertext (linked) libraries, create and manipulate text and graphics, send and receive messages, and structure information intuitively. Users were able to create linkages between ideas and explore these linkages using a variety of features that facilitated developing and tracking interconnections. These were the first systems to articulate the potential of computers to create cognitive and social connectivity (Harasim, 1990a).

Licklider (1968), one of the key developers of ARPANET(Advanced Research Project Agency), and the forefather of computer networked communities (Hauben, n.d.), appreciated the potential entailed in Computer Mediated Communication (CMC), and perceived it to be much more than a mere tool for transferring information. He believed that: "When minds interact, new ideas emerge" (Licklider, 1968), and was among the first to perceive the spirit of community created among the users of CMC.(Hauben, n.d.). Licklider's vision of the potential entailed in CMC implied collaborative knowledge building through communication and interaction within online social environments.

THE NEW FEATURES OF DISTANCE LEARNING

Computer networks and particularly the Internet permeated many facets of our lives, introducing the vowel "e", for Electronic. Distance Learning(DL) as an historically mediated form of learning adopted the new technologies to become 'e-learning' (Ghosh, n.d.).

Computer networks and particularly the 'discussion media' technologies, now available for use in distance learning, not only introduced 'e- learning' as a new term in the DL arena, but drawing on literature, it signalled three major changes in the perception of DL:

1. *New technology Affording New Opportunities* The new technological infrastructure facilitated social participation, which presented DL with the opportunity to integrate social theories of mind and learning, and perceive those as processes of learning and knowing(Pulkkinen, 2003).

2. *Breaking Isolation* The introduction of the social concepts of learning signified an important turning point for DL learners, enabling them to break the isolated image of the distance learner, connecting learners to teacher and peers. Adopting the social concept of learning had altered the perception of the learning environment of DL, shifting from its historical highly individual activity(Holmberg, 1986), to a socially interactive learning environment often referred to as a 'learning community' (Pulkkinen, 2003).

3. *Teaching through Dialogue and Reflection* The arrival of e- learning, using CMC was accompanied by great expectations for 'quality learning', as it was argued that CMC is the ideal vehicle for avoiding the danger of earlier forms of Distance Learning where knowledge was packaged and sent out as a product. CMC could break this package and facilitate processes of reflection and dialogue. The technology offered by CMC meant that a tutor working only part time as usually is the case in higher education, will be able to hold continuing tutorials for the duration of a course with a small group of students, encouraging and modelling a deeper engagement with the issues of the course(Mason & Kaye, 1990). This model of teaching small groups allowing for reflection and dialogue and engagement in

the learning is aligned with the quality learning
modelled by Oxford and Cambridge where teaching was
based on a one-to-one tutorial where students received
immediate feedback from their tutors(Gibbs &
Simpson, 2002).

The constructivist theorists who contested the old one- way communication
formats practiced in Distance - Learning could now explore the new technologies for
their envisaged role as facilitators of interactive exchanges and collaborative
constructions of knowledge. Furthermore, the leading theorists in distance learning, for
example, Homberg, Wedemeyer, and Moore, put the learner and his or her interactions
with others at the centre of the education process(Moore & Anderson, 2003). Harasim
(1990a), presented a formal view of the practice of CMC, or in its more recent name e-
learning, that highlighted its social nature, collaborative environment and capability to
amplify intellectual discourse and foster the social construction of knowledge (Harasim,
1990a; Moore & Anderson, 2003).

The new technologies sparked new perceptions of distance learning, and, in
turn, these perceptions aspiring to foster intellectual discursive environments, guided
the primary use of the technologies available. The new social nature of distance learning
suggested a special focus on the use of 'discussion media', and in this particular study,
the use of discussion forums.

THE NATURE OF DISCUSSION FORUMS

The term 'Discussion Forum', as a linguistic idiom, entails two linguistic
expressions that form its nature. In the literature, the word '*discussion*' denotes
"discourse - an extended communication often interactive, dealing with some particular
topic" (Miller, n.d.). The term 'forum' is defined as "a space (physical or intellectual)
for people to meet and converse, or alternatively it can be a medium of open discussion
or voicing of ideas, such as a newspaper, a radio, a television program, or the Internet
(Allen, 1990). The combination of the two denotes a space, in the case of this study,

23

virtual /intellectual, where people can interact and voice ideas with each other about some topic. Using discussion forum environments in the context of e-learning can be seen to align with DL theorists i.e. (Harasim, 1990a; Moore & Anderson, 2003) who advocate intellectual discourse in the context of e-learning. Applying this type of practice implies that the learning model aspired by the theorists of DL is the one advocating interactive dialogue and feedback enabling collaboration and social construction of knowledge, rather than favouring the traditional 'sage in the box'[2] model promoting practices in which an authoritative source of information controls the learning situation.

The New Distance Learning Environment: Interactions, Dialogue, Feedback Collaboration Construction of Knowledge

Contemporary perceptions expressed by , researchers such as (Richardson, 1997; Van Ments, 1990; and,Wertsch, 1991),associated with Postmodern philosophy, and social-constructivist theories of learning, perceive learners not as passive recipients of knowledge, but as active reflective critical thinkers able to explore different perspectives, and construct knowledge from their own resources. Learners are expected to act through social interactions, hence, an important aspect of this approach involves interactions and dialogues (Van Ments, 1990). In the following sections I review the applicability of the various components entailed in the theories of learning described here to the online learning environment

Interactions, Some Definitions

Traditionally interactions were considered in the context of a classroom-based dialogue between students and teachers. With the advent of communication technologies the concept has been expanded to include mediated synchronous and a-synchronous discussions(Anderson, 2003)

---

[2] Adaptation of the "sage on the stage" metaphor to educational computer programmes

Wagner(1994) identified interactions in distance education contexts as "reciprocal events that require at least two objects and two actions. Interactions occur when these objects and events mutually influence one another"(,p.8). This definition could be regarded as the general description of the kind of interactions which occur in online discussion forums requiring two people and two messages or a messages and its response. Simpson and Galbo (1986), argue that the essential characteristic of interaction "is reciprocity in actions and responses in an infinite relationship"(p38). Dewey (1916) defines interaction as a component of the educational process that occurs when the student transforms the inert information passed to him/her from another and constructs it into knowledge with personal application and value.

Simpson and Galbo's definition allows for including various responses to a specific message, each creating a different type of relation unique in its contextual environment of actors and topics of discussion, created in a specific message - response situation. This contextualisation of interactions holds the potential for Dewey's concept of interactions to evolve into an educational process involving the social construction of knowledge.

The Importance of Dialogue

The perception of dialogue as an essential component of learning has become a well- established notion throughout the history of education, (Lai, 2001; Laurillard, 1993). Burbules (1993) points to a few examples beginning with Socrates and the 'Slave'(Plato, 1986),to Freire and 'the oppressed peasants'(Freire, 1970).

The use of dialogue as a technique for teaching and learning centres around the notion suggesting that it is above all else a means of escaping from our own individual perceptions of the world. It adds to the richness of understanding and enables people to make a contact with the mind of others in the most direct way possible (Van Ments, 1990). This concept of dialogue as a banquet of shared human thoughts, is granted an additional perspective by Collis(1996). The author argues that an important source for learning lies within the realm of informal interactions with colleagues and peers, who provide the necessary communication partners for the argument, debate, brainstorming and discussion that are crucial to the social construction of knowledge.

Borje Holmberg has been recognized as a prominent theorist in distance education. Central to Holmberg's (1989) theory of distance education is the concept of "guided didactic conversation" (p.43), which refers to both real and simulated conversation. Holmberg (1991) emphasised simulated conversation which is the interaction of individual students with texts and the conversational style in which pre-prepared correspondence texts are written. According to his theory of didactic conversation, which he developed while seeking an empathy approach to distance education, course developers are responsible for creating simulated conversation in self-instructional materials. The role of the teacher is largely simulated by written dialogue and comments (Holmberg, 1991).

Garrison (2000) questions whether an inert learning package regardless of how well it is written, is a sufficient substitute for real communication with the teacher. Homberg's theory of guided didactic conversation while closely associated with the correspondence movement and the industrial organisation of distance education introduces an empathy approach focusing on the importance of discourse both real and simulated (Gunawardena & Stock McIsaac, 2004).

The Importance of Human Feedback, and 'Customised Learning Assistance'

Since the days of Plato through to Dewey the importance of interactions between students and teachers have held an important role as supporting students' motivation and providing feedback (Anderson, 2003). Feedback is considered by students as the highest factor supporting quality learning, and determining the quality of courses, as is shown in a survey conducted by McCollum, Calder, Ashby, and Morgan (1995). The linkage between quality of teaching and learning and feedback is further discussed by researchers highlighting various aspects of this relation. For example Rowntree (1997) describes feedback as the key to quality in education and accentuates the fact that it is important that the feedback is given as a personal response by "another human being that challenges or confirms their understanding and helps them overcome errors or encourage them towards new insights" (p.58). The importance of the human feedback is further discussed by Laurillard (1993), who in her analysis of university teaching, emphasises the importance of providing feedback through dialogic interactions where tutors can provide intrinsic and adaptive feedback. Laurillard argues against any attempts to automate feedback in e-learning systems, and stresses that:

> "No simulation or technology is able to give truly intrinsic or fully customised feedback, the closest they can manage is 'extrinsic feedback'. Online tests self assessment questions and other artificial sources of formative feedback cannot provide the degree of depth or insight required for customised learning assistance.... in the ways a human tutor can" (Laurillard, 1993p.153).

The emphasis Laurillard puts on human dialogue and feedback highlights the importance of granting e-tutors with the necessary tools for providing what Laurillard refers to as 'customised learning assistance'. Customisation of the learning process provides an opportunity for students to have course materials interpreted in ways meaningful to them. This is why tutors need to be aware of students' conceptual processes and difficulties (Ramsden, 1988).

As the literature acknowledges the importance of feedback for learning, e-tutors involved in implementing constructivist learning approaches in online environments would benefit from having analysis tools that would help them identify significant instances of 'customised learning' that lead to meaning construction so as to be able to better support these.

What is Collaborative Learning?

The interactive environment and the social constructivist approaches imply the need for collaborative learning environments. In his study of collaborative learning Dillenbourg (1999) highlights a wide variety of notions attributed to collaborative learning , some of which I note here:

- Some scholars include any collaborative activity within educational context, such as studying course material or sharing course assignments
- Others view the activity as joint problem solving, where learning is expected to occur as a side-effect of problem solving, measured by the elicitation of new knowledge or by the improvement of problem solving performance
- Some theories address collaborative learning from a developmental perspective, as a biological or cultural process which occurs over years
- One perception of 'collaborative learning' used by the 'Computer Supported Collaborative Learning (CSCL) identifies collaboration as a situation where for example a group of 40 subjects follows a course over one year.

The common denominator of all these elucidations argues Dillenbourg (1999) is their focus on 'collaborative' notions rather than 'learning', hence the author proposes his own definition of collaboration using three major criteria:

1. Interactivity- usually focusing on the extent to which these interactions influence the peers' cognitive processes.

2. Synchronicity- 'doing something together', which in a-synchronous discussion media has been developed by the users to produce conversational rules for coping with the delay of the technology, to keep the floor, to initiate turn taking and so forth.

3. Negotiability- interactions are about negotiation rather than authoritarian situations

Identifying these three criteria paved the way to the study of learning in a collaborative environment. In her study of computer supported learning Di Eugenio (2001) argues that it is the interactions and collaboration that foster learning. Approaching learning from this perspective acknowledges the existence of a non-authoritative, decentred dialogue even when there are discrete teacher and student roles (Burbules, 1993). Furthermore, Dillenbourg (1999) suggests collaboration fosters negotiable rather than hierarchical interactions in which one partner will not impose his/ her views on the sole basis of authority, but will to some extent argue for his/her standpoint, through processes of justification, negotiation, and persuasion. However, it is important to acknowledge that not all interactions can automatically be classified as 'collaborative learning'. Collaborative learning involves groups working together in solving problems, and in sharing and clarifying ideas around those problems (Kemery, 2000).

In a non- collaborative learning situation teachers tend to use a 'tutorial dialogue' in which they present the learners with packages of information or alternatively with a set of instructions or tasks that the learners need to perform. A tutorial dialogue usually does not involve many participants or multiple interactions. The structure of collaborative dialogue on the other hand is expected to be more complex and will include tutors and students collaborating, and negotiating to build a shared understanding, so as to enable students to construct knowledge by themselves rather than be instructed or given the 'correct information'(Di Eugenio, 2001; Dillenbourg, 1999).

What is Social Construction of Knowledge?

The notion of constructivism is comprised of several schools of constructivist thought, sharing a common understanding that the building of knowledge is a recursive process, in which blocks of new knowledge are the products of previous constructions. Thus, the structure and content of knowledge are inextricably interwoven in constructivism(Beniam, 1995). Ernst Von Glasersfeld(Von Glaserfeld, 1989) defines one school of constructivist thought, Radical Constructivism in which knowledge is not passively received either through the senses or by way of communication, but is actively built by the cognising subject. Another school of thought, social constructivism, is mostly associated with the Russian psychologist and philosopher Vygotsky, who emphasised the influence of cultural and social contexts in learning. Vygotsky's theory argues that people construct meanings actively and continuously in a social context, and meanings emerge from the patterns of our social experiences that occur over time in a contextual, situated, and continually changing synthesis. Social constructivism asserts that knowledge is grounded in the relationship between the knower and the known, and is generated through social interactions, which in turn enable learners to gradually accumulate and advance their levels of knowing. Social constructivists believe that knowledge is constructed socially using language (Vygotsky, 1962), and is therefore sometimes regarded as symbolic social interaction, using conversational language for negotiation of meaning and conceptual delimitations (Kanuka & Anderson, 1998). From the social constructivist perspectives the construction of knowledge is a socio-linguistic process (Kanuka & Anderson, 1999).

Constructivist learning ventures far beyond the mere movement of information from instructors' minds to students' notebooks and instead focuses on meaning making activities requiring articulation and reflection involving internal and social negotiation. Constructivists aspire to foster personal meaning making and discourse among communities of learners socially negotiating meaning, rather than to instruct intervene, and control the learners (D. Jonassen, Davidson, Collins, Campbell, & Bannan Haag, 1995).

Constructivism -Not Only for Children

Among the two widely accepted constructivist learning theories: *critical constructivism and social constructivism*, *social constructivism* is currently the most accepted epistemological position associated with online learning(Kanuka & Anderson, 1998).The social -constructivist approach perceives teaching as an act of assistance offered at points of the 'Zone of Proximal Development' (ZPD) at which performance requires assistance.(Bliss, Askew, & Macrea, 1996; Tharp & Gallimore, 1991). The Vygotskian (ZPD) defines "the difference between the development of the individual's performance in 'independent problem solving', and in 'problem solving under adult guidance or in collaboration with more capable peers"(Vygotsky, 1978p.86). While Vygotsky's setting refers to adult-child pairs, other paradigms, such as 'reciprocal teaching'(Palincsar, 1986) introduce situations in which one learner plays the role of the teachers and this role shifts between learners(Dillenbourg, Baker, Blaye, & O'malley, 1996). This enables the expansion of constructivist notions beyond the adult-child situation, to include peer situations, which could imply child-child interactions or adult-adult situations. In a similar way, Gadamer,(1975), argues that language is the core of understanding, and that communicative dialogue is its basis. He argues that an individual's present 'horizon' of knowledge and experience can be transcended though exposure to others' discourse and linguistically encoded cultural traditions because others' horizons convey views and values that place one's own horizon in relief (Nabudere 2002).

Gadamer's concept can be seen as bearing some similarity to Vygotsky's ZPD, referring to mediation processes occurring between the immediate, as different from the emergent horizon of understanding, placing discourse at the centre of how learners understand their environment, transcending the child –adult formation. This model enables investigating constructivist notions in an all-adult environment such as the data set investigated in this study.

COLLABORATIVE AND CONSTRUCTIVIST LEARNING IN ONLINE DISCUSSION FORUMS

Kanuka and Anderson(1998) describe Online Discussion Forums(ODF) as complex learning environments where group collaboration is practiced in a technologically mediated environment in which the interactions occurring between its participants can lead to the creation of communities of learners. The technology of ODF enables, as Preece (2000) suggests, new opportunities for learners to work together, exchange information, comment on each other's work, share resources, and meet people from across the world. Preece's perceptions imply collaborative work and the sharing of knowledge. Conceptually, collaborative learning encompasses Vygotskian socio- constructivist notions in which learners use language(D. Hung, Chen, & Tan, 2003) for constructing knowledge in a primarily socio-linguistic process (Kanuka & Anderson, 1999). In online discussion forums these socio linguistic processes can be observed by investigating the written interactions posted between participants in the discussion.

Deconstructing the complexity of online learning environments entails issues of socio linguistic interactions; collaborative learning; and social construction of knowledge, mediated through written messages posted on computer networks. Studying such complex environments prompts methodological questions as to the methods needed for observing and investigating the issues entailed.

In this section, I have outlined the components comprising the e- learning environment as envisaged by visionaries and educational theorists aspiring to move towards an interactive collaborative environment where learners interact with tutors and peers, and away from the traditional model of one-way communication. However, the literature of e -learning seems to presume that the technology in itself will instigate educational change, reassigning traditional roles and contexts. For example, changing the role of the teacher, to that of a facilitator. It also presumes that constructivist e-learning is effective, desirable and real (Salmon, 2000).

Returning to Wellmans'(2003) notion of going beyond the sheer admiration of the technology, there is a need for deeper research and verification of the existence of the processes and activities required for achieving the potential, vision, and goals expected of the e-learning environment in becoming dialogic, collaborative socio constructivist learning settings.

In the following section, I review the existing research done in the area, focusing on online discussion forums within learning contexts, or in other words Online Learning Discussion Forums (OLDF).

Part Two- Section One: Online Learning Discussion Forums (OLDF) as Interactive Learning Environments: A Critical Overview of the Available Research

In this section I review a number of research studies conducted in the field of online discussion forums in an attempt to acquire a general overview of the various perspectives and research methodologies in the field. The aim of this brief review is to identify what is perceived as relevant to the study of online communicative, interactive, learning environments, and to attempt to discover what is needed for the study of this field. The section will begin by a brief review of research studies followed by a review of the prevalent methodologies used in the field.

Research of the growing phenomena in which people exchange messages, using the various computer mediated 'Discussion Media' for communicating with other people across computer networks, is constantly expanding to engulf issues ranging from technological aspects of usability and accessibility, to a vast range of contexts (Preece, 2000).

Roberts(2004) in his book "Online Collaborative Learning Theory and Practice", identified five categories of studies, which form a framework for the various perspectives used for the study of communicative online learning environments.

1. Instructional and technological issues

This category includes studies focusing on the effectiveness of different online learning tools, environments and techniques for collaborative learning, and their implications for students' outcomes. For example, a study evaluating two collaborative dialogue games found that they produce significant improvements in students' conceptual understanding(Ravenscroft & Matheson, 2002; Roberts, 2004). Another example is a study investigating the ability and effectiveness of online learning environments used in tertiary education for supporting collaborative learning, focusing on the groupware technology in terms of supporting creative group work at a distance, and found them wanting, as they experienced limitations in the available technology(Villalba & Romiszowski, 1999).

The effectiveness of technology rather than focusing on its own merits or limitations is tested in relation to its effectiveness in supporting students' learning outcomes.

2. *Evaluation of e- learning*

Much of the literature reviewing studies of Online Collaborative Learning (OCL), show an implicit focus on evaluation. Often these implicit notions are descriptively oriented toward the students' experience of learning. The majority of these studies tend to draw on ethnographic methods, focusing on the students' perceptions and experiences of the online learning, as for example the study of Sanders and Morrison-Sjetlar(2001). However, according to Roberts(2004) not many studies focus on the value of the students' collaborative learning.

3. *Socio-Cultural issues*

Roberts (2004) found that literature tends to classify these studies into three broad clusters: *pedagogical studies; linguistic studies; and cross-cultural studies.*

Pedagogical studies An example of a pedagogical study can be observed in the study of Ronteltap and Eurelings(2002), who used a quantitative approach for quantifying types of learning issues that generate most interactions, alongside qualitative approaches for studying which types of learning issues generate the highest level of information processing. The authors note that although tools and functionality are important, they do not necessarily produce interactions of a quality that lead to learning(Roberts, 2004; Ronteltap & Eurelings, 2002).

Linguistic studies In most cases these studies focus on identifying features of the dialogue and discussion, examining processes that take place online and sometimes comparing them with off line processes(Roberts, 2004). Many of the linguistic studies are situated within a theoretical framework that endorses the socially constructed and socially mediated processes of learning and meaning production, drawing on ethnographic approaches. These approaches stress the social context, rejecting *'a-priori categories'* of analysis, attempting to focus on the learning processes at hand(C. Jones, 1998). In most cases, rather than developing a theoretical model for the analysis of communicative practice in Online Collaborative Learning (OCL)(Gunawardena, Lowe, & Amderson, 1997; Roberts, 2004), studies claiming to focus on such social processes mediated by online communication tools explore the exchange of personal communication and effects of communication channels on self-disclosure, question asking, and the reduction of uncertainty between online partners(Tidwell & Walther, 2002).

4. *Cross-cultural Studies*

These studies focus on demographic differences and cross-cultural factors in OCL, as it increases its prevalence through flexible web- based learning programmes encompassing diverse populations across the globe. A study conducted across cross-cultural groups discovered differences in the participants' perception of collectivism(Gunawardena, Wilson, Lopez-Islas, Ramirez-Angel, & Megchun- Alpizar, 2001). Such studies challenge pedagogical assumptions and highlight issues of generalisability across different cohorts and individual differences(Roberts, 2004). Furthermore, these studies seem to focus on differences rather than collaborative notions.

Summary of Review of Perspectives:

This section, albeit encompassing a brief and limited review, elicits the variety of perceptions and interpretations attributed to the notion of 'collaboration', and what perspective are perceived as relevant for its study. This brief review implied the need for three principles required for the investigation of technology mediated communicative learning environments:

- Investigating the technological tools in a communicative learning environment should investigate the implication the technology has for people's activities, i.e. learning, rather than focus on the technology itself

- The investigation of communicative practices cannot be limited to the perspectives of individuals, and social environments and entities need to be perceived as more than a mere backdrop for individuals to act in

- E- Learning as a potentially interactive environment needs theoretical models for analysing communicative practices, and discovering the social aspects of collaborative activities

KEY RESEARCH METHODS USED FOR STUDYING ONLINE DISCUSSION FORUMS (ODF)

A substantial body of research has attempted to establish the suggestions and assumptions relating to the ability of online discussion forums to support and facilitate collaborative learning and social construction of knowledge. Research studies in the field have applied a variety of research approaches using a variety of methods ranging from quantitative measurements of login frequencies, and the number of contributions per student (Monroe, 2003), to qualitative 'content analysis' approaches, focusing on the quality of the messages as artefacts of critical thinking and argumentation content (Jeong, 2003).

LOGIN COMPUTER GENERATED DATA ANALYSIS

Computer networks supporting online discussion tools record automatically any access and activity performed by participants, automatically creating a tracking database recording every activity. Analysing these login records enables the evaluation of participation providing data relating to frequency, length of time spent on the activity, order in which activities were performed, and spaces, or particular forums accessed by the participant. This type of data has its merits; however, it does not convey any information regarding the content conveyed by the participants, or the existence of collaborative activities as such, as it focuses on individual activity(Roberts, 2004).

CONTENT ANALYSIS

Content analysis is a research technique which can be defined as both a quantitative as and qualitative method. It is a technique which requires critical qualitative skills for assigning content to a number of variables that are later to be analysed quantitatively through calculating relationships between the identified variables. Content analysis can be used as an analysis tool for any type of artefact of human discourse or activity. It is often associated with the analysis of text documents.

In e-research these text documents are often found in email and discussion forums. The technique of content analysis begins by defining variables for analysis. There are 'Manifest Variables' and 'Latent Variables'. Manifest variables provide a wide variety of descriptive information that can help in the understanding of the nature and scope of the online activity. For example, one can analyse the length of the average email message, or the frequency of the use of personal nouns, or the average number of responses to a request for help. The descriptions obtained in this type of analysis enable the researcher to describe and quantify typical patterns of interactions, discourse, and participation. Manifest variables are about quantification, placing content analysis under its quantitative hood. Defined over fifty years ago by Berelson(1952). He argued that Quantitative Content Analysis (QCA) is "a research technique for the systematic objective, and quantitative description of the manifest content of communication" (p.18). Primarily QCA involves segmenting communication content into units, assigning each unit to a category, and providing tallies for each category. For example, Bullen(1999) studied participation and critical thinking in an online discussion by counting the number of times each student contributed to the discussion and by assigning each contribution to one of four categories of critical thinking(Bullen, 1999).

However, not all the information can be obtained by focusing on the manifest or surface content. For example, educational research would be interested in obtaining information showing evidence of creative or critical thinking, or the effect of teacher's behaviour on students' achievement, or the measurement of student motivation, or in the case of this study, the achievement of high quality collaborative, socio constructivist processes. Exposing these not so obvious issues requires 'Latent Variables' which according to Potter and Levine-Donnerstein(1999) can be classified into two types. The first type is latent "pattern variables", identifiable by "recognising patterns across elements" (p.261). An example of latent pattern variables would be focusing on the way in which an online facilitator signs off his or her messages. In this case the variables would focus on the closing statements of the messages, looking for a pattern of use that would provide information about the function of these statements(Anderson & Kanuka, 2002). The second type of latent variables is the 'latent projective variable'(Potter & Levine-Donnerstein, 1999) identified by "judgments based on a 'projection' of an abstract concept by the researcher"(Anderson & Kanuka, 2002,p.175). In an educational context this could be used to investigate the provision of effective teacher interjection (ibid), or in the case of this study, the existence of 'high quality of collaborative learning'.

Qualitative content analysis is usually associated with research of latent variables, thereby allowing the researcher to work with the meanings that underlie the content rather than directly with the actual content under investigation(Anderson & Kanuka, 2002). Recently researchers have developed protocols for conducting meaningful qualitative analysis(Marra, Moore, & Klimczak, 2004). Qualitative content analysis as an approach of empirical, methodological controlled analysis of texts within their context of communication, following content analytical rules and step-by-step models, without rash quantification, Mayring (2000) describes two such models, one inductive and the other deductive. The inductive model begins with the determination of category, and definition of criteria, continuing with the formulation of inductive categories out of the material; formative check of reliability; summative check of reliability and finally interpretation of results. The deductive model starts with a theoretical based definition of the aspects of the analysis, followed by a theoretical formulation of categories , and finally formative and summative check of reliability (Mayring, 2000). Another example using 'qualitative content analysis', is Mason's study(Mason, 1991) of behavioural indicators as seen through types of communications in which students participated.

'Content Analysis' is said to be applied to the analysis of the 'self transcribed conversations' stored and archived by Online discussion forums (Kanuka & Anderson, 1998; Levin, Haesun, & Riel, 1990). However, not many researchers define exactly what they mean by the term content analysis. Furthermore, not many adhere to its long tradition largely developed within communication studies(Rourke, Anderson, Garrison, & Archer, 2001).

Research studies addressing such issues as educational quality in discussion forums are usually defined as using content analysis methodology. These studies range from 'quantitative content analysis', measuring the frequency of criteria assessed contributions per student i.e. (Meyer, 2004; Weiss & Morrison, 1998),through to inferring learning processes in online contexts from quantitative content analysis for assessing (Kanuka & Anderson, 1998), or alternatively applying 'qualitative content analysis' techniques for studying the quality of the messages as artefacts of critical thinking and argumentation content(Jeong, 2003). Additional studies applying content analysis techniques, to name but a few are Anderson's investigation of issues of teaching presence and its assessment(Anderson, 2001), and Poole's investigation of student participation(Poole, 2000).

In spite of the abundance of data accessible in Online Discussion Forums (ODF), there seems to be a relatively small amount of research on the actual content of messages, such as sharing ideas, constructing knowledge, solving problems and critical thinking(Marra, Moore, & Klimczak, 2004). This scarcity may reside in the fact that analysing and measuring the educational quality of online discussions is a complex and time consuming procedure(Roberts, 2004; Rourke & Anderson, 2004), or it may be that the lack of proven research paradigms in the field is impeding the emergence of such research studies(Marra, Moore, & Klimczak, 2004).

Furthermore, content analysis tends to focus on the analysis of single messages, or in other words, the utterance of an individual within the group. However, this focus is without reference to the relationships and interactions between messages and the people constructing them. It may be that an approach able to venture beyond the single message, such as conversation and discourse analysis would provide the missing paradigm.

CONVERSATION ANALYSIS

One of the fields of ethnomethodology, is 'Conversation Analysis' (CA), sometimes even considered an autonomous field, separate from ethnomethodology. CA is the study of structures and the formal properties of language considered in its social use. Conversations are organised; they respect an order, which is essential for making them intelligible. The utterances are locally organised, providing the participants with the thread of conversation and enabling them to understand it and pursue the exchange. People talk in turns and questions and answers are paired, which Sacks called "adjacency pairs" (Sacks, Schegloff, & Jefferson, 1974,p.16)This adjacency may be disturbed in Online Discussion Forums (ODF) because of two of the inherent features of these communication tools. First, their a- synchronous nature creating a time lag between a message and its response disrupting the 'turn adjacency', and second, their one- way conveyance of the content, relaying messages in one bulk, rather than by key strokes or singular sentences(Herring, 1999). Furthermore, the single bulk in which messages are relayed creates a situation in which messages are transmitted linearly, not representing multi participant interaction and creating a situation in which a message may be sequentially separated from its previous one (Herring, 1999).

Coulon (1995) suggests that the analysis procedure in Conversational analysis is based on the notions stating that:

- Interaction is structurally organised
- The contributions of the participants to this interaction are contextually oriented; the indexing process of utterances to a context is inevitable
- These two properties are actualised in every detail of the interaction, so that no detail can be disposed of as being accidental or inaccurate

The inherent nature of ODF that disturbs the adjacency turn taking and the linear conveyance of messages, prevents the discovery of multi participants' interactions, and in so doing creates difficulties in identifying interconnected messages and their responses. Hence it is difficult to construct the context of the interactions created by the participants' interactions. Therefore there are limitations to the application of conversation analysis for the analysis of ODF, in the context of collaborative, and constructivist learning.

DISCOURSE ANALYSIS

Discourse analysis draws upon a variety of disciplines, including linguistics, philosophy, psychology, pragmatics, rhetoric, and sociology, to study language use. Within discourse analysis research, attention is typically focused on texts, both oral or written, and on the roles and strategies of the *speakers* (*writers*) and the *hearers* (*readers*) who participate in that text, and the ways in which speakers construct and how hearers interpret discourse(Prideaux, 1997).

Computer networks are changing the way we think and interact. They are redefining the spatial and temporal parameters of the interactions they mediate so that online discourse is taking new directions, particularly in the way people write. One important observation made by a number of researchers is that new conventions are evolving and blurring the past distinctions between writing and talking. Tornow(1997) describes the written interactions that occur in electronic discussion forums as a kind of "written talk"(Tornow, 1997), or as Grifin et. al. 1989[3] cited in (Voiskunsky, 1997) call it "Written speech". An extended stretch of language, such as we find in conversations, narratives, polemical statements, political speeches, etc., is not just a string of sentences, one following the other, but rather it exhibits properties which reflect its organization, coherence, rhetorical force, and thematic focus. In written discourse, unlike more casual oral discourse, the writer constructs the text through the use of various linguistic, stylistic and rhetorical devices and presents it in a more formal and coherent structure (Prideaux, 1997).

Discourse analysis addresses language use, language in context and coherence(Norrick, 2001). It attempts to study the organisation of language above the sentence or above the clause, and therefore to study larger linguistic units, such as conversational exchanges or written texts. Discourse analysis is also concerned with language use in social contexts, and in particular with interaction or dialogue between speakers(Stubbs, 1983). An example of the use of discourse analysis techniques can be observed in Dythe(2002), and Jones(1998)whose studies investigated issues of knowledge construction and the building of learning communities.

Attempting to apply Discourse analysis techniques to online discussion forums would encounter the same difficulties I have described earlier in relation to Conversation Analysis. Unlike Content Analysis which typically treats each message as an individual unit of analysis, discourse or conversation analysis require that the researcher investigate a complete conversation. A complete conversation constitutes a series of several exchanges, comprising the contexts of a number of related messages(Thomsen, Straubhaar, & Bolyard, 1998).

Generally, conversations in online discussion forums are perceived as the group of messages posted within a 'discussion thread'. Studies have attempted to use these as units of analysis. For example, Simoff (1999)studied discussion threads for the evaluation of the degree of collaboration, and Lipponen(2002) explored the validity of

---

[3] Grifin's article is in Russian therefore I can only refer to the citing in Voiskunsky's paper.

computer supported collaborative learning. However, Lipponen's study found that discussion threads tend to be short and hold divergence topics, and unequal participation patterns. A study investigating learners participation and its implication to learning found that the *branching structure* of online discussion threads often leads to a lack of coherence and unity in the discussion(Thomas, 2002). These findings cast doubts on the ability of discussion threads to serve as units of analysis, as they are not able to clearly indicate the conversation scope and the separation points in the thread when the conversations evolves into another topic. This inability results from the problem of disturbed adjacency and the way in which computer systems record the conversations. I shall return to this issue in greater detail in chapter four of this study.

ACTIVITY THEORY

Activity Theory (AT) offers a set of perspectives on human activity and a set of concepts for describing that activity. Engeström's (1987)framework shown in *figure 2-1* below depicts, an *Activity System* in which all activity is treated as part of a rich dynamic in which the relations among the actors (subjects) and the objects they act upon are mediated by tools, rules, communities, and divisions of labour. An 'object', according to AT can include social and cultural properties and connects the individual actions to the collective activities(Nardi, 1996).

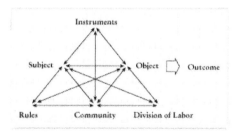

Figure 2-1 Activity system

The illustration of the activity system elicits the meditating principle of AT depicting that all actor/s > object relations are mediated by the tools, rules, community and the division of labour, making AT an effective tool for investigating the introduction of a new component into an activity system. Issroff and Scanlon(2002) suggest that AT provides an effective framework for understanding and describing learning. It is no wonder that AT is quite popular with educational design, assisting in the design and testing of new educational tools and systems, and the investigation of the effects these have on various components of learning, particularly e- learning where mediation is primarily reliant on new and yet to be tested technologies. AT is used for analysing and informing the design of online spaces of collaborative learning evaluating a peer- to- peer interface for learning objects, designing online learning communities, supporting inquiry based learning and more. For example, Barab and Schatz (2001) used AT for the design of online community; Dobson LeBlanc, and Buroyne (2004) used the AT framework for evaluating the design of a peer- to -peer interface for online learning objects, and Hung and Chen(2002) applied AT for investigating the formation of identity within communities.

As valuable and helpful as AT may prove, critics such as Davydov(1999), and Engestrom (1999) argue that AT involves a certain technicist activism that has no humanistic origins. Davydov goes as far as saying that AT is actually changing reality without taking into account the historical interests of humans and realistic possibilities of the reality itself. Engstrom(1999)argues that in spite of its cultural –historical roots, AT research often tends to neglect the concrete historical analysis of activity under investigations. Ratner (1999) further argues that the AT framework tends to perceive culture as an external independent variable rather than as system of relationships and processes which organise psychological phenomena in a particular manner.

The mediation principle of AT creates dynamics of interchangeability. For example, the community in AT is perceived as an aggregation of individuals bearing an identity which assume a role in the community. The community on the other hand is a source of identity creating mechanisms, as it contributes to the formation of rules, and roles. Similar interchangeability can occur in relation to tools, rules and the division of labour. However, this interchangeability is not extensively discussed within online related literature working from within the AT framework. Instead, AT acknowledges the interrelations between its components, however, it tends to encourage the compartmentalisation of reciprocally defining and interacting components(Barab & Schatz, 2001).

The research reviewed in this section approached Online Discussion Forums from a number of perspectives, and in search of various issues. In all of these perspectives however, there seem to be very little attention to collaboration. While some of the research studies reviewed claim to investigate ODF for their collaborative learning features, their research goals and methodological approaches raise queries as to their perception of 'collaborative learning'. Studies concerned with the instructional /technology perspectives showed an interest in the 'effectiveness' of the tools and the implications for students' outcomes. Roberts (2004)found that much of the literature of online collaborative learning focuses on students' experiences with very little regard to actual collaboration. Pedagogical studies focus on types of learning issues that would generate interactions, although they are not able to indicate which interactions will lead to learning. Linguistic studies look at features of dialogues comparing online with off line features. Demographic differences are investigated by the cross-cultural studies(Roberts, 2004). To summarise, these studies appear to view collaboration as the communication between individuals, a view which I will argue is erroneous.

Rourke and Anderson (2004) suggest that educational technology researchers may have to expand their role to include the role of a communication researcher, as prevalent educational research perspectives and methodologies seem to fall short of investigating the communicative/interactive aspects so fundamental to collaborative and socio- constructivist e-learning

The prevalent methodologies used in the studies reviewed in this section seem to be limited in their ability to address issues of collaboration, and although Activity Theory primarily deals with the connection of the individual's actions to the collective activities, it tends to compartmentalise the interacting components. Furthermore, AT primarily describes occurrences rather than follow processes such as the emergence of roles.

Login analysis and Content analysis techniques are equipped to study individuals; their login patterns of behaviour or the content they produce, and the pattern of their use of language. Studies applying content analysis techniques use the self-transcribed records of messages as their data; however, the abundance of this type of research data does not seem to attract large numbers of research studies. Reasons for this scarcity of research are said to arise from lack of procedures, and proven research paradigms(Marra, Moore, & Klimczak, 2004; Roberts, 2004; Rourke & Anderson, 2004), and the propensity of educational research to focus on the individual rather than interactions and the social entities these construct.

In the next section I will review the issue of studying interactions and the supra-individual nature of collaborative and social constructivist learning.

Part Two Section Two- Online Discussion Forums (ODF) as Collaborative E- Learning Environments

Viewing online discussion forums as computer applications for building 'learning communities,(Palloff & Pratt 1999; Simoff, 1999) developing collaborative learning, (Daradoumis, Marques, Guitert, Gimenez, & Segret, 2001; Guitert, Daradoumis, Gimenez, & Marqus, 1999; Palloff & Pratt 1999) , and applying social constructivist learning approaches, (Kanuka & Anderson, 1998; Kanuka & Anderson, 1999; Morrison, 2003), is no longer a novelty; however, achieving these aspired notions is still an on-going quest, beginning with needing to understand what is entailed in these aspirations. In this section I will unfold the issues entailed in online discussion forums in relation to collaborative learning.

Historically, interactions, dialogues, and feedback have long been accepted as essential ingredients for quality teaching/learning processes(Gibbs & Simpson, 2002; Rosenberg, 2001). The literature argues that collaborative learning and social interaction play a major role in cognitive development, enabling the "acquisition of knowledge, skills or attitudes that take place as a result of people working together to create meaning, explore a topic or improve skills" (Graham & Scarborough, 1999,p. 20).

Discussion forums as communication tools are primarily places of interaction, discussion and communication, hence they attract proponents of collaborative and constructivist learning eager to apply the two- way communication tool for creating collaborative socio-constructivist learning environments.(Kanuka & Anderson, 1998; Preece, 2000; Romiszowski & Mason, 2004). As a communication tool enabling *many –to-many* communication that structures information exchange and group interactions(Anderson & Kanuka, 1997; Harasim, 1990b; Kanuka & Anderson, 1998), discussion forums are deemed by the constructivists and pro-collaborative theorists to facilitate students' construction of knowledge through active learning and collaboration, that presumably increases the effectiveness of the learning (Bonk & Cunningham, 1998; Romiszowski & Mason, 2004).

Although OLDF have the technological and communicative structural ability to support such features and provide a social constructivist learning environment(Ferdig, Roehler, & Pearson, 2002), as I have shown earlier in this chapter most studies conducted within the realm do not seem to devote much attention to the interactions and the social dynamic processes occurring in OLDF, and the learning progression these portray (M. Collins & Berge, 2001; Jeong, 2003).The growing acknowledgement and expectations of the new technologies to support quality, active, collaborative, constructivist learning, still remains to be investigated, explored and evaluated for their effectiveness and ability to support processes of meaning making and advancing of levels of knowing. Although some research has attempted to address issues of collaborative knowledge building i.e. (Chan, Lam I. C.K., & van Aalst, 2003), no empirical evidence has been provided to support practitioners in the field. Furthermore, no clear criteria were outlined for identifying, let alone assessing constructivist social construction of knowledge. The key feature of collaborative learning is that it involves social interaction. In order to establish whether real collaboration is taking place the researcher needs appropriate methods of empirical analysis(Cox, Hall, Loopuyt, & Carr, 2002).

Introducing online discussion forums to learning environments was not an attempt to force collaborative learning, but rather an effort for improving the conditions for facilitating and supporting what is defined as "ideal learning"(Cox, Hall, Loopuyt, & Carr, 2002). According to Habermas(1984) "Ideal Learning" is a situation where "communicative practice is free from any kind of distortion, any form of coercion and ideology, and does not involve any force, except the force of a better argument"(p.25). From a constructivist approach, this notion represents the collaborative construction of knowledge through social negotiation(Cox, Hall, Loopuyt, & Carr, 2002; D. Jonassen, 1994)

In this section I have highlighted some of the notions related to the practice of collaborative learning. In the next section I will look at issues relating to the study of collaborative learning in OLDF.

THE MEANING OF RESEARCHING COLLABORATIVE LEARNING ONLINE DISCUSSION FORUMS – OR THE RESEARCH PROBLEM

Treleaven(2004) suggests that the collaborative learning expected to happen in OLDF should be looked at as a 'state' creating situations in which productive interactions between learners can be generated. This is a different concept of productivity or learning outcomes as perceived in traditional learning environments(Treleaven, 2004). This conceptualisation implies that there is a need for looking at the *interactions* between the learners to gain understanding of the 'state' surrounding and supporting the emergence of collaborative learning, alongside the investigation of the action and outcomes of individuals in a group (Dillenbourg, Baker, Blaye, & O'malley, 1996).

Researching for collaboration and constructivism in online discussion forums entails addressing issues of interactions going beyond the message- by -message concept utilised in Content Analysis to encompass a whole conversation. Defining the scope of a conversation in online discussion forums requires analysis tools that would illustrate and map the 'branching structure'(Thomas, 2002) of conversations within discussion threads.

Venturing beyond the single message unit indicates the supra individual nature of the inquiry, as it is no longer limited to the study of the behaviour of an individual, but is investigating indications of behaviour occurring between individuals. Mason(1992) argues that ascertaining the quality of the conversations requires investigating what is being said, using a method of analysis that would not be constrained by the specifics of course content(Mason, 1992). Furthermore, if evidence of research is to support practitioners, then the method of analysis would need to exceed the parameters of any specific course, context or content.

A study of the conversations in OLDF is accessible through the self transcribing feature embedded in their technology, recording every conversation and storing it. In the next section I take a closer look at this feature.

Unique Data Collecting Method – the Self Transcribing Conversations in Online Discussion Forums

Online discussion forums hold a unique feature that allows them to automatically record and archive discussions, producing self-transcribed, actual transcripts of each and every step in the processes occurring within them. As I have mentioned before, this self transcribing feature provides powerful data corpus for understanding learning conveyed through the recorded interactions(Kanuka & Anderson, 1998; Levin, Haesun, & Riel, 1990). Although various researchers (Blake & Rapanotti, 2001; Cox, Hall, Loopuyt, & Carr, 2002; Zaiane & Luo, 2001) have developed models and tools for facilitating the analysis of this unique data form, the use of these tools is still not widely exhibited. Jones (1999), in his extensive study of the range of theoretical and practical aspects associated with researching the Internet, concluded that most studies stop short of using the Internet for collecting data(S. Jones, 1999), resorting to the use of questionnaires, interviews, and logging data.

Online discussion forums as a- synchronous systems contain what Lueg and Fisher(2003) refer to as "persistent conversations", because of their ability to archive conversations. Persistent or archived conversations are visible for an extended time on computer servers, and can be viewed by people at different times. They enable people to join a "persistent conversation" at any point, presenting 'late comers' with historical messages, as well as on going conversations, making the progression of the conversation visible. Lueg and Fisher(2003) suggest that "Persistent conversations" create "a-synchronous online social information spaces"-places where users can engage in conversation, make their presence known through contributions, can share ideas, develop a growing dimension of 'place-ness', and gain a shared social knowledge(Lueg & Fisher, 2003p. 6). The 'place-ness' and shared social knowledge are notions articulated in definitions attempting to capture the concept of 'online communities'. Lueg and Fisher(2003),argue that the a- synchronous social spaces are a rich source for research because of the availability of the data.

REVIEW OF RESEARCH METHODS ATTEMPTING TO STUDY ONLINE INTERACTIONS

Exchange Structure Analysis (ESA) is primarily a method of dialogue analysis(Kneser, Pilkington, & Treasure-Jones, 2001) that enables the researcher to observe basic patterns in the nature of a conversation(Cox, Hall, Loopuyt, & Carr, 2002). ESA can be used to "identify some of the characteristics of Computer Mediated Communication (CMC) dialogue and its effectiveness for educational interaction", and allows the researcher to "investigate the inclusiveness of participation and the distribution of participant roles"(Kneser, Pilkington, & Treasure-Jones, 2001,p.65).

The ESA method has proved successful in identifying the key features of on-line chats and forums, and in comparing the two communication tools. ESA enabled the determination of the roles being played out and the manner in which these were affected by the orientation of the student and facilitators (Cox, Hall, Loopuyt, & Carr, 2002).

ESA is focused on the minimal unit of dialogue and has been used for looking at basic patterns in the nature of online conversations (Cox, Hall, Loopuyt, & Carr, 2002; Kneser, Pilkington, & Treasure-Jones, 2001) , a feature which may depict a dyadic interaction in great detail, providing important information. However, this minimalistic outlook may hinder the method from looking at the wider social contexts within which the dyad operate, influence, and are being influenced by.

Levin and others (1990)attempted to study interactions by developing an approach they titled 'inter-message Reference Analysis', in which messages were analysed by coders who determined whether a message was referring to a previous message. In this study, the researchers attempted to collect information about the interactions themselves, attributing less importance to their content. The study noted responses to messages and reference to other messages, investigating the identity of the responder, their motivations and role. The study refers to the referenced messages as indicating a 'human mesh', or a network. In their study Levin and others attributed 'influence' levels according to the number of references to a message- the more references, the more influential the message. Some of the ideas in this study indicate perceptions used in Social Network Analysis, which I shall investigate in detail later in this section. However, the researchers themselves admit that the coding system used to analyse the messages proved ambiguous in some cases(Levin, Haesun, & Riel, 1990; Wang, 2000).

ONLINE INTERACTIONS AND LEARNING

Henri (1992)makes a significant contribution to understanding the relationship between interaction and learning by proposing an analytical framework for assessing the learning process through the facilitation of interaction in a collaborative computer conferencing environment. She proposes a system of content analysis that involves breaking messages down into units of meaning and classifying these units according to their content. The model consists of five dimensions of the learning process: participation, interaction, social, cognitive and the meta-cognitive. This framework has informed studies of collaborative learning providing the field with a potential structure for coding CMC messages to study the nature and quality of the discourse.

However, a later study using Henri's model found that Henri's definition of the concept of interaction was unsuited for the interactions that occur in a computer conferencing environment(Gunawardena, Lowe, & Amderson, 1997). Gunawrdena and her research associates proceeded to define interaction within the CMC environment and develop a framework of interaction analysis that would be more appropriate for analysing the debate transcript(Gunawardena, Lowe, & Amderson, 1997). The authors suggested that the metaphor of a patchwork quilt describes the process of shared construction of knowledge that occurs in a constructivist learning environment. They referred to the process by which the contributions are fitted together as 'interaction', and the pattern that emerges at the end, revealing the accumulated interactions, is the newly created knowledge or meaning. They defined interaction as the essential process of putting together the pieces in the collaborative creation of knowledge. Their development of an interaction analysis model to examine the negotiation of meaning that occurred in the online conference is based on social constructivist theory (Gunawardena, Lowe, & Amderson, 1997; Gunawardena & Stock McIsaac, 2004). The efficacy of the Gunawardena et. al.(1997) interaction analysis model was tested in other studies, such as the one of Kanuka and Anderson (1998) who used the model for analysing a professional development forum.

THE PROBLEM WITH RESEARCHING COLLABORATIVE LEARNING

For many years, theories of collaborative learning tended to focus on the individuals and the ways in which they function in a group. In this type of theory, a dyad of learners is viewed as comprising two relatively independent cognitive systems which exchange messages. A collaborative view of a dyad would consider it a single cognitive system with its own properties, portraying a supra-individual entity(Dillenbourg, Baker, Blaye, & O'malley, 1996). The individual approach views the individual as the unit of analysis. Research in this case would focus on how one cognitive system is transformed by messages received from another. The collaborative approach would view the group as its unit of analysis, and the research in this case would focus on understanding the ways in which the cognitive systems merge to produce a shared, supra individual understanding(Dillenbourg, Baker, Blaye, & O'malley, 1996). The whole notion of this shared understanding or social construction of knowledge raises the question of whether knowledge building is an individual or a group activity. Dillenbourg argues that most of the research done in the field of collaborative learning is actually concentrating on individual cognitive processes (Chan, Lam I. C.K., & van Aalst, 2003; Dillenbourg, 1999).

Dillenbourg(1999) summarises the different approaches to collaborative learning as: "a situation in which particular forms of interaction (i.e. affecting cognitive processes, and fostering negotiability) among people are expected to occur, and that these would trigger learning mechanisms" (ibid p.5). However, the author states that there is no guarantee that the expected interactions will actually occur, hence there is a general concern to develop ways of increasing probability of the certain types of interactions to occur. This concern inspired a large body of empirical research on collaborative learning, however, Dillenbourg(1999) found that beyond a few main results research has been unable to produce any conclusive solutions. Collaborative learning is still considered difficult to observe and ascertain its occurrence, and effectiveness, as well as identify ways of encouraging it, or studying hindering aspects (Roberts, 2004).

FROM INDIVIDUALS CONVERSING TO NETWORKS AND COMMUNITIES

Much of the research done on virtual communities is in fact analysing various discussion media. Research of online discussion forums encompasses social, cultural, and educational uses of discussion forum, gradually moving the focus of study from the technological aspects to the social potential and the social changes induced by the new social capabilities This shift in the focus of research attracted researchers from disciplines other than computer sciences and information technology, to include social scientists, who began treating online discussions as social entities, social places, and communities, in which interactions and collaborative actions occur. The social scientists introduced social sciences methodologies to the research of online environments, one of which is Social Network Analysis (SNA).

Social Network Analysis(SNA) is a fundamental intellectual tool for the study of social structures, suggesting that the key to understanding structural analysis is recognising that social structures can be represented as 'networks' –as sets of nodes and sets of ties depicting their interconnections(Wellman & Berkowitz, 1988).

Studies using Social Network Analysis (SNA), investigated issues of knowledge construction and sharing , (Aviv, Erlich, Ravid, & Geva, 2003; Cross, Parker, & Borgatti, 2002), and the creation of Learning Communities(Haythornthwaite, 2002). The introduction of SNA to the online learning research arena indicated a significant shift of this research corpus from the individualism common in social science towards a structural analysis, facilitating the identification and investigation of patterns, and their organisation as systems(Scott, 2000). SNA suggested redefinition of units of analysis, focusing on relationships rather than individuals and the development of new analytic methods, based on 'graph theory', used to describe the pattern of connections among points and mathematical calculations(Garton, Haythornthwaite, & Wellman, 1999; Scott, 2000). These mathematical ideas made possible a crucial breakthrough in the theory of group dynamics. This breakthrough consisted of moving from the concept of *cognitive* balance in individual minds to that of *interpersonal* balance in groups, opening the way for research of collaborative- interpersonal and social constructivism to investigate whole systems rather than groups or sums of individuals(Scott, 2000). The mathematical foundation of graph theory incorporated into SNA provided a much needed empirical stature to the collaborative learning research arena(Romiszowski & Mason, 2004; Warschauer, 1997).

In an attempt to gain better understanding of online conversations, Sack(2000), developed a mapping interface that enables visual representation of online conversations. Applying Social Network Analysis principles, the 'conversation map' interface converts the data of online discussion forums into social and thematic networks. The maps illustrate participants in the discussion as 'nodes' or 'actors' in the network, linked together in a 'tie' by a reciprocating quotation or reference to other actor's message. Sack's(2000) conversation map interface enables following the discussion through two different maps:

- A social network, representing ties between participations, showing who responded to whom. The ties are based on lexical cohesion, collating words appearing in a group of messages to produce a category of, for example, words associated with music.
- A semantic network, showing emerging metaphors or definitions of ideas and their evolvement through the discussion, permeating the vocabulary of the participants, and homogenising the manner in which they are used by the participants in the group.

'Figure 2-2' is an example of Sack's maps showing the two networks on each side of the screen and the themes discussed listed in the middle column between the maps.

Figure 2-2 Sack's conversation map version 0.01

Sack's 'conversation map' approach is a seminal breakthrough in the arena of the discussion forums research, as it facilitates detailed information into the occurrences in discussion forums. However, the notions underpinning the analysis framework of both the lexical and the semantic networks may jeopardise the objectivity and generalisability of the conversation map, as these are prone to subjective interpretation of the coding processes applied by the researchers.

INFORMATION EXTRACTION AND MEANING MAKING IN ONLINE DISCUSSION FORUMS

Trailing meaning making and knowledge advancement processes in online discussion forums can be perceived as extracting meaning making information from a vast data corpus (Chibelushi, Sharp, & Salter, 2004). The data gathered in online discussion forums is comprised of the self- transcribing conversations recoded by the technological platforms running online discussion forums. Extracting meaning making information from this type of data presents a unique analytic challenge, because individual messages in online discussion forums are incomplete entities, and messages are dependent on each other to form a context. Individual messages in online discussion forums carry a limited amount of information(Murakami, Nagao, & Takeda, 2001). The uniqueness of the situation requires an analysis framework that would enable trailing meaning making and knowledge advancement processes in a way that would address the fragmented environment where messages are interdependent.

COLLABORATIVE LEARNING - LESSONS LEARNED

Researching online collaborative learning is proving to be a complex task. The Fifth International Conference on Computer Support for Collaborative Learning (2002), attempted to address and articulate a new paradigm for 'a distinctive form of learning research'. Surprisingly, perhaps, a browse through the conference proceedings soon revealed that only a small minority of more than 50 long papers focused on the issues and practicalities of researching learning in networked environments(Lally & de Laat, 2002). Although this is a disappointing result, it is at the same time understandable. The challenges posed by this field of research are attractive, but at the same time formidable(Lally & de Laat, 2002). The mediated, self-transcribing learning environment supporting online discussion forums and communities can create the comforting feeling, for unsuspecting researchers interested in learning processes, suggesting that the transcripts of discussions taking place in these online environments contain easily accessible and significant evidence of learning among the participants. There is no need for any manual transcription as these are already available, and the computerised organisation of the conversations into discussion threads illustrate quite clearly who said what, and when. This comfortable setting suggests that all that is needed for gaining understanding of learning processes in these environments is to content analyse the written messages. This is often the first, (and sometimes the only) analytic solution proposed by researchers. However, this approach poses a range of problems and limitations as suggested previously. Content analysis is hard to administer, particularly in large data sets, moreover, it is time consuming. Notions of coding and categorising are complex issues in themselves, but they also raise generalisability and objectivity issues. Furthermore, content analysis focuses on individual messages rather than systems of messages comprising conversations(Thomsen, Straubhaar, & Bolyard, 1998).

The emerging reality is that the nature of learning interactions among participants in advanced learning communities is very complex and multi-dimensional, and hence is not researchable using any single research method(Lally & de Laat, 2002). In (de Laat, 2002) "Network and content analysis in an online community discourse", the author applies a combined approach using social network analysis and content analysis for studying interaction patterns among the members of a community of practice, and the way they share and construct knowledge together.

SOME EMERGING CONCEPTS

The growing interest in OLDF and their potential for facilitating and supporting quality collaborative learning and social construction of knowledge has generated a growing body of research attempting to study these assumptions. However, until recently it was said to lack a unifying and established theoretical framework, agreed objects of study, methodological consensus, or agreement about the concept of collaboration, or unit of analysis(Lipponen, 2002).Furthermore, a substantial portion of the research was comprised of practice based reports, hence deemed anecdotal rather than empirical(Romiszowski & Mason, 2004; Warschauer, 1997). The available research data that would confirm the claims and assumptions of the theorists and educationalists is scarce and inconclusive. Furthermore, the theoretical position seems to support online learning mainly because it offers tools for collaboration with no clear evidence of the contribution of the tools to the actual processes (Romiszowski & Mason, 2004).

Recently the 'International Conference of the Learning Sciences (ICLS 2004)', has dedicated a special issue to *"Community-Based Learning: Explorations into Theoretical Groundings, Empirical Findings and Computer Support"* where empirical findings were presented(Klamma, Rohde, & Stahl, 2005). In this special issue the authors have tried to address methodological issues and produce a theoretical framework for researching online collaborative learning. The studies presented in this special issue position the investigation of collaborative learning well within the theoretical realm of the socio-cultural and constructivist learning theories, perceiving learning as a "knowledge creation process"(Klamma & Spaniol, 2005). They also investigated the implication of the technological environment supporting the collaborative learning to enhance our understanding of technologically mediated collective learning processes, referred to in the literature as CSCL (Computer Supported Collaborative Learning). The studies addressed the notion of 'Community' as a mediated learning environment, arguing for a methodological focus on small groups within communities, as the site where knowledge building can most likely take place in communities. Stahl(2005) refers to small groups as the "engines of knowledge building," creating the basis for both individual internalization and collective externalization of knowledge in cultural artefacts and procedures of social communities. Stahl investigates the spectrum between individualistic and social concepts of learning in communities, arguing for an analytical perspective focused on the intermediate level of small work groups within larger communities(Stahl, 2005). These recent studies begin to outline a theoretical field within which learning occurs in mediated; in this case, Internet based groups. By addressing issues of mediated learning in social environments these studies set the scene for critical academic debates around notions of learning in mediated social environments.

Stahl touches on one of the key issues surrounding learning in social environments, the tension between the individual and the social. Stahl's solution is an intermediate stage of focusing on small groups within the larger community. Later in this chapter, I will address this issue arguing that we need to go further, than the individual versus social model, or in other words explore beyond what is known in the social science literature as the '*Structure Agency Debate*' (Giddens, 1984).

Herring (2004), argues that over the past fifteen years, social scientists, and educators have been trying to understand the nature of Computer-Mediated Communication and the ways in which society can optimise its use. Investigation of these communication environments can be supported by the fact that the activities in online forums leave a textual trace, making the interactions more accessible to scrutiny and reflection than is the case in ephemeral spoken communication, and enabling researchers to employ empirical, micro-level methods to shed light on macro-level phenomena. Despite this potential, much research on online behaviour is anecdotal and speculative, rather than empirically grounded. Moreover, the research often suffers from a premature impulse to label online discussion in broad terms, categorising all groups of people interacting online as "communities" (Herring, 2004).http://ella.slis.indiana.edu/%7Eherring/cmda.html - _edn1

In view of the research one can say that there is a need for a supra individual approach to the study of OLD as collaborative social constructivist learning environments, and to achieve this notion there is a need for clarifying the unit of analysis suitable for the purpose of exploring learning in OLDF .

SUMMARY

The review of the research has enabled me to identify three key issues needed for the investigation of collaborative and constructivist learning environments:

- The need to identify the unit of analysis in collaborative and socio-constructivist learning environments, where meaning making is dependent on interrelated messages (Murakami, Nagao, & Takeda, 2001).
- The need to address and expand the research beyond the individual versus the social
- The need to harness the self-transcribing conversations for facilitating empirical study of the micro for understanding the macro

The first two items are interrelated as they both refer to the need to go beyond the individual, and I will address these in the next part of this chapter. I will address the third issue identified in the methodology chapter of this study.

Social scientists refer to groups as structures moulding and constraining the activities of individuals within them. This perception focuses research of activities in groups either on the individual – the *agency*, or the group- the *structure*. The bulk of the research attempting to investigate collaborative learning investigates the actions and artefacts produced by individuals, attributing the nature, level, or the quality of the actions and artefacts, either to the personal attributes of members in the group or as resulting from the context and constraints set by the structures surrounding, or within which the activity took place(Dillenbourg, 1999; Dillenbourg, Baker, Blaye, & O'malley, 1996). Stahl (2005), in his study of group learning refers to the dichotomy found in knowledge building theories focusing on two extreme scales: the individual as the acquirer of knowledge, and the community in which the participation takes place(Stahl, 2005).

The social nature of e- learning invoked questions relating to the role of the individual versus the role of the group, and the blurring of boundaries introduced by the notion of knowledge building interactions challenging the traditional divisions between the inside/outside boundary of the individual(Y. Rogers, 2004). In studying people's actions, in this case, learning through an online discussion forum, one is faced with the question of 'what is at play'- the given environment, shaped by the technology, the participants' personal attributes and their affiliation to certain social groups, i.e. gender, professional status and the like, or, is it a reality constructed by its participants, and if so what is contributing to its construction. In social theory questions similar to these are discussed in the 'agency-structure debate'[4], which is primarily concerned with the question of to what extent are people active in the

---

[4]   The agency-structure perspective is sometimes considered as the European alternative to the micro-macro perspective in America; however, the two are not identical. Ritzer(2004), attributes the difference between the two to the behaviourist tendencies detectable in the micro-macro behaviourism, whereas the agency-structure theory places an emphasis on conscious creative action(Ritzer & Goodman, 2004).

shaping of their social environment or are they acted upon by the *'social structures'* surrounding them.

In sociology, the term *Social Structure* appears as early as the writings of the eminent sociologist Durkheim(Durkheim, 1938). As a term, social structure is sometimes widely used as a blanket term or synonymous for 'system', 'organisation', 'complex', 'pattern', 'type (of groups)', and indeed does not fall short of 'society as a whole'(Nadel, 1957). However, in anthropology, the term 'social structure' was approached from a more precise definition, mostly because of the work of Radcliffe-Brown(Nadel, 1957). Radcliffe- Brown explains that 'in social structure the ultimate components are individual human beings, thought of as actors in the social life, that is, as *persons,* and structures consists of the 'arrangement of persons in relation to each other (Radcliffe-Brown, 1965(1952),p.198). Furthermore Radcliffe-Brown argues that a social structure is made of 'human beings', which are considered not as organisms but as occupying positions in social structure (Radcliffe-Brown, 1965(1952)). The 6th edition of "Notes and Queries on Anthropology" defines social structures as the 'whole network of social relations in which are involved the members of a given community at a particular time'(Royal Anthropological Institute of Great Britain and Ireland, 1951,p.63). Nadel(1957) defines 'structure' as an abstraction of *relational* features from the totality of the perceived data, ignoring all that is not 'order' or 'arrangement', in other words, separating structure from content. Nadel defines the positions relative to one another of the component parts. Adopting this abstract approach one can describe the arrangement of a musical fugue or sonata without making any musical sounds. This is a significant feature as it implies that structures can be transposed irrespective of the concrete data manifesting it. It can be alternatively said that 'the parts composing any structure can vary widely in their concrete character without changing the identity of the structure'(Nadel, 1957). However, Nadel recognises the problematic implications that could arise from such an open ended definition, hence the author proposes a revised definition: "structure indicates an ordered arrangement of parts, which can be treated as *transposable,* being relatively invariant, while the parts themselves are variable(Nadel, 1957pp.7-8).

An observation of a social environment may reveal certain structures, such as. A is related to B in a mother son relation. This illustration describes the observed situation in an abstract form. It is important to make the distinction between structure as actually existing concrete reality, to be directly observed, and structural form describing a dynamic continuity like that of the organic structure of a living body. An organic structure is constantly renewed, and similarly social life constantly renews the social structure. Thus, the actual relations of persons and groups change from time to time as new members come into a community and others leave. However, although the actual structure changes, the general structural form may remain relatively constant over a longer or shorter period. Changes to a community's membership occur but not much changes in the kinds of relations that can be observed(Radcliffe-Brown, 1940[2002]). Social structures are not only persistent social groups such as nations, but all social relations of person to person(Radcliffe-Brown, 1940[2002])

This brief discussion about social structure asserts a key notion, which spawns a number of important realisations. Social structure as defined here is an entity that exceeds the mere aggregation of people, to describe an entity comprised of relations linking roles and positions rather than particular individuals. This key realisation opens the way for social structures to be conceptualised in the following ways:

1. They are transposable maintaining their structure in spite of changes in their components and the specific contexts in which they operate.

2. The perception of roles rather than particular individuals allows for the abstraction of social structures, hence it becomes a *'form'* rather than a specific reality observed enabling the observation of dynamic continuity allowing the form to remain across time and changes it brings.

3. Human beings are the occupants and at the same time creators of the structure, as they are perceived as role and position figures, which imply that the structure is reliant on their role, however, at the same time implying that since the roles are held by humans then they have the potential to alter the structure.

The notion of participants contributing to the creation of structure and at the same time affected by the existence of the structure is an idea that has been debated and contested at length in e social theory. In the next section I will touch on some of the historical roots of this debate

THE MEANING OF COLLECTIVES, AND THE INDIVIDUAL VERSUS SOCIAL

Throughout his writings Durkheim(Durkheim, 1938, 1952), suggest that social phenomena are not reducible to the level of the individual or individual psychology. Durkheim opposed the idea that had long influenced thinkers in which individuals' wills are thought to contribute to social processes and that society "is no more, nor less than what man makes of it"(Hatch, 1973,p.166). Inherent in this position is a reaction against the role of human agency in shaping society(MacLeod, 2002).

Durkheim argues against the role of the individual influencing or shaping the collective ideas of a group - "[t]he individual can no more create collective beliefs and practices than he can a live oak tree"(Hatch, 1973.p.168). Collective social processes are distinct from the individual(MacLeod, 2002). Durkheim's positioning of a sharp distinction between collective representations and the individual negates the possibility of the individual's will as a useful, functional element of social phenomena, suggesting that this confusion occurs because collective representations are voiced by individual members of the group thus giving expression to the collective beliefs (MacLeod, 2002). In his doctrine Durkheim focuses on the social structural determinants of society(Coser, 1977). Durkheim argues that social phenomena are 'social facts', and can be defined as "every way of acting, fixed or not, capable of exercising on the individual an external constraint"(Durkheim, 1938,p.13). However, Durkheim's later writing problematises the notion of constraint, perceiving social facts as guides and controls of conduct only to the extent that they become internalised in the consciousness of individuals, while continuing to exist independently of individuals. In this definition, constraint is no longer a simple imposition of outside controls on individuals, but rather a moral obligation to obey a rule. In this sense, society becomes "something beyond us and something in ourselves"(Durkheim, 1953,p.55)

Durkheim attempts to study social facts not only as phenomena "out there" in the world of objects, but as facts that the actor and the social scientist come to know"(Parsons, 1968a). Durkheim argues that a social phenomena, arises when interacting individuals constitute a reality that can no longer be accounted for in terms of the properties of individual actors(Coser, 1977). In this statement Durkheim touches on the essence of the notion of 'reality', as something constructed by individuals, but then existing independently of them, suggesting that there is a reality 'out there' however, that it is the creation of interacting members, which surpasses their existence as individuals. Indeed Durkheim argues that a social group cannot be perceived solely as an aggregation of individuals, but rather as a structural whole(Coser, 1977). Durkhiem focused on the characteristics of groups and structures rather than on individuals and their attributes. Durkheim's doctrine has averted the focus of social study from the individual traits, to the characteristics of a group or a structure. It also enabled to focus on the rates of occurrence of a specific phenomena rather than on an incidence, which in turn enabled Durkheim to engage in comparative analysis of various structures(Coser, 1977). The shift in the focus of vision proposed by Durkheim opened a new way of looking at social phenomena, focusing on structure rather than the individual.

Weber perceived sociology as a comprehensive science of social action(Coser, 1977). His initial theoretical focus is on the subjective meaning that humans attach to their actions and interactions within specific social contexts. Weber created a topology that distinguishes between four major types of social action, which are intended to be a comprehensive list of the types of meaning and underpinning motivations attributed by people to their conduct across socio-cultural systems:

1. Zweckrational- roughly translated "Technical thinking" defines action in which the means to attain a particular goal are rationally chosen. (Elwell, 1999).

2. Wertrational- or value-oriented rationality is characterized by striving for a goal which in itself may not be rational, but which is pursued through rational means. The values come from within an ethical, religious, philosophical or even holistic context--they are not rationally "chosen."(Elwell, 1999)

3. Affective action- is based on the emotional state of the person rather than in the rational weighing of means and ends(Coser, 1977).
4. Traditional action - action is guided by custom or habit. People engage in this type of action often unthinkingly, because it is simply "always done." (Elwell, 1999)

As an advocate of multiple causation of human behaviour, Weber was well aware that most behaviour is caused by a mix of these motivations(Elwell, 1996).

Adams and Sydie(2001) argue that while Weber also wrote about structural issues, he added some different element to sociological analysis. His primary focus was considered to be the social actor, his or her uniqueness as an individual, and interaction among social actors at the individual and small group level. In their book the authors argue that Weber developed an approach that attempted to understand and interpret social actions of the individual actor, arguing "that sociology must never lose sight of human agency" (Adams & Sydie, 2001,p.168).

The Durkheim versus Weber approaches have traditionally been perceived as the roots of what is referred to as the *structure* versus *agency* debate. However, this seemingly Cartesian divide has long been problematised and eventually blurred as I will show in the next section.

BLURRING THE BOUNDARIES OF STRUCTURE AND AGENCY

Micro –Macro Sociologies

'*Structure*' and '*Agency*' can be viewed as entities each conceived by a different social theory. Structure is typically attributed to macro-sociologies, whereas Agency is seen to belong under the micro- sociologies. Traditionally micro-sociology seems to avoid the study of large-scale social organizations, and tends to see the micro level as the essential reality of social life, whereas macro-sociology tends to search the broader scope of social life for what it values as significant issues, dismissing the study of day-to-day social activity as trivia(Giddens, 1984). This apparent divide between micro and macro is what Giddens conceptualises as the 'unhappy division of labour'(1984,p.139). Micro-sociology is usually perceived to be concerned with the activities of the "free agent" whereas macro-sociology is presumed to be concerned with the study of structural constraints which set limits to free activity(Giddens, 1984). This conceptual division of labour is the main reason for the perception of the divide between the two, and is being reinforced by the philosophical dualism. Functionalism and Marxism perceived social relations as predominantly determined by broader structural factors, whereas micro-sociology predominantly addressed by phenomenology and ethnomethodology, celebrated the 'free agent(Giddens, 1984).

In a less traditional view of the micro-macro distinction, micro is extended beyond the traditional model of the conscious creative actor regarded by many agency theorists, to include less conscious behaviour. Similarly, the term macro is referred not only to large-scale social structures but also to the cultures of collectivities[5]. Thus micro may or may not refer to 'agents' and macro may, or may not refer to 'structures'(Ritzer, 2000; Ritzer & Goodman, 2004). These perceptions of structure and agency are blurring the definitions of each of the two entities. This blurring provokes additional inquiries into the relevancy of the divide between structure and agency.

Giddens contests the notion that 'structure' is relevant only to macro-sociology, and asserts that activity in micro contexts has shown structural properties, as ethnomethodology has successfully sustained(Giddens, 1984).

Giddens, quoting Collins(1981) suggests that the step forward for social science is to reconstitute macro-sociology on micro foundations(Giddens, 1984).Collins suggests that structural situations are often simply sheer numbers of people in various kinds of micro-situations. Following this notion, social reality becomes 'micro-experience'; it is the numerical temporal and spatial aggregations of such experience,

---

[5]   Collectivity - When two individuals interact in the mutuality of orientation defined in terms of shared patterns of normative culture, known as values, and in so far as their behaviour is distinguishable from others by their participation and not others, they form a collectivity(Parsons, . Shils.E., Naegele, & Pitts, 1961) however, Simmel argues that a super-personal life or a collective action can only occur in a formation of three and above participants(Coser, 1977)(pp. 186-189). Simmel's concept is the more relevant one to this study as I will show in the findings and analysis chapter

which make up the macro-sociological level of analysis. In other words, Collins suggests that the 'structural' qualities of social systems are the results of conduct in micro situations; independent of what he defines as the macro variables such as number, time and space. Collins' concept suggests a micro-translation of 'structural phenomena'(Giddens, 1984).

STRUCTURATION APPROACH

Blurring and eventually converging the notions of structure and agency appear in the work of two prominent social theorists- Anthony Giddens, and Pierre Bourdieu, the former working in Britain and the latter in France. Both theorists are referred to as structurationists, aiming at finding ways of converging the notion of 'structure' and 'agency(Parker, 2000).'

Parker(2000) suggests that the term Structuration has been used in two related ways:

- The generation of structures
- The rejection of the dualism of subjective(agency) and objective(structure)

The two aspects are intertwined, as the conceptualisation of the Structuration approach of notions of 'structure' and 'agency', already entails the rejection of the dualism. Giddens embraces Collins' notions of systems being the result of micro situations, and proceeds to establish his own way of converging structure and agency in his 'Structuration Theory'(Giddens, 1984; Ritzer & Goodman, 2004). Giddens' main claim for his theory is that it draws together the two principal strands of social thinking. The structuralist tradition emphasises the structure, and perceives it to be a constraint, whereas the phenomenological and hermeneutic traditions focus primarily on the human agent, perceiving it as a 'free agent'. Structuration theory attempts to recast structure and agency as a mutually dependent duality(Rose, 1999).

Similar ideas are expressed by Pierre Bourdieu(1985), in his theory of 'Generative, or Constructivist structuralism' in which he attempts to describe, analyse and acknowledge the genesis of the person, and of social structures and groups. In his 'Habitus and Field' approach, Bourdieu proposes a dialectical analysis of practical life, and attempts to offer the potential to exhibit the interplay between personal practice,(agency) and the external world of social practice(structure) (Bourdieu, 1980/1990; Harker, Mahar, & Wilkes, 1990)

The Generation of Structures- Giddens' Style

Giddens argues that Structuration "refers abstractly to the dynamic process whereby structures come into being"(Giddens, 1976,p.121). This concept depicts structuration of structures as '*process*', and as such, suggests that it should entail a series of events with temporal duration, among which would be found systematic relations with the cumulative effects which could explain the existence of the structure in question(Parker, 2000). Establishing the origins of structures involves investigating their structuration, irrespective of the kinds of structures or the kind of structuring processes being investigated. The definition of 'structure' in this respect incorporates anything which can be conceptualised as composed of relations between parts(Parker, 2000).Giddens' perception suggests that it is the practices of actors that create the structures in which they exist, and furthermore, the practices of the actors forge the construct of the structure. Structural properties of social systems should not be perceived as 'social products' as this would imply that pre-constituted actors somehow come together to create them. In reproducing structural properties, agents also reproduce the conditions that make such action possible(Giddens, 1984). Structure is not external to individuals, it is more internal than exterior to their activities in a Durkheimian sense(Giddens, 1984,p 25).

Giddens argues that the basic domain of study of the social sciences is neither in the experiences of individual actors, nor in the existence of any form of social structures, but in the social practices ordered along space and time. Human social activities are not brought into being by social actors but are continually recreated by them through the very means they use for expressing themselves as actors. In and through their activities agents (actors) reproduce the conditions(structures) that make their activities possible(Giddens, 1984). This two-way action is what Giddens refers to as the 'duality of structure', which entails the core of his 'Structuration Theory'. According to the duality of structure, the constitution of agents and structures are not two independently given sets of phenomena-a dualism, but represent a duality, in which the structural properties of social systems are both **medium and outcome** of the practices they recursively organise. 'Structuration Theory' claims that the moment of production of action is also one of reproduction in the contexts of the day-to-day enactment of social life(Giddens, 1984).

While Giddens acknowledges that structure can be constraining to actors, he argues that the importance of these constraints have been over exaggerated by sociologists. Giddens argues that structures can enable actors to do things that they would not otherwise have been able to do, and that a social system is a set of reproduced social practices and relations between actors. The concept of structuration accentuates the interdependence of structure and agency, suggesting that there can be no agency without structures that shape motives into practices, on the one hand, but on the other hand, there can be no structures independent of the routine practices that create them (Ritzer & Goodman, 2004).

Giddens' Structuration Theory and Online Collaborative Learning

Giddens argues that structure and agency cannot be conceived as divorced from one another(Ritzer, 2000). His 'Structuration Theory' is one of the best- known efforts to integrate agency and structure(Ritzer & Goodman, 2004). Structuration means studying the ways in which social systems are produced and reproduced in social interaction (Giddens, 1984). Collaborative learning, viewed through the lens of Structuration theory, opens new ways of bridging the extremities mentioned by Stahl(2005), and going beyond the division of labour between the individual acquiring the knowledge and the structure, the context, or the community in which this acquisition takes place, as the actions of individuals within the context are at the same time acquiring and structuring the context around them.

Bourdieu and the Generation of Structures

Bourdieu in his 'Constructivist structuralism' attempts to describe, analyse and consider the genesis of the person, and of social structures and groups(Harker, Mahar, & Wilkes, 1990). According to Bourdieu(Bourdieu & Wacquant, 1992), social structure is a system of *'relations'* and differences rather than a set of attributes or *'essences'*. Subjects, whether they be individuals or institutes, derive their social meaning from their positions with respect to one another in a social field and not from their intrinsic characteristics(De Nooy, 2003). The *relational* thinking so central to Bourdieu's theory(Bourdieu & Wacquant, 1992; De Nooy, 2003), is not a new idea, as it appears in the broad structuralist tradition tracing back to Durkheim and Marx(Bourdieu & Wacquant, 1992), however, what is unique to Bourdieu is relentless deployment of this concept as is evident in both his key concepts *'habitus'* and *'field'*. A *'field'* consists of a set of objective, historical relations between positions anchored in certain forums of power (or capital)(Bourdieu & Wacquant, 1992), it is a network of social relations among the objective positions within it. It is not a set of interactions or inter-subjective ties among individuals(Ritzer & Goodman, 2004). A *'habitus'* consists of a set of historical relations 'deposited' within individual bodies in the form of mental and corporeal schemata of perception, and action(Bourdieu & Wacquant, 1992).Bourdieu argues that the *habitus* both produces and is produced by the social world. People internalize external structures, and they externalize things they have internalized through *practices*(Ritzer & Goodman, 2004). It is *practice* which relates all the elements referred to by the traditional dichotomies: individual, society; material, ideal, mind, body, subject, object, being and becoming. The reference to the concept of *'becoming'* is crucial because it focuses attention on practice as relating to moments of time and levels of history. Through *'practice'*, we 'become', through constant movement, as practice unfolds through time.

These notions offer a new perspective for the study of collaborative learning and the emergence of communities of learners, as it enables us to depict learning as something learners *'become'* through constant movement. In the context of online discussions, this notion could be detected through the conveyance of an idea from one participant to another or the movement of a participant from one relation to another, creating a trail of interactions, and in so doing constructing the structure and facilitating the further conveyance of ideas and the ongoing of interactions and further movement. Hence, *'becoming'* develops into a *'perpetuum mobile'* of movement and evolvement of the individual, the interactions, and consequently the structure.

The task of sociology according to Bourdieu is "to uncover the most profoundly buried structures of the various social worlds which constitute the social universe as well as mechanisms which tend to ensure their reproduction or their transformation"(Bourdieu, 1989,p.7. and; Bourdieu & Wacquant, 1992).

Central to Bourdieu's work is the notion of relationalism, viewing social structure as a system of relations and differences rather than a set of attributes or 'essences'. (De Nooy, 2003), a notion which sits comfortably with the relational approach mentioned by Giddens viewing 'structure' as comprised of relations between parts(Parker, 2000).

Bourdieu's approach to 'relations' aligns with structuralist analysis notions of viewing 'relations' as networks of social positions rather than of interactions among individuals, emphasising the role and positioning of the individual within networks as the defining factor in the formation of the network or the structure rather than the attributes of the individual moulding the structure.

STRUCTURAL ANALYSIS

Structural analysts, like Bourdieu(Bourdieu & Wacquant, 1992) believe that the main business of social scientists is to study social structure and its consequences. They study social structures directly and concretely, by analysing the ordered arrangements of relations that are dependent on exchange among members of social systems. Structural analysts map these structures and describe their patterns, using tools derived from mathematical 'graph theory', and seek to uncover the effects of these patterns on the behaviour of the individual members of these structures. Structural analysts argue that social categories such as class and gender and bounded groups are best discovered and analysed by examining relations between social actors, to reveal their roles as they unfold in the interactions. Rather than beginning with *an* a priori classification of the observed world, they begin with a set of relations, from which they derive maps and typologies of social structures, thus drawing inferences from wholes to parts, from structures and relations to categories and from behaviours to attitudes (Wellman & Berkowitz, 1988). This kind of approach applies R*elational Data*. Social sciences have developed distinct types of data to each of which distinct methods of analysis are appropriate. The principal types of data are ***Attribute Data*** – which relates to the attitudes, opinions and behaviour of agents, as long as these are regarded as the properties, qualities or characteristics that belong to them as individuals or groups. The items collected through various data collecting methods are often regarded as the attributes of particular individuals that can be quantified and analysed. Attribute data uses *variable analysis*, where attributes are measured as values of particular variables, such as income, age, education etc.(Scott, 2000,p.2). *Relational Data* on the other hand, are the contacts, ties and connections, the group attachments and meetings, which relate one agent to another and so cannot be reduced to the properties of the individual agents themselves. Relations are not the properties of agents, but of systems of agents. These relations connect pairs of agents into larger relational systems. The methods appropriate to relational data are those of *network analysis*, where relations are treated as expressing the linkages running between agents. While it is possible to undertake quantitative and statistical counts of relations, network analysis consists of a body of qualitative measures of network structure(Scott, 2000,p.3).

In the 1950s structural researchers began constructing formal and mathematical techniques to be combined with Radcliff-Brown's concept of 'social structure', and began using networks as a tool for mapping patterns of ties among individuals. These researchers investigated individuals and groups beyond the boundaries of the kinds of organised subgroups that sociologists and anthropologists had traditionally identified within populations, such as classes, families, tribes, etc. These studies sometimes referred to as 'structural analysis studies' were descriptive and did not use the mathematical tools developed by the other group of researchers. In the early to mid 1960s, the two research traditions – the formal and analytic and the descriptive and phenomenological, came together. The result was the formulation of what Wellman refers to as 'social network concept' ,and the formation of its methodology, Social Network Analysis(Scott, 2000). Network analysis is a means toward a structural analysis which aims to explain phenomena in terms of the network's form(Degenne & Forse, 1999). The idea driving social networks is that social structure is best understood in terms of a dynamic interplay between the relations between and among persons, or institutions on the one hand, and the positions and roles they occupy within a social system on the other(Berkowitz, 1982).

Social Network Analysis (SNA) assumes there is no way of knowing in advance how groups or social positions come about, or how combinations of relations are formed. SNA attempts to identify behaviour patterns and the groups that correlate with those patterns. Then it sorts out the pertinent groups a posteriori and identifies the concrete constraints of structure on behaviour at the same time as it uncovers constraints on structure from group interactions. Structure is a network of relations, as well as a constraint. Networks operate as a constraint on the personal preferences, behaviour patterns, opinions and so on individuals(Degenne & Forse, 1999).

Early Durkheimian notions suggesting that structures exert all- powerful control over action have been contested even by Durkheim himself(Giddens, 1979), and indeed the strong determinism is incompatible with *structural analysis* for two reasons: First, it leads to an a priori identification of structures, which involves establishing an abstract causality between structures and individuals, where actual relations are disregarded. Second, it does not necessarily avoid the atomisation of individuals, which contradicts the relational principle. Network analysis argues that the function, and ability to exercise control, depends upon the structural position of a relation(Degenne & Forse, 1999).

Network analysis starts with the idea that relations do not arise at random and tries to explain why *birds of feather flock together*, strictly in terms of the network (Degenne & Forse, 1999). According to SNA principles, it is essential to know the complete form of the network of relations in order to understand its structural features. Structural differences may appear in form, or average distances between individuals. These differences may affect the permeation of new ideas. Structural position of individuals within a network may differ, which may have an affect on their

73

communication possibilities, control and accessibility to information or resources. On the one hand, structure has every chance of affecting exchanges on the other hand it is also the product of elementary interactions. Structural analysis considers this circularity essential since it constitutes the living framework of a structure which both determines and is determined by interaction(Degenne & Forse, 1999), a notion shared by both Giddens and Bourdieu.

To Summarise the Key Points about Structures

In summarising the key points I have observed through the review of the various approaches to structures, it appears that these imply the application of the following notions:

- Using neither positivist nor phenomenologist approaches, avoiding the 'what is' in favour of 'what could be', in other works, the possibilities.
- Using **no** a priori categories relating to the participants of the research
- Perceiving social structure as a 'form' or an 'abstract' of social reality, hence enabling the application of structural forms across situations, transposing structures irrespective of concrete data

SUMMARY OF PART THREE

Stahl (2003)argues that conceptualizing communities as complex systems, rather than the sum of isolated parts, calls attention to several important processes. The theoretical frameworks of Giddens and Bourdieu offered a way of reconciling the agency structure divide, and shift the focus of study of collaborative learning to the interactions between individuals, and the structures these interactions create. Giddens refers to this as the 'duality of structure(Giddens, 1984). This notion can be viewed as an alternative way for investigating collaboration, arguing that wherever collaboration exists, it acts as a living proof of the duality of structures as entities structured by the activities of individuals.

In this section, I have outlined theoretical concepts allowing the shift from individual versus structure, to viewing structures as constructs of interactions between individuals. In the following section, I will investigate methodological frameworks and tools enabling the investigation of such concepts.

Part Four- Approaches and Tools for Studying Online Networks: And the Collaborative Construction of Knowledge

Garfinkel(1967), the man behind ethnomethodology argues that actors take an active part in the definition of the situation. According to this approach people define their daily lives, and the institutions in which they live through their interactions. Ethnomethodology tries to understand how people see, describe, and jointly develop a definition of the situation (Coulon, 1995). Garfinkel's Documentary Method of Interpretation (DMI) contributes to the study of these definitions.

Benson and Hughes(1983), suggest that in response to classical sociology, Ethnomethodology advocates two major principles:

1. Human beings are not merely acted upon by social facts or social forces but are constantly shaping and creating their own social worlds in interaction with others
2. Special methods are required for the study and understanding of these uniquely human processes.

Furthermore, classical, Durkheimian sociology is in the business of explaining *social facts*, (social phenomena), the effort of ethnomethodology is directed towards the clarification of their creation. While the interests of most qualitative researchers is in wanting to know the world 'as practitioners see it', ethnomethodology prefers the 'how, by the use of which procedures and methods any particular 'world' is produced and perceived. The most common way to do ethnomethodological research is to observe naturally occurring situations as closely as possible, which sometimes involves recording and transcriptions of these(Have, 2004).

Ethnomethodology clearly broke away from traditional sociological modes of thinking. More than a theory, it is a research perspective, a new intellectual posture shifting from a sociology that strives to explain to a sociology that strives to comprehend,(Coulon, 1995). People's daily actions consist of acting, interacting and understanding the meaning of what they do. This simple phenomenon seems to be difficult for social theorists to understand(I. J. Cohen, 2000). Ethnomethodology looks at everyday activities as indications of members' methods of making those same activities visibly rational and reportable for all practical purposes(Garfinkel, 1967).

THE DOCUMENTARY METHOD OF INTERPRETATION

Garfinkel(1967), who borrowed from Mannheim[6] the notion of 'Documentary Method of Interpretation' (DMI), argues that the DMI is common to both commonsense and sociology, and refers to the way in which people join together past, present and future events in order to produce a coherent interpretation of their interactions with others. In particular, it can be used to assemble a body of knowledge of social structures -'decisions of meaning, facts, method, and causal texture' (78). Mannheim [sic] offered a description of the DMI as 'the search for "... an identical, homologous pattern underlying a vast variety of totally different realisations of meaning"... treating an actual appearance as "the document of," as "pointing to," as "standing on behalf of" a presupposed underlying pattern'7 (78). The process works in several ways, and the underlying document is both derived from and used to interpret new events. We all use

---

[6] Karl Manheim, "On the Interpretation of Weltanschauung" in Essays on the Sociology of Knowledge, pp.53-63

[7] Either in the mind or a required pattern like the clerk in the uncle's story

this method every day to interpret words and actions, and sociologists use it too (78). To reveal the work of the DMI Garfinkel devised an experiment 'designed to exaggerate the features of this method in use and to catch the work of "fact production" in-flight' (79). In the experiment, a group of ten undergraduate students were told that they would receive counselling through an intercom system. The students were asked to pose questions through the intercom and received a yes/ no answer. What the respondents in this experiment were not aware of is the fact that the responses given to them were predetermined and randomly placed, so they were not genuine responses to their questions. On hearing the response, subjects were asked to record their comments as they attempted to interpret it. They then recorded their overall impressions, and were subsequently interviewed. The subjects of the experiment made every effort to interpret these random answers in a way that made coherent sense to them, even when the answers were surprising. They were also extremely forgiving of what appeared to be contradictions in the answers, and seemed to find some genuine meaning in them(Garfinkel, 1967)

Wilson(1974),summarises the 'Documentary Method of Interpretation' as follows:

> Documentary interpretation consists of identifying an underlying pattern behind a series of appearances such that each appearance is seen as referring to, an expression of, or a 'document of' the underlying pattern. However, the underlying pattern itself is identified through its individual concrete appearances so that the appearances reflecting the pattern and the pattern itself mutually determine one another in the same way that the 'part' and the 'whole' mutually determine each other in Gestalt phenomena(p.68).

Individuals unveil social reality to each other, making it 'readable' by building up visible patterns. Using the DMI allows viewing the actions of research participants as the expressions of patterns and to perceive these patterns as descriptions or explanations of their actions. The actions are continuously interpreted in terms of context, context being in its turn understood through those actions (Coulon, 1995). This perception implies that in applying the DMI the analytic stance shifts from asking *what* social reality *is* in the perspective of the actors to asking *how* this reality is produced or accomplished in practice. Asking for the *how*, is asking for the *modus operandi*, for the *habitus*, which is basic to the practice in the sense of Pierre Bourdieu (Bohnsack, 2002).The *habitus* is the mental structure through which people deal with the social world. It can be thought of as a set of internalised schemes through which the world is perceived, understood, appreciated, and evaluated. A *habitus* is acquired as the result of the long-term occupation of a position in the social world. Depending on the position occupied, people will have a different *habitus*. The *habitus* operates as a structure, but people do not simply respond to it mechanically. When people change positions, their *habitus* is sometimes no longer appropriate. Bourdieu argues that the *habitus* both produces and is produced by the social world. People internalise external structures, and they externalise things they have internalised through practices. The *habitus* is constituted by the *field* in which it is created(Bourdieu & Wacquant, 1992). The concept of *field* provides the objective complementing notion to the *habitus*. The *field* rather than being a set of interactions or intersubjective ties among individuals, is a *network* of social relations among the objective positions within it(Bourdieu & Wacquant, 1992; Ritzer, 2002). This concept of 'relations' imply a conceptual similarity between Bourdieu's 'constructivist structuralism' and 'structural analysis', in their perception of roles and positions within a network. This concept is a liberating idea, as it directs analysts to look at linked social relations freeing them from thinking of social systems as collections of individuals(Berkowitz, 1988). The perception of relations as roles and positions is one of the key aspects of Social Network Analysis.

SOCIAL STRUCTURES, SOCIAL NETWORKS, ROLES, RELATIONS AND THEIR MEANING

Social Network Analysis (SNA), is neither a method nor a metaphor, but a fundamental intellectual tool for the study of social structures. Social Network Analysis (SNA) maps social structures, and describes their patterns using tools derived from mathematical *Graph Theory*. Graph theory illustrates social structures as 'networks' in which *nodes* (actors) are connected by sets of *ties* (relations) depicting their interconnections(Berkowitz, 1988)

Graph theory permits the visualisation of networks, providing analysts with images that call attention to structural properties of networks that might not be apparent otherwise(Freeman & White, 1993). The illumination of structural properties triggered ideas and mathematical mechanisms that allow researchers to measure the social actions and relationships constructing them (Wellman & Berkowitz, 1988). For example, Graph theory can illustrate a situation in which a certain actor (node) seems to take a central position in the network. SNA can pursue this central position and calculate the amount of influence the actor in question may have, and the role he or she may hold in relation to other actors in the network.

CENTRALITY AND ITS MEANINGS

One of the uses of graph theory in SNA is the identification of the 'most important actors', or the 'central' actors in a social network, or in other words, identify his or hers 'Centrality'. Centrality is a role an actor holds in the network. Calculating an actor's centrality will show his or her ability to convey information, or act as a gatekeeper, controlling the flow of information within the network.

Using the graphs enables visual representation of the network, depicting different patterns. These patterns, or structural properties as I have referred to them earlier in this chapter, imply different centrality levels of the actors in the network. For example, a *circle* graph indicates that all actors ('nodes') illustrated in the figure below, as points identified by 'n^{x}', are interchangeable, and hence are equally central. However, in a *star* graph, one actor outranks the others, and the others are interchangeable. In the *line* graph the nodes centrality decreases, as nodes are further away from the centre.

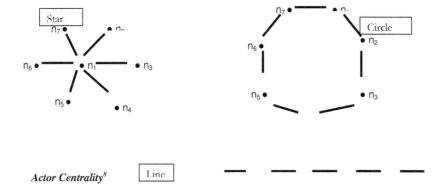

Actor Centrality[8]

The simplest definition of actor centrality is that central actors must be the most active in the sense that they have the most ties to other actors in the network or graph. This can simply be done by looking at the pattern of the graph i.e. circle versus star. The first actor in the star is clearly the most active and will have the *maximal centrality index*. In the circle graph all actors will have the same centrality index(Wasserman & Faust, 1994).Prominent actors are those that are extensively involved in relationships with other actors. This involvement makes them more visible to the others. Within the framework of SNA analysts are not concerned with whether this prominence is due to the receiving (recipient) or the transmission (source) of many ties, what is important is that the actor is simply involved. This focus on involvement leads to consider non-directional ties where there is no distinction between receiving and sending. For non-directional relation, Wasserman and Faust(1994) define a central actor as one involved in many ties.

Group Centrality

Group level is an index of how different the levels of centrality of actors in the group are. It records the extent of which a single actor has high centrality and the others low centrality. It can be viewed as a measure of inequality of individuals. For example,

---

[8]   In the context of this study, I shall consider Actor centrality as the EC centrality – the EC being the unit of analysis of this study, as I will show in the methodology chapter.

the 'star' graph is maximally central, since its one central actor n^1 has direct contact with all others who are not in contact with each other(Wasserman & Faust, 1994)..

Betweenness Centrality

Interactions between two non- adjacent actors might depend on the other actors in the set of actors, especially the actors who lie in the path between the two. These 'other' actors may have some control over the interactions between the two non adjacent actors. If the *geodesic* (the shortest path) has to go through two other actors then we could say that the two actors contained in the geodesic might have control over the interaction. One could say that the 'actors in the middle' have more 'interpersonal influence' on others. An actor is central if it lies between other actors on their geodesics, implying that to have a large 'betweenness' centrality the actor must be between many of the actors via their geodesics(Wasserman & Faust, 1994).

A central actor occupies a "between" position in the geodesics connecting many pairs of other actors in the network. As a cut-point in the shortest path connecting two other nodes, a between actor could control the flow of information or exchange of resources, perhaps charging a fee or brokerage commission for transaction services rendered. If more than one geodesic links a pair of actors, each of these shortest paths has an equal probability of being used.

Actor betweenness centrality for actor i is the sum of the probabilities, for all pairs of actors j and k, that actor i is involved in the pair's geodesic(s)

$$C_B(n_i) = \sum_{j<k} \frac{g_{jk}(n_i)}{g_{jk}}$$

(Wasserman & Faust, 1994).

Flow Betweenness

Calculates the flow betweenness and normalized flow betweenness centrality of each vertex and gives the overall network betweenness centralization(Borgatti, Everett, & Freeman, 2002).

Stephenson and Zelen(1989) introduce a technical measure of centrality that will make use of all paths between pairs of points. They argue that if we assume that communication only occurs along the shortest possible path (the Geodesic), then we neglect to measure communication occurring along reachable, however, non-geodesic paths. Information" in the context of 'centrality', equals the level of ability to transmit, to communicate.

When measuring information flow, it would be probable to assume that information will take a more indirect route either by random communication or may be intentionally channelled through many intermediaries in order to 'hide' or 'shield' information in a way not captured by geodesic paths. These considerations raise questions as to how to include all possible paths in a centrality measure. Stephenson and Zelen(1989) argue that earlier measures of centrality had limitations, which would have significant ramifications for understanding 'total' network processes particularly in large networks.

Stephenson and Zelen(1989) propose a measure of centrality that uses all paths, but gives them relative weighting as a function of the 'information' they contain. Information is technically defined in their development. For example, consider a network with n points or nodes and m lines or edges in which non -directed networks are where all pairs of points are reachable. If two points are connected by the **same line** they are said to be **incident** and the path is referred to as an **incident path** the distance between them will be taken as one unit.

If i,j refer to a pair of points there may be paths other than incident paths that connect them. Suppose for points i,j there are K_{ij} paths connecting i, and j. These paths will be denoted by $P_{ij}(1)$, ... $P_{ij}(Kij)$ P denotes all paths geodesic and non geodesic. In Stephenson and Zelen 's(1989) measure of centrality all paths are taken into consideration as influencing communication and information. They define a distance measure of a path as the number of lines in the path. D_{ij} is defined as the number of lines in path P_{ij}. They define an information measure I_{ij} to be the reciprocal of the distance measure for example: $I_{ij} = 1/ D_{ij}$

Information is defined by Stephenson and Zelen (ibid) according to the theory of statistical estimation, which states that information of a single observation is the reciprocal of the variance of the observation. To illustrate their theory the authors use the figure below:

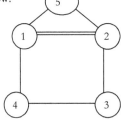

Path $P_{12}(1)=1$-2 can be envisioned as a 'signal' from point 1 to point 2. The 'noise' in the transmission of the signal is measured by the variance (the number of incident paths) of the signal going form point 1 to point 2.

The path $P_{12}(2) = 1$-5-2 may be interpreted as the transmission of two independent signals 1to 5 , followed by 5to 2. Since two transmissions are required for a signal from point 1 to reach point 2 through point 5, we can rewrite the path as the sum of two incident paths (1-5)+(5-2) since the variance of a sum of independent signals is additive then :

Variance $[(1$-5$) + (5$-2$)]$ =variance (1-5) + variance (5-2)

If the variance of any signal is unity, then the variance of a path simply counts the number of incident paths. Thus the variance $[(1$-5$) + (5$-2$)]$ =2. The increase variance reflects the condition that there is more 'noise' in two transmissions than in one transmission. The length of any path is simply the variance of transmitting a signal from the first point of a path to the last point in the path. The measure of information of this transmission (using the statistical estimation theory) would be the reciprocal of the variance. Since there may be several paths going from i to j the article introduces the idea of a combined path, which is a weighting function of the individual paths. The optimal combined path for points 1, 2 is obtained by weighting each path proportional to its information. The result would show that the combined path would have more information than the incident or geodesic pair alone.

A combined path for i to j may be interpreted as a signal originating with point i targeted for point j. The signal at i is transmitted to all the incident paths associated with point i and will reach point j from each possible path. The estimate of the signal at point j is obtained by weighting the signal from each path proportional to its information. The optimal weighting has the property that the information of the combined path is equal to the sum of the information from each path(Stephenson & Zelen, 1989).

The authors' interpretation of 'information' is that every path can be evaluated for its information content. Generally the information is inversely proportion to the distance of a path (the longer the path - the less information), and the information in a combined path is equal to the sum of information of the individual paths.

Information measure of centrality shows that the points (nodes) which are at the periphery of the network are ranked lowest (points having only one path are regarded as peripheral points)

The central individuals in the network may represent those who can transmit information relatively easily, whereas those on the periphery of the network have a smaller probability of transmission.

Comparing information centrality measures to other measures shows that the closest measure is that of 'distance'.

The 'betweeness' measure is not measuring centrality, but ranks points according to the 'control nodes exert in the network. One way to measure control is to count the number of nodes in a smaller sub-network that is generated when removing a node that exert control in the network(Stephenson & Zelen, 1989).

Why Do Flow Betweenness Routines?

Suppose two actors want to have a relationship but the geodesic (shortest) path between them is blocked. If an alternative pathway exists, the two actors are likely to use it even if it is longer than the geodesic path. The flow approach to centrality expands the notion of betweenness centrality. It assumes that actors will use all pathways that connect them.

I chose to apply the flow betweenness because of its acceptance of all available paths not just the geodesic. My data is based on messages, which means that the content of a message may reveal a situation where people while addressing the message to certain member or members may relate to additional members in the actual content of the message. This kind of context suggests that there may be distant links beyond the geodesic paths connecting members.

For triangulation reasons I applied 'information flow' measuring what Stephenson and Zelen(1989) refer to as 'the level of ability to transmit, to communicate'.

THE RATIONALE BEHIND THE VISUALISATION OF NETWORKS

As I have shown earlier in this chapter, Graph Theory enables the visualisation of networks, and the measuring of relations within it. This mathematical tool enabled social sciences to study social structures in a way that would elicit the system of relationship among its parts. The use of mathematical tools in social sciences is not a new idea, however, the tools introduced by graph theory shift the focus from statistical measurements representing the physical world, to the study of abstract forms **representing** reality rather than **presenting** it. This notion is similar to Nadel's(1957) idea mentioned earlier in this chapter, where he defines 'structure' as an abstraction of relational features. Shifting away from the statistical attempts or presenting reality, to abstract forms representing it, requires a shift in our understanding of the function of mathematics as a measuring tool. In the next section I introduce Graph Theory with its geometrical notions facilitating the abstraction of structures.

PATTERNS, OR MATHEMATICS AS ABSTRACTIONS OF THE WORLD

The empiricists perceive mathematical measurements as representations of the physical world, and treat them as absolute truths. Principles of 'graph theory[9], allow this study to perceive mathematical forms, or geometrical forms as abstractions of the physical world.

In the perceptual experience of common everyday occurrences within the world in which we live and act, the *Umwelt*, sometimes referred to as the **Lebenswelt**, we encounter bodies whose special forms are only typically determined, or determined in a more or less vaguely circumscribed range of variability(Gurwitsch, 1966).

Geometry provides a method of definitively overcoming the relativism of perceptual experience and the limitation of the practical art of measurement, idealising real life situations. Geometry arises by the process of idealisation, as it is there to overcome the lack of precision and should I say imperfectness of real life. Special forms as given in the perceptual experience may be referred to the geometrical figures as ideal poles which the former approximate to a greater or lesser degree.(Gurwitsch, 1966) However, Lebenswelt, is prior to, and underlies geometry as a 'foundation of sense', therefore, when geometry is taken as an established method, it is no longer understood as a 'mental accomplishment of a higher order', involving the process of idealisation and therefore founded upon the presupposing pre-geometrical experience of the Lebenswelt upon which idealisation is performed(Gurwitsch, 1966).

Using geometry as idealisation of a concrete world is not the same as applying geometrical measurements in order to discover the real world, in fact, it is right the opposite. And this is the great difference between empirical science and the ethnomethodology stance suggested by Gurwitsch(1966). Galileo inherited geometry as an established science, with an absolute and universal validity, which he considered as a model and standard of knowledge. Consequently, geometry was applied to life experience in order to discover the reality as it is in itself(Gurwitsch, 1966). Galileo's application of mathematics and geometry to the real world has exchanged the real experience for the mathematical system that validates its existence by manufacturing

---

[9] 'Graph theory', used to describe the pattern of connections among points

perfect measurements. The real world according to the scientific method emerging from Galileo is a mere subjective phenomena, and bears any significance only as far as they serve as indications of the true, mathematical condition of things(Gurwitsch, 1966).

The notion of geometry as idealisation of reality allows using geometrical forms created by idealising, or should I say abstracting the social interactions occurring in my data-set. However, choosing to apply graph- based illustrations of social relations does not automatically imply that the graphic patterns emerging from a specific data-set are presentation of the reality of the social interactions occurring, but rather an abstraction of these. Conceptualising data representation this way suggests issues of local versus generalisable representations of research findings.

Using mathematical abstractions allows researchers to generalise while at the same time acknowledge the differences in local context bound situations. The abstraction allows incorporating local situation within its geometric – theoretical forms. The geometric forms serve as my analytic frames rather than representations of the actual reality(Gurwitsch, 1966).

SUMMARY OF SECTION

In this section, I reviewed possible methodological routes for investigating relations in a social network; in an attempt to understand how information and meanings are conveyed. Using ethnomethodology as a starting point, I was able to break from the individual- structure frame of mind, and explore ways of investigating interactions, and relations acting as driving the activities occurring in online discussion forums. Applying SNA tools enabled the translation of the theoretical concepts into visualised, measurable, and analysable data, representing mathematical abstractions of the reality under investigation.

SUMMARY OF CHAPTER

In this chapter, I attempted to sketch the milieu of the study by first describing the field, and the changes it has undergone. Next, I attempted to elucidate the terminology used in the literature related to the field of distance collaborative learning. The second part of the chapter reviewed the research conducted in the field, first by looking at studies relating to communicative, interactive online learning environments, and later focusing on, the problems facing the study of collaborative learning in online discussion forums. The review revealed a myriad of research approaches and their strengths and limitations. One of the key problems I have identified in the review of the research is the limitations of the methodologies applied in the field in addressing learning as a supra-individual, collaborative activity. I then attempted to investigate alternative analytical frameworks that would address the problems identified in studying collaborative learning in OLDF. Finally, I described various analytic tools that would enable applying the theoretical framework identified in the previous section.

In the following chapter I will search for a methodology that would enable me to address some of the issues raised in this review.

A methodological quest and the introduction of an alternative analytic
approach to the study of online discussion forums

Introduction and Organisation of Chapter

The benefits of social interactions, dialogue, and the collaborative construction
of knowledge are well studied and documented by (Ferdig, Roehler, & Pearson, 2002;
Rogoff, 1995; Vygotsky, 1978; Wertsch, 1991). Since the dawning of the Internet
people were inspired by its technological ability to connect people, and facilitate
collaborative knowledge building. However, in this study I argue that there is a need for
more investigation into the processes occurring throughout these much revered
technological spaces, so as to further explore, the activities and practices of participants
in online discussion forums and communities.

This chapter can be perceived as a guided tour revealing the paths and routes of
my mind as they evolved throughout the quest defining this study. Here I describe the
process of the development of a new method of investigation of the occurrences in
online learning discussion forums. The route leading to the development of the new
method is scattered with clues and snippets of data guiding my thinking.

The first part of this chapter describes the pilot study I conducted prior to
embarking on the present study. It then proceeds to describing my first attempts at
obtaining a handle on the data collected in the present study. In the second part of this
chapter I describe the search for a methodology that would address the issues I
encountered throughout my pilot study and later in my preliminary explorations into the
data of this study. In the third part of this chapter I describe the development of the new
method and exhibit its application on a small mock data-set.

In this section I describe a pilot study I have conducted prior to the current study. I will them proceed to describe preliminary analysis attempts conducted using the data-set collected for the current study.

T h e   P i l o t   S t u d y

Before embarking on the present study, I conducted a pilot study at a college of education in Israel. In the study, I followed a group of ten experienced educators, who participated in an on-campus in-service Information and Communication Technology (ICT) course, which involved online activities in addition to the face-to–face (FTF) meetings. The incorporation of the online discussions component in the course was to provide an alternative learning environment, which would facilitate and support professional discourse among the course participants, beyond the FTF meetings. The a-synchronous[10] platform supporting the discussion forums was to enable participants to choose the time slots convenient for them to participate in the discussions, either from the comfort of their home or other accessible locations.

The pilot study set out to find whether the provision of a technology that afforded a flexible temporal and contextual environment would encourage professional related discussions among educators participating in a higher education course.

The findings of the pilot study revealed some correlation between the temporal - contextual environment and the evolvement of discourse; however it was the unexpected findings which provoked my curiosity for further study. The analysis of the participants' postings to the online discussion forums revealed an interesting phenomenon, suggesting a link between social interactions and course related discussions as an increase in social interactions was accompanied by an increase in

---

[10] Does not require simultaneous presence of the participants

course related contributions. The figure below (*figure 3-1*) illustrates this link, particularly marking two considerable swells in levels of social and course related interactions, once towards the end of January (end of first semester – in the north hemisphere), and the second one towards June (end of second semester– in the north hemisphere). Although the participants of the pilot study were required to submit an assignment at the end of each semester, *figure 3-1* highlights a difference between the two peeks. At the end of semester one, a high level of contributions was related to assignment submission issues, whereas the end of the second semester (around June), revealed a towering swell in discussions related to course materials reaching an all high of 56 contributions, with a mere 2 assignment submission related contributions.

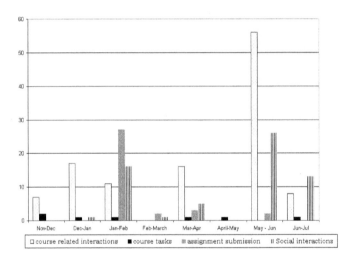

Figure 3-1 –Course Related and Social Interactions Ratio

The link between course related and social related interactions flared my curiosity as to the role of interactions in Online Learning Discussion Forums (OLDF), and the possible affect they may have on learning processes. I wondered whether the difference between the end of the first and the second semester indicated a possible difference in the perception of learning exhibited by the participants. The assignment related interactions exhibited at the end of the first semester (January) could imply a perception of learning as a product oriented activity, focusing on the assignment submission. The end of the second semester (June) marked by high levels of course related interactions but not necessarily assignment oriented, indicate a different perception in which learning is perceived as an exchange and sharing of opinions and views between peers, implying some, if only rudimentary level of collaboration.

These findings may suggest that the foresights and expectations I have mentioned earlier about the Internet becoming a conducive environment for collaborative learning and the evolvement of learning communities, might be seen to materialise in some instances, confirming the potential predicted. However, at this stage this potential seems to materialise quite haphazardly, and the circumstances enabling its realisation are not widely understood. In this study I explore possible ways of detecting and analysing activities in online discussion forums, in an attempt to better understand the circumstance leading to the application of different perceptions of learning, and the occurrence of collaborative learning activities in certain instances.

The Current study- Preliminary Attempts

The pilot study suggested a link between levels of course- related interactions and those of social interactions. It also suggested *time* related differences in the perceptions participants had about learning, implying that changes in the perceptions generated different types of activities, conveying different content.

In the current study I attempt to pursue these notions furtherby observing a Distance learning Masters Course, which took place at a College of Education in New Zealand. The course incorporated online activities which took place in a number of online discussion forums. In my preliminary investigations of the data collected for the current study I chose to first address the aspect of *time* and changes in activities along a time line.

The preliminary analysis revealed a single temporal distinguishable phenomenon in the form of a peak level of contributions to the online discussion forums during the month of March which was the second month of the course[11]. '*Figure 3-2*' depicts the peak contributions levels in March.

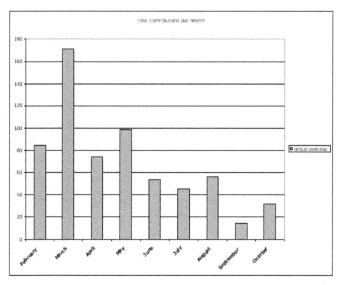

Figure 3-2-*Total Monthly Contributions*

Exploring the reasons behind this peak activity revealed that March was the most prolific month in terms of activity opportunities. All through the duration of the course observed in this study, the facilitator of the course set up discussion forums. Some were to serve as social spaces; others were set up as course oriented discussions. On some occasions the facilitator closed down a forum after some time, and on other occasions she left the discussions open. Some continued to attract activity, others dwindled away, and ground to a halt of actions.

The illustration below shows the number of forums active in each month of the course

---

[11] Some early birds logged on to the site as early as January, but the official starting date was February

93

Month	January	February	March	April	May	June	July	August	Sept	Oct.	Nov.
Number of forums	1	8	13	9	7	5	6	2	4	3	3

March holds the highest number of discussions active at one time, which could provide some explanation of the peak in activity. Eight of the thirteen forums active in March bore a social context. However, during that time, two of the course content modules were running concurrently, each generating and feeding into a content module discussion forum. In addition, three course- oriented forums were active, two of which began their activity in March.

Looking for further time related changes in activity I followed levels of contributions to the discussion forums, measuring the number of messages sent by each member each month. *'Figure 3-3'* depicts my findings.

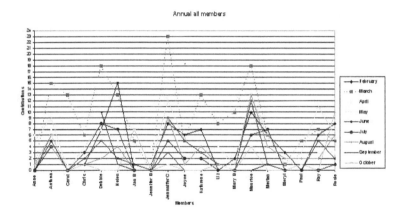

Figure 3-3- *Frequency of Monthly Contributions*

'Figure 3-3' shows no identifiable patterns in Individual contributions as they seem quite random, with the exception of a peak in contribution during March, which

94

incidentally is aligned with the peak of group contributions I have shown earlier in *'Figure 3-2'*.

Having exhausted the time related phenomena and levels of contribution measurement routes of analysis; I now turned to exploring another analytic route implied earlier in the pilot study, the *'type'*, or *'nature'*, of the activities and contributions to the discussion forums

The computer network system supporting the discussion forums observed in this study requires every contribution to the online discussions to declare its nature, or *'nature of post'* as it is referred to by the computer system. The system provides a list of a number of *'nature of post'* choices, out of which contributors are able to select the one expressing the nature of their contribution. For example, a contribution labelled 'formal task' would indicate that the contribution would include some course requirement product i.e. course assignment. Following the *'nature of post'* feature could provide some information as to the content, or intent of the contribution.

The discussion forums I observed in the current study were initially set up by the course facilitator with the intent to create two types of discussion forums: *'course related'* forums, and *'social related'* forums. These different roles assigned to different forums provided me with some criteria for categorisation of the current study's rather large data-set, making it more manageable.

With this categorisation in hand, I attempted to study the *'type'* or *'nature'* of contributions, and find whether the two different roles assigned to the various forums affected the choice of the 'nature of post' format used in them. I analysed this feature in an attempt to discover possible differences between the nature of contributions posted to social forums, and the course related ones. As the only temporal phenomena I could detect so far was the peak contributions in March, I proceeded to explore the 'nature of post' contributed during that period. The figures *'3-4'*, and *'3-5'* depict the two types of forums, each exhibiting the choice of 'nature of post' selected in them

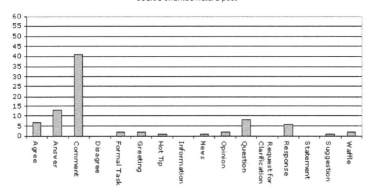

Figure 3-4 Course Oriented 'Nature' of Post

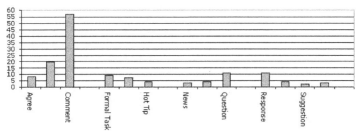

Figure 3-5 -Social Oriented 'Nature of Post'

The two charts show no distinct difference in the use of the 'nature of post' feature, however, they do exhibit a similarity of preference in the use of the 'comment' format of the 'nature of post', as in both cases this format exceeds all the others. The term 'comment' in itself could be interpreted very differently by different contributors; hence attempting to follow its use could prove rather illusive and inconsistent.

Having concluded the route of *'nature of post'*, with no significant findings, I turned to the only remaining route of investigation indicated earlier in the pilot, - the *'content'* of interactions.

The data-collected in the current study reached a total of 1104 messages. Pursuing to analyse the content of each message on a data-set of this magnitude would prove unmanageable, as this approach is very labour intensive and time consuming beyond the resources of a single researcher. Applying such an intensive analysis route to the current data -set required choosing a manageable sample from the data.

The obvious choice of a sample would have been a temporal one, simply sampling a number of messages every pre determined time interval. However, as *'figure 3-2' and '3-3'* showed, the only significant temporal pattern of activity detected is a surge of contributions during March, indicating that attempting to define a sample according to time intervals, may not result in any significant findings. Any other options for choosing a sample would need some kind of sorting or categorising the data beyond the classification observable at this stage of analysis.

SUMMARISING THE PRELIMINARY ANALYSIS ATTEMPTS OF THE CURRENT DATA-SET

The proliferation of contributions in March, during which a total of 13 forums were running, eight bearing a social role, and five holding a course related role could be seen to further support the findings of the pilot study, implying a link between social interactions and discussions related to course materials, however, this was still only an observation bearing some indication, alas with no underpinning explanation of the occurrences, their interrelations, and the affects they may have on each other.

My attempts to establish a *temporal* progression of perceptions of learning were not successful, nor could I detect any differences in the *nature* of the contributions as both were similar in social as well as the course related forums. Furthermore, the similarity of the 'nature of post' showing a significant preference to the 'comment' form in both the social and the course related forums, appeared as an illusive attribute to follow, as the term 'comment' could entail different things on different occasions. Attempting to analyse the *content* of a data-set of this magnitude is beyond my means as a single researcher. Any content analysis attempts would require a sampling system beyond those apparent at this stage of the study.

My attempts in this preliminary phase could be described as focusing on the *product*, the contributions made to the discussion forums, however, with no reference to the agency, the actor/s producing these online messages.

Having failed to discover any significant findings so far, I now turned to a different route of analysis, quite common in social research the *'attribute data'* route (Scott, 2000,p.2). Here, I focused on the study of individual attributes, and group characteristics, in the hope of discovering patterns of behaviour that would help me search for ways of detecting learning activities, the perceptions of learning exhibited and the circumstances supporting these activities.

Who Are My Participants – Attributes

In the beginning, there were nineteen educators from all walks of the educational system in New Zealand, who while participating in a Distance Learning Masters level course, "Critical Reflection" agreed to participate in my research. Five were from early childhood, two from primary, four from secondary, and six from tertiary education. Some were teachers or lecturers, some were principals, and others were educational consultants.

Some research participants came from the North Island, some from the South Island, some from small rural towns and others from the big cities.

Some wanted to get into *"more philosophical discussions about postmodern ideas, and the ways they relate to praxis"*. Others wanted *"a place where we are all trying to take part - where we support each other in making contributions - and where we can test out our tentative ideas"*.

Diverse as my research participants may seem, this variety could in fact be contained within three distinct categories:

- Geographical regions and contexts of residence- categorising participants according to their living surroundings;
- Professional affiliation - categorising participants according to the educational sector they work in.
- Learning surroundings – as expressed by the participants;

This almost instinctive impulse to categorise and classify any assortment of entities seems almost the natural thing to do. Benson and Hughes(1983) argue that ordinary members of society regularly make use of categories in order to describe the world around them. Similarly, sociologists make use of categories in order to map out their phenomena of interest; these usually refer to types of social actors (i.e. teachers, institutions, or activities). For both sociologists and lay persons, it is presumed that these categories are visible, describable and detectable(Benson & Hughes, 1983).

Looking at the course Website, I was able to experience Benson and Hughes(1983) theory suggesting an all human impulse to categorise and classify everything that comes across our path, when I detected an almost identical categorisation of the course participants done by the course facilitator - Elaine. This categorisation impulse not only compels us to put people in pre- determined 'boxes', but also often lures us into making assumptions, or anticipating certain behaviour from people we have grouped into a certain category.

The course Website revealed that after a short period during which the participants introduced themselves online in small groups, populated simply in the order in which people enrolled and logged on to the course site, Elaine regrouped the participants. Assuming that participants would welcome the idea of conversing online with people living in geographical proximity, Elaine set up regional groups, in which participants were grouped online according to their physical address. These groups were segregated, allowing only designated members access to the discussions occurring within them. However, these did not encourage much activity, and after a short while Elaine re-grouped the participants, this time according to the educational sector they worked in, but with a difference. The sector groups were not segregated and participants could wonder around; so for example, participants working in the primary sector could move outside their own sector forum to access and contribute to all other sector forums. Arriving at the decision to open up the forums was preceded by Elaine's consulting the participants. This consultation was triggered by snippets of ideas sounded by participants at various discussions throughout the online forums. A small excerpt of these snippets indicates some of these ideas:

> I applaud you for joining the course, and would love to keep this correspondence going, even though you're not part of "my" NorthIslanders group and I'm not part of "your" group... .

(Posted in 'Mary's teacup'; thread subject – 'why I like on-line learning')

This message refers to the separation created by the segregated regional groups, and implies a will to communicate across these borders.

In an interview I conducted with Elaine a short while after the course had ended I asked her about her reasons for grouping the participants in her online classroom. I was particularly interested in her reflection on the criteria she chose when she was setting up the groups, as well as the choices she made about access to the forums– either as open to all participants, or restricted to designated members. In response to my questions Elaine commented that:

> The regional groups were not very successful, and some of them were actually nonexistent for example the Nelsonians, hardly had any activity, and the CHCH group met face- to- face, and abandoned the online context, apart from using it as a bulletin board for arranging their face-to-face meetings. ......The sectorial groups experience was much more successful, here; the participants asked not to be segregated within their working sector and be allowed to drift from one sector group to the other with no restrictions. These groups acted very much like

real life situations where people drift in and out of a community, at their will……. (Interview 3rd Feb 03 Mary-Elaine)

My participants seem to express three main points regarding group affiliation, first, they wish to exercise the choice of groups to which they belong; second, they wanted to be granted the ability to move freely between groups, which implies or generates a third notion and that is that people are able to participate in several groups

One explanation for these notions can be found in Bougle's article 'what is sociology' (Bougle 1897), in which he suggests that the routine classification we practice in our everyday life tends to pick out a single attribute of our subject of classification, and group them accordingly. However, the individuals in the group are not only specimens of the categorisation they have been classified under. The attributes used for the classification do not encompass all their attributes. People do not belong to one social circle, i.e. primary teachers, or young mothers, but to several which sometimes overlap(Bougle, 1897 as cited in \Degenne & Forse, 1999)[12]. Bougle's observation of individuals belonging to *overlapping groups* or categories can provide an explanation to the movement of my research participants between the groups defied by Elaine's classifications, that was based on a single attribute, whereas the participants perceived themselves as belonging to several social groups, as the attribute used for their specification does not encompass all their attributes.

Another explanation can be found in Simmel's work "Die Kreuzung sozialer Kreise", ("Intersection of Social Circles") in its English title "The Web of Group Affiliation"(Simmel, 1955(1922))[13]. In this work Simmel talks about the analogy between the formation of individual personality and the emergence of social structure, as both consist of the development of representations of reality which go beyond what is immediately experienced by the subject. Diani(2000) in analysing Simmel's work suggests that this formation, both in the case of individuals and groups, is a matter of growing differentiation between what is immediately perceivable/ or available and what

---

[12] Bugle 1897 'Qu'est-ce-la sociologie'- the original source is in French, hence I had to rely on Degenne & Forse's translation

[13] In this work Simmel uses the term 'circle' as synonymous for the term 'group'.

is identified as relevant to the actor. For individuals the process consists of their awareness of the existence of a reality beyond the group to which they may currently belong (i.e. family, of a work, or study assigned team); for groups the analogy consists of the passage from forms of association based on similarity, and/or proximity, to forms based on free choice. Simmel also talks about the overlapping affiliation phenomena and suggests that an individual may belong to many groups and can be perceived as standing at the intersection of social circles(Simmel, 1955(1922)).

These observations may explain my participants' choice of groups, their opting to participate in multiple groups and move around different groups. Simmel's notion of people standing at intersection of groups is an interesting notion in the study of online forums as it would provide a framework for studying the interconnections and relations between different discussion threads, and in a situation where various discussion forums are activated under the same umbrella context. Thus, in the situation of this study, it would be interesting to follow any connections between various discussion forums. However, this would be beyond the scope of this study. Instead, I shall focus on the relations and interrelations within single discussion threads.

Further exploring my participants' attitudes toward categorisation, I discovered that some messages, like the one I have chosen to show below, refers to the greater society and the ways in which society classifies and categorises people:

> Hi Mary .... I actually like on-line learning because you are not judged on your age, ethnicity, abilities / disabilities and so on.

(Posted in 'Mary's teacup'; thread subject – 'why I like on-line learning')

The manner in which the participants in my study referred to the all too common categories of age, gender, abilities, and other prevailing labels we so often use in our everyday life, as well as in social science research propelled me to question the role, and indeed the validity of categorising people by attributes that bear little or no relevance to the online environment I am investigating. The specialised nature of the online environment I am studying, allowing access only to the members of the masters course in reflective teaching, and the fact that through the online environment the participants are able to transcend geography and the need for physical presence, challenges some of the notions of categorisation applied throughout sociology and mass communication research methods (Thomsen, Straubhaar, & Bolyard, 1998).

In our everyday life we constantly classify people we encounter. At times we base our classification on physical attributes, i.e. age; gender; ethnicity; and so forth. Alternatively we classify people by their trade related attributes, so, for example, a person carrying a ladder wearing overalls would probably be classified as a 'painter'. Social status attributes are also commonly used for classifying people, for example, we would probably classify a person driving an expensive car, as 'wealthy'. Conducting an online study means physical, trade, or status attributes are at best concealed, if not totally unobtainable. Furthermore, the online arena is unique in its approach to identities. Judging by the reactions of my participants it is quite clear that they resented the attempts to classify them according to their real-life identities. One participant went as far as saying that:

> …….. I am a young Māori woman and I actually found meeting people at the block course [a short face-to-face section of the course] has now hindered my desire to talk on-line. Perhaps people will not take me seriously because I am young and I don't have as much to offer as them in terms of experience.
>
> Some may disagree, but it is interesting how people approach you differently once they have placed their assumptions on you - often without knowing it.
>
> Just something to ponder on - the fact that it is so easy to interact when there is no book cover.
>
> (Mary's Teacup – why I like online learning)

Online, "there is no book cover" said this participant, which once again suggested to me that when conducting an online research, there is a genuine need for distancing our perceptions of people from the real-life based groups and categories we so commonly tend to use.

Turkle in her book '*Life on Screen: Identity in the Age of the Internet*'(1995), suggests that the internet is changing our psychological lives and our evolving ideas about minds, bodies, and machines. Turkle suggests that there is an- ongoing evolvement process through which a new sense of identity-as de-centred and multiple is emerging, creating a dramatic shift in our notions of self, and the other(Turkle, 1995). Addressing the changes in the notion of identity when confronted with the online social environment is a fascinating topic; though it is beyond the agenda of this study. However, Turkle' s (1995) observation of the online identities reflects my own deliberations, provoked by my observations in regard to the relevancy of the traditional real-life social environment and its social groups and identities when applied to the online environment.

Adhering to the agenda of this study, I will choose to explore this issue from the methodological, rather than the sociological perspective, extending the issue of relevancy of specific, in this case real-life categories, to questions of approach and methods used for choosing the categories.

WHY CATEGORISE IN THE FIRST PLACE?

Radcliffe-Brown(1940[2002])argues that when studying social phenomena one can only make direct observations of the set of actually existing relations at a given moment of time which links together certain human beings. These observations seem to construct the concrete reality with which a study is concerned; however, the particularities of this reality are not what a scientific study would attempt to describe. Unlike history or biography, science is concerned with the general and reoccurring events. The actual relations of Tom, Dick and Harry, or the behaviour of Jack and Jill, may be recorded in the field notes, and may provide illustrations for a general description. However, a scientific study would require an account of the form of the structure. Mooney and Singer (1988), suggested that searching for regularity in social phenomena could prove valuable as the search for reoccurring patterns could elicit possible causes. The authors argue that causal knowledge is important for predicting events and enabling intervention for the production of desired effects(Mooney & Singer, 1988).

Acknowledging these notions, I would like to add that establishing patterns of participation in an online discussion forum would be of significant importance for e-researchers, as patterns could suggest possible generalisations of the observed phenomena. The identification of patterns could also prove valuable for e-educators, as patterns of activities could form the basis for prediction and anticipation of behaviour in similar situations, an important factor for e-educators in their planning of teaching, and ongoing support of learners.

REAL –LIFE PERCEPTIONS PUT TO THE TEST IN THE ONLINE ENVIRONMENT

The online environment in which this study is situated has challenged some of the real-life issues we tend to take for granted in our real-life everyday life experiences, as well as in traditional research. My preliminary attempts challenged my perceptions of:

1. *'Time'* and its meaning or relevancy in the online environment
2. 'Identity' relating to real-life physical attributes, i.e. gender, and race, and its perception and relevancy to the online context
3. 'Contextual *attributes'*, i.e. workplace; and geographical location and the relevancy to the online environment

The Meaning of 'Time'

Our real-life perception of *'time'* refers to some progression or continuity over a number of measurable units of days, weeks, etc., however, this concept may be deceiving when applied online. *'Figure 3-1'*, referring to the pilot study, measured activities over a time-line, revealing two significant occurrences, indicating two different styles of activities. As the two appeared at two distinct periods of the academic year, one at the end of semester one, and the second one at the end of semester two, I assumed them to be time related. Establishing a progression of time elapsing between a single occurrence to the next can lead us to form a link between time progression, and process (mental or social) progression. Time related progression is linear; linking process progression to time frames assumes linearity of the progression of the process. This assumption is debatable in any environment whether it be online, or real-life, however, it is a commonly found link[14]. Reflecting on the ideas guiding my preliminary attempts at the data of this present study, I admit to applying this link and pursuing some evidence to it. The results of my pursuit depicted in *'figure 3-2'*, and *'figure 3-3'*, revealed no such link as I could not establish any visible time related progression. These findings made me revisit the notion of *'time'* in online discussion forums. By their nature, or should I say technology, online discussion forums are a-synchronous communication tools, which means that participants in the discussion are not necessarily present, or in online terms, logged-on to the forums in the same time. This a-synchronous feature in itself puts a new perspective to the notion of time of participation and activity in these forums. In our everyday or real-life environments we refer to 'time' as something that measures progression from an earlier to a later point in 'time'. A-synchronous online environments, however, can only exhibit progression between contact points, which materialise on the event that a participant in the discussion contributes a message to the forum. Being a-synchronous, the contribution relates to a message, irrespective of the time in which it was posted. In spoken conversations there is the normal expectation that 'turns', or contributions that "belong together"—meaning that they are intended as responses or follow-ups to previous turns—will occur adjacent to one another in temporal sequence(Herring, 1999). However, in online contexts, the adjacency of response is not time bound, the response relates to content and any context a message or a group of messages created as a repository stored on the discussion forum's network server. Contributing to online discussions is a bit like *thawing a conversation, responding and re-freezing it for further contributions*. Following any progression in online a-synchronous discussion forums is similar to linking between dots on a paper, and drawing lines between them to complete the picture of who talked to whom and about what.

---

[14]   Some educational theorists such as Piaget believe that biological and psychological progression is linear, linked to biological age(Piaget, 1997)

106

The Relevancy of Identity

Unless a participant shares their real-life physical *identity* with the rest of the discussion group, online we cannot tell whether a participant is young or old, fat or thin, Māori (indigenous New Zealand people) or Pakeha (European descent New Zealanders). Some, as I have shown in one excerpt from the data, find this physical obscurity liberating, enabling new opportunities and contexts for interacting with others. When studying online environments one must be aware of these liberating feelings, which may contribute to the creating of a maze of social groups which are comprised of people who in their physical life may have not been communicating.

The Relevancy of Contextual Attributes'

Contextual attribute relate to issues like workplace, and geographical location. The movement between the externally imposed grouping, and the will to shrug off the physical, and contextual attributes and affiliations expressed by my participants and supported by Elaine's observations, have contributed to the establishing of the notion that any reference to the real-life attributes my participants may bear may prove as irrelevant, negligible, and at times even undesired when dealing in the online context.

My attempt to follow the grouping and categorisations applied throughout the course as a framework for this study proved ineffective, as the participants' movement between groups suggested the existence of either alternative, and at this point unknown groups, a total lack of characteristic groups, or a perpetual evolvement of groups.

P a r t   T w o

In Part One of this chapter, I questioned the *relevancy* of 'real – life' approaches to the online context. In this section, I will expand this notion to investigate not only the issue of transferring a situation from one context to another, but also investigate the wider notion of imposing a presupposed context or preconceived classification on the observed context. In particular I investigate the methodological implications elicited by these issues, and search for theoretical and methodological frameworks that would accommodate such notions. This study is primarily about people interacting with others; hence, in this section I pursue the meaning of social interactions in the context of Online Learning Discussion Forums.

Introduction

Choosing presupposed '*a-priori*' contexts would at times guide the study down well-treaded trails of social science investigation, rather than invoke new paths. Investigating relevant research paths beyond the trodden trail is of particular significance for this study as it investigates the relatively new research context of the online environment.

My preliminary attempts and first glances at my participants not only challenged any attempts to transfer real-life perceptions to the online environment, but also alerted me to the necessity of this study to be rooted in the online occurrences rather than applying any real-life based assumptions, categorisations and grouping. This emerging awareness of the necessity of the online rather than the real-life perception has ramifications for my choice of research design, or methodology, as well as my choice of data collecting methods.

I would summarise all my early analysis attempts as 'relevancy challenged', as they failed to acknowledge the differences between real-life and online contexts. Studying online environments is a comparatively new research arena, and as McLuhan and Fiore(1967) put it, "When faced with a totally new situation, we tend always to attach ourselves to the objects, to the flavour the most recent past. We look at the present through a rear-view mirror. We march backwards into the future" (,p. 74-75). Attempting to avoid the '*rear view mirror*' pitfall, I would need to search for a new and preferably a more relevant approach more befitting to the uniqueness of the online environment. This would undoubtedly mean that I would also need to extend the notion of relevancy to issues concerning the role of the researcher, the research design and the data collecting methods

Questioning the relevancy of real-life categories for the online context raises a much wider notion questioning the validity of any imposed, pre supposed, or *a priori* categorisation on observed events.

Degenne and Forse(1999) argue that most sociologists accept the notion that individual behaviour and opinions are rooted in the structures to which people belong. However, most researchers handling empirical data will ignore this reality choosing to construct *a priori* categories into which individuals will be aggregated according to sex, age, or occupation, to determine the relevance and significance of these descriptive categories to the variable under investigation, for example, learning practices. Furthermore, the authors argue that *a priori* defined categories cannot predict the type of actions or behaviour in which individuals aggregated in the category will engage. One can only assume that a group of tertiary educators or a group of early childhood teachers, will each exhibit definable learning practices, however, the mere categorisation of individuals working in, for example, a certain educational sector, does not predict, nor can it guarantee their anticipated behaviour or actions(Degenne & Forse, 1999).

Degenne and Forse(1999) agree with the fact that people's actions may indeed be rooted in the structures to which they belong, however, they argue that the problem lies in the perception researchers have as to the origin of these structures. The authors challenge the prevalent assumption guiding social science studies in which structures are based on over generalised assumptions, or using their term - 'conventional wisdom' for grouping people according to for example, age or gender, or occupation. In challenging these groups based on conventional wisdom, the authors imply the need for observing concrete situations for detecting the structure emerging. In a way, the challenges raised by the authors can be said to engage in some aspects of the 'structure, agency debate', as they question the origins of the structure implying that it may be formed by the actions of the people observed(Degenne & Forse, 1999).

STRUCTURE, AGENCY, AND WHAT IS AT PLAY?

In studying people's actions, in this case, learning through online discussion forums, I am faced with the question of 'what is at play'. Is it the given environment, shaped by the technology, the participants' personal attributes and their affiliation to certain social groups, such as, gender, professional status and the like, that affects the actions of individuals or, rather is it the other way around, in which case, the environment is constructed by its participants, their actions and behaviour. However in the latter case, I wonder what is contributing to the construction of the environment.

Long lasting philosophical debates revolved around the question– is social action motivated by individual self-interest or communal obligations? Is action freely willed by the individual or determined by cultural socialisation and or available material resource(I. J. Cohen, 2000). These questions later became known as the 'Agency Structure Debate', which can be seen as represented by two perspectives in social theory. One perspective focuses on social structure, arguing that the individual is acted upon and influenced by the social structures. In his doctrine Durkheim argues that it is the social structure which determines and exercises external constraints on the individual (Coser, 1977; Durkheim, 1938). According to MacLeod(2002) Durkheim argues against the role of the individual influencing or shaping the collective ideas of a group. The other perspective focuses on the individual, arguing that it is the individual who is responsible for the generation of their social environment; therefore the individual's actions are driving and affecting the creation of social structures. According to Adams and Sydie (2001)Weber and Simmel developed an approach that attempted to understand and interpret social actions of the individual actor, arguing that "sociology must never lose sight of human agency"(as cited in Adams & Sydie, 2001,p.168).

Investigating 'what is at play' in the 'structure agency debate' context could be said to inquire whether my participants are free to act, or are they constrained by some structure. To investigate these questions I would first need to ascertain whether the environment studied exhibited any online- borne forms or patterns that could be defined as a social group or structure.

Judging by the evidence emerging from my early analysis attempts I would suggest that my participants exhibited the ability to act as 'free agents' and seem to have wandered outside their designated real-life embedded groups. However, the question remaining is whether the boundaries of these designated groups were broken to enable an entirely borderless environment, or were alternative groups and boundaries constructed, and if so, what was their impact on the activities of the participants?

Identifying patters of behaviour would enable me to establish structures, or groups that share these patterns. The idea that the participants in my study were acting in random with no apparent reoccurring patterns has crossed my mind, however, before taking the path of 'chaos theory'[15], I attempted to find an observation framework that would enable the observation of the activities online. Underlying my search was the desire to find a way that would help me establish patterns of behaviour, which would hopefully help me search for ways of detecting learning activities, the perceptions of learning exhibited, and the circumstances supporting these activities.

Reaching for a Methodology – Discovering Ethnomethodology

My search for a methodology entailed a search for an approach that would address my data with no pre-existing notions, enabling me to address emerging, rather

---

[15]   The very name "chaos theory" seems to contradict reason; in fact it seems somewhat of an oxymoron. The name "chaos theory" leads the reader to believe that mathematicians have discovered some new and definitive knowledge about utterly random and incomprehensible phenomena; however, this is not entirely the case. The acceptable definition of chaos theory states that chaos theory is the qualitative study of unstable a-periodic behaviour in deterministic non-linear dynamical systems. A dynamical system may be defined to be a simplified model for the time-varying behaviour of an actual system, and a-periodic behaviour is simply the behaviour that occurs when no variable describing the state of the system undergoes a regular repetition of values. A-periodic behaviour never repeats and it continues to manifest the effects of any small perturbation hence, any prediction of a future state in a given system that is a-periodic is impossible(Donahue, 1997).

than a-priori contexts. My goal was to reveal the roots of patterns representing emerging structures. In other words, I set out to find a methodology that would enable me to investigate the occurrences in the online discussion forums as they emerge, and discover reoccurring events and emerging patterns through my observation of the data rather than any external assumptions, rules, or presupposed structures.

Ethnomethodology (EM) often associated with Garfinkel (1967; , 2002), has affected social thinking and shifted it from a sociology that strives to explain, to a sociology that strives to comprehend. EM argues that the 'real' is already described by people. Ordinary language tells the social reality, describes it and constitutes it at the same time(Coulon, 1995). Garfinkel (1967,also see; Koschmann, Stahl, & Zemel, in press) argues that it is useless to assess action by applying rules that come from outside the situation at hand; thus refusing to seriously consider assessing practical activities by using rules or standards obtained outside the actual setting within which it was produced, and talked about by its participants (Garfinkel, 1967; Koschmann, Stahl, & Zemel, in press). For example, this approach would not consider the 'culture of secondary teachers' when investigating their behaviour beyond the school, in this case, in cyberspace.

OBSERVING PATTERNS IN THE ACTIONS AND PRACTICES OF ONLINE LEARNING DISCUSSION FORUMS (OLDF)

Approaching the data from a non- deterministic view may imply The 'agency approach', which is sometimes twinned with 'methodological individualism' identified with scholars like Mises, and Popper (Udehn, 2002), who argue that the only reality we can grasp is the deeds/actions of individuals, not classes . However, to be able to generalise about action in any way or approach, theorists must assume that action is never entirely random, which implies that it is possible to find sociologically significant patterns of action if we look for them. The theoretical enigma is to **locate the source of the patterns** that we want to find. Contemporary theories of action typically locate the source of sociologically significant patterns of action in one of the two dimensions of social conduct. Some theorists maintain that action is best understood in terms of its subjective (existential or phenomenological) meaning to the actor or actors involved. These are viewed as 'Action' theorists; scholars such as Weber and Parsons, and tend to perceive the actor as determining the significance of their actions, focusing on conscious social action and the mental interpretation of the actor(I. J. Cohen, 2000; Gingrich, 2003). Other theorists, such as Mead, Garfinkel , and Giddens, locate the source of significant patterns in the way conduct is enacted, performed, or produced, and are referred to as 'Praxis' theorists (I. J. Cohen, 2000). Praxis theorists emphasise the process of enactment, examining the way social actions take place, changes and the forms they take. It recognises people's ability to adjust to each other, making conscious and sometimes unconscious decisions, and thus creating social structures. Theorists of praxis believe that although human actions are versatile and can be quickly adapted to unpredictable situations, there are patterns and regularities in human social action and interaction, which they attempt to understand and explain in terms of the ways patterns emerge and change(I. J. Cohen, 2000).

Theorists of praxis perceive social action as part of an interaction in situations. Action theorists, such as Weber and Parsons recognize this, but do not develop the implications of this as fully as theorists of praxis such as Simmel, Mead, Goffman, or Garfinkel, who focus on action as part of interaction (I. J. Cohen, 2000; Gingrich, 2003).

Action and praxis both refer to social conduct; however, there is a difference between the two. Action refers to what actors mean or intend by what they do, whereas praxis refers to what goes on when people act(I. J. Cohen, 2000)

In choosing the 'action theory' perspectives I would need to investigate what people meant or intended when they posted a message to one of the discussion forums I observed in this study. On the other hand, choosing the 'praxis theory' perspective would allow me to understand the processes occurring when people act. In this study Praxis theory would be more suitable as I would like to investigate what happened when my participants interacted in the online learning discussion in relation to learning. I see praxis theory as potentially enabling me to observe the following:

- Ways in which learning in online discussion forums can be detected
- The perceptions of learning observable

- The circumstances facilitating the various perceptions of learning

Furthermore, studying the meaning and intentions of people would have meant moving the focus of the study from the observation of practices, to the study of reflection on motivation and intentions, which would entail following interviews, journals, and personal narratives. Garfinkel would have argued that this approach would result in what he referred to as 'the Gap'(Lynch, 1993,p.289).

Garfinkel's 'Gap Theory'

Garfinkel argues that researchers attempting to reconstruct the relationship between the reported procedures and the results frequently encounter a gap of insufficient information. He goes on to suggest that even when the most rigorous scientific accounts are applied, there will still be a gap between the evidence, observable in the data, and the conclusions drawn from it (Garfinkel, 1967). To demonstrate the *gap* theory, Garfinkel uses the story of his uncle and a government clerk, in which his uncle's narrative was transcribed in a way that would produce a product that from the standpoint of the clerk would comply with administration and rules of the office, as shown in Garfinkel's original version:

> During the war my uncle had occasion to go to a government office because he wanted an increase in his allotment of fuel oil. There he complained to a clerk that his allotment was insufficient. He had a long story with which to justify his request for an increase. He described his circumstances at home. It was cold in the house; his wife was unpleasant because it was so cold; there was that large dining room which was always hard to heat even when you could buy as much fuel oil as you could afford; he was living in a particularly cold part of town; the children were down with one illness after another, one giving what ailed him to the next, so there was no rest for anyone; and so on.
>
> After several minutes of this the clerk stopped him. "How large is your house?" The story started again describing how large the house

was; how it had always been a burden; that his wife and not he had wanted the house. The clerk interrupted again. "Excuse me, how many rooms do you have in the house? How many square feet?" My uncle told him. "What kind of heater do you have?" and "What was your allotment last year?" And so it went. Out of the flow of material with which my uncle described his situation the clerk established about four or five points.

The clerk understood of course that the situation as my uncle described it was a fix in which a person could be. But the clerk consulted the rules of office operation, and in terms of these rules, exemplified in the information that was asked for on the form that the clerk filled out, the clerk undertook the process of selection, of classification, and the rest such that the clerk came up finally with what from the standpoint of the administered form was "the case."

There was one description of the social structures that my uncle furnished the clerk. The transformed description of my uncle's circumstances found in the form described a world which did not include complaining wives, or a house whose size and expense were regretted. Such features, though known to the clerk, were not relevant. Instead the clerk described a social situation which included instances of houses with certain square footages, with certain types of heaters, that would on the average produce certain units of heat over a unit period of time, with the expected result that some expected amount of a scarce commodity would have been used up by one instance of a "home owner"(Garfinkel, 1959).

The uncle's story was quite different from the clerk's description of the uncle's story. The uncle's narrative was translated by the clerk into an intelligible and defensible bureaucratic document, where a social situation was described in functional uses and material needed(Lynch, 1993). The gap Garfinkel refers to occurred between the 'natural accountability' of the life-world and the formal renderings produced by bureaucratic functionaries and professional scholars. This gap is produced through a transformation of locally accomplished, embodied, and 'lived' activities into **disengaged textual documents**(Lynch, 1993,p.287).

When transcribing a participants' narrative one must be aware of Garfinkel's gap, and the pitfalls of applying a participant's narrative to fit the interviewer or researcher's pattern/s, using the narrative to fill out slots in the pattern. Garfinkel argues that the way to overcome this gap is to use of 'the documentary method of interpretation (Zeitlyn, 1990).

The Workable Facets of the Documentary Method of Interpretation

Garfinkel(1967), argues that social order is constructed in the minds of social actors. He suggests that the way individuals bring order to or make sense of their social world is through a psychological process, which he calls the Documentary Method of Interpretation (DMI). The interpretation is done by the interlocutor's ability to infer their sense from the actions of others around them as they are performed. The sense making of an action or a series of actions is not determinate, but rather is always open to new interpretation (Garfinkel, 1967). DMI primarily consists of participants selecting parts which they would treat as relevant, and elect to choose those from a social situation(Garfinkel, 1967; Koschmann, Stahl, & Zemel, in press). These choices seem to conform to a pattern which can then be used to making sense of these facts in terms of the pattern. Once the pattern has been established, it is used as a framework for interpreting new facts, which arise within the situation (Poore, 2000). To demonstrate these notions Garfinkel conducted the experiment I have mentioned in chapter two in which he engaged a group of students and told them that they would receive counselling from training counsellors. To communicate with the counsellors they were asked to pose questions in an either/or format. The communication was done via an intercom system through which the students received a yes/no response to their questions. However, they were not made aware of the fact that the yes/no responses were supplied in a predetermined random sequence. Through the experiment Garfinkel was able to detect a number of interesting findings, some of which are of particular relevance to this study. The subjects perceived the answers as relevant to their questions, despite the fact that these were predetermined random responses. The identical utterance responded to several different questions simultaneously and of constituting an answer to a compound questions although they consisted only of a yes/no(Garfinkel, 1967)

Both these findings indicate that people will infer any response to their own circumstances, so much so that even randomly given yes/no responses made sense to the participants. Furthermore, their reflection on the responses as recorded in the experiment showed that they constructed for themselves a meaningful dialogue(Garfinkel, 1967; Zeitlyn, 1990).

Following these notions, attempting to study the emerging social order of the actions and practices of my participants enabled me to trail the order in which my participants make sense and construct meaning from their online contexts and experiences in the course. The *'documentary method of interpretation'* applied by my research participants is made visible through the choices they make in selecting which messages and even more specifically , which themes within a message they will respond to. Furthermore, in the context of online discussion forums, where messages are also representations of their authors, the choice the participants make not only depicts their choice of content but also their choice of social contacts. The manner in which participants choose to respond reveals an emerging pattern induced by the participants' interpretation of a situation or sequence of actions. Choosing to respond in a 'question answer' format would indicate the participants' interpretation of a situation in which, for example, a specific content or a certain member is involved. These choices which are helping participants make sense of their online world are also charting the structure of the discussion thread in which they are participating, creating patterns representing structures of social encounters. These structures represent the participants' understanding of what and how a situation needs to be addressed, such as a situation requiring a 'question answer' type of interactions, or alternatively, a situation inviting a sharing of ideas and collaboration with others.

The primary assumption guiding DMI is that behaviour, whether verbal or not is assumed to be connected to a hidden state of affairs(Zeitlyn, 1990). DMI treats actual appearance as "the document of' , 'pointing to', **standing on behalf of' a presupposed underlying pattern** (Benson & Hughes, 1983,p.90; Coulon, 1995,p.32). I hope to be able to use these emerging patterns, as underpinning my participants' perceptions of the use of the discussion forum either as a place for extracting and disseminating information or as a social sphere for exchanging, negotiating, and debating topics and ideas.

DATA COLLECTING - GOING EXCLUSIVELY ONLINE- THE SELF TRANSCRIBING CONVERSATIONS

Although I have collected data using interviews and questionnaires I feel that in view of the relevancy issues I have raised earlier in this chapter, and the '*gap*' Garfinkel refers to occurring between the 'natural accountability' of the life-world and the formal renderings produced (Lynch, 1993), I chose to use the data available through the online discussion forums as my primary data source. Although I will make use of the data collected in the interviews and questionnaires, these would act as a supportive source enabling the triangulation of the data observed online.

Opting to resort primarily to the information having direct relevancy to the occurrences in the online learning discussion forums meant relying largely on the online messages posted to the observed discussion forums, as my primary data source.

Technically, online discussion forums are a-synchronous communication tools, which enable people to communicate and interact with each other using text-based messages. Participants in online discussion forums contribute to the discussion by posting messages which are sent via a Web-based server. The server automatically stores the messages, so as to enable people to access and read each other's messages and respond to them, by posting responding text messages. All messages and responses are automatically stored on the server for further access and reference. This storing feature creates a data- base containing all the interactions, creating a self transcribed resource of automatically recorded conversations and processes. This abundance of information captured in these 'written conversations' portray an incredibly valuable resource for understanding online occurrences, in this case, possible learning processes (Kanuka & Anderson, 1998; Levin, Haesun, & Riel, 1990). As I have shown in the literature review chapter, few studies have used these self transcribing resources, even though these enable following the Documentary

Method of Interpretation processes, and hence portray accurate and almost true to real life accounts of online interactions, addressing issues raised in Garfinkel's 'gap theory'. Perhaps the reasons for the scarcity of studies using this lies in the methodologies used so far for the study of online discussion forums.

IN SEARCH OF A THEORETICAL FRAMEWORK FIT FOR ONLINE LEARNING DISCUSSION FORUMS (OLDF)

When I first embarked on this study, I set out to identify, investigate, analyse, and evaluate, learning processes in online learning discussion forums. However, having conducted a sample analysis of my data, I realised that before addressing these goals, I would first need to look for a way of observing, processing, representing, and analysing information generated by participants in online discussion forums in a way that would enable me to achieve my initial goals. The pilot study highlighted the need to establish the existence of certain activities and processes to be associated with learning, before proceeding to attempting to understand their meaning through analysis and evaluation of the processes at hand.

Ethnomethodology, with its commitment to the study of everyday procedures and practices used by members of a society(Garfinkel, 1967), enables the researcher to listen to "naturally occurring conversations in order to discover how a sense of social order is created through talk and interaction"(Gubrium & Holstein, 1997,p.7)

EM through its 'Documentary Method of Interpretation' (DMI) suggests that the empirical base of research is in the knowledge of those under research and in their relevancies, however, this does not mean that the observer is committed to their subjective intentions and common sense-theories. Furthermore, the observer is able to find an access to the structure of action and orientation, which exceeds the perspective of those under research(Bohnsack, 2002).

The notions embedded in the methodological stance of ethnomethodology offer a way of attempting to pursue my research objective in opening the way for the identification and study of learning dynamics, and preparing the way for further investigations and interpretation of the observed phenomena.

THE RESEARCH OBJECTIVE AND THE ANALYTIC IMPLICATIONS IT DENOTES

In attempting to explore possible materialisation of the historical and educational aspirations for collaboration in online discussion areas, my research objective is to:

- Explore possible ways of obtaining visual patterns representing online interactions in an attempt to identify different learning dynamics implying different learning perceptions and processes

For a more focused view of the objective of the study I phrased my objective as a research question:

- How can I identify, observe, and represent learning dynamics and processes in online discussion forums?

Traditional social sciences methodology would have probably approached this question using one or more of the following analysis perspectives:

1. Analyse the texts of the conversations, in search for evidence of learning within the content conveyed by these online contributions.

2. Analyse the environment in which conversations occur.

3. Analyse the ways in which the actions and behaviour of the research participants constituted learning.

Analysing Texts

Analysing texts would have most probably involved research techniques such as quantitative or qualitative content analysis, which could both provide valuable information about learning processes. Rourke, Anderson, Garrison, and Archer, (2001) however argue that content analysis techniques present researchers with a number of difficulties. Some of these difficulties are of pragmatic nature, as content analysis is a time consuming technique(Rourke & Anderson, 2004), particularly in online situations where data available can reach great magnitudes in terms of quantity of texts comprising a data set. Other difficulties are of a methodological nature, for example:

1. **'Objectivity'** - the extent to which categorization of sections of transcripts is subject to influence by the coders.

2. **'Reliability'** - The extent to which different coders, each coding the same content, come to the same coding decisions.

3. **'Replicability'** - the ability of multiple and distinct groups of researchers to apply a coding scheme reliably

(Rourke, Anderson, Garrison, & Archer, 2001).

Analysing Environments

Social structure is the aspect of environment in social science contexts. Analysing the environments or social structures surrounding the online conversations in this research would have probably situated this study in the arena of the 'structure – agency debate'. This debate has its place in the online context; however, issues of relevancy raise the question of locating the source of structures. Garfinkel's 'gap theory' would have questioned the effectiveness of structure oriented research in producing accurate accounts of the real life situation experienced.

Analysing Actions and Behaviour

Analysing the actions and behaviour patterns of my research participants in search for actions constituting learning could be interpreted as a study of actions of individuals, under 'action theories'. However, action theories approach would have raised the question of intention and relevancy issues for studying it. Intentions can be exposed through the study of the actors' own personal accounts, in the form of personal reflections, which may be situated outside the actual processes occurring in the discussion forum, and obtained by using reflective journals or interviews and questionnaires. These would raise the question of relevancy of these accounts as authentic, true to life representations both in terms of their origin, situated outside the actual occurrences, and in terms of Garfinkel's 'Gap' would be **disengaged textual**

documents, produced through a transformation of locally accomplished, embodied, and 'lived' activities (Lynch, 1993,p.287).

In this study I perceive the three analysis perspectives I have outlined in this section, as representing three focal points of study:

a. Text – the content of the messages comprising my data set
b. Environment – designated or created social and thematic structures
c. Behaviour – actions and reactions of my participants to each other's messages

Indeed each of these focal points could evolve into a study in its own rights; however, I would like to approach all three points as components of the whole process under investigation- the occurrences in Online Learning Discussion Forums (OLDF). One could argue that many studies used more than one perspective for studying similar situations. However, I would attempt to apply all three as components of a single, unified focus of study – 'what goes on in online learning discussion forums', which entails texts, created by actions and behaviours, to construct an environment. In searching for an approach that would enable me to approach the study from this perspective I turned to '*praxis*' theory.

The 'Praxis theory' approach focuses not so much on the meaning of the actions of actors, but rather on 'what happens when people act', or in other words, the relations between actions and their interaction with the environment. The praxis approach examines and emphasises the process of enactment of social conduct, how "we act (through our bodies) and the word reacts, our minds register and respond to the world, and then we act again"(I. J. Cohen, 2000,p.84). In this perspective on social action, sociologists examine what social action is, how it takes place, how it changes, what forms it takes, how people adjust to each other, and the social institutions that emerge from social action. Praxis theory assumes that there are patterns and regularities in human social action and interaction, hence the sociology of praxis attempts to understand and explain the various ways that these emerge and change (I. J. Cohen, 2000; Gingrich, 2003).

Adopting the praxis approach with its focus on the occurrences when people act, would enable me to amalgamate some of the aspects presented by the three approaches I have portrayed earlier as it looks at actions, in the case of my study through the posting of text messages, which invoke actions and reactions from others, and in doing so creating and changing the environment.

SUMMARISING THE GUIDELINES LEADING TO MY METHODOLOGY CHOICE

My search for methodology was initially triggered by questioning the relevancy of the real-life contexts to the online environment. Summarising my early analysis attempts, I was able to conclude that the real-life perceptions were irrelevant to the online context. This realisation pointed my investigation in the direction of a *priori*, versus '*a- posteriori*' categories, raising the question of 'what is at play'- some, a priori structure, represented by the categorisation into some pre- determined groups, imposing on the participants, or the participants, the actors, generating and forging the structure. Consulting my early analysis I was able to detect actions, which indicated activities beyond the designated groups. These observations suggested not only the possible irrelevancy of these groups, but also the ability of the participants to act freely, implying that they could either be acting in complete random, or alternatively they could be forging groups and structures, which in turn could imply that some a-*posteriori* structures could be emerging, led by the actions of my participants.

Three questions emerge from my observations so far:

- How can I detect these possibly emerging patterns of behaviour that would constitute structures in the online context of a learning discussion forum?

- Are the participants in the online discussion forum I am observing generating any patterns of behaviour that would indicate the formation of a social structure[16] describing systems of role attributed relations?

- What would constitute these patterns?

It is becoming clear that in this study I will be referring to the online environment as the reality of my participants, hence issues of relevancy do not stop at real-life versus online categories, but extends to issues of the observation of real- life situations and the formal accounts of the actions. The object of this study, searching for ways of detecting learning in online discussion, suggests a 'theory of praxis' approach enabling the analysis of 'what goes on, or what happens when people act in the forums'. Studying 'what happens when people act' implies looking at the data for revealing what is worth studying, rather than setting a priori hypotheses, or as ethnomethodologists would put it "the researcher's job is to document what the participants of the study ARE doing, rather than what they SHOULD be doing based on some a-priori expectations"(Koschmann, Stahl, & Zemel, in press).

Approaching an investigation from the data perspective, may entail the necessity of constructing an account of even the most obvious of actions. Ethnomethodology is a theoretical framework which can be described as a way to investigate the 'relationship between social practices and accounts of those practices'(Lynch, 1993,p.1)

ETHNOMETHODOLOGY – KEY POINTS

Ethnomethodology offers a fresh approach to social science: "systematic analysis of how members of a society build the events they participate in…"(Goodwin

---

[16]   According to Bourdieu, social structure is a system of relations and differences. Subjects, whether they be individuals or institutes, derive their social meaning from their positions with respect to one another in a social field and not from their intrinsic characteristics(De Nooy, 2003). (Garfinkel, 1967; Parsons, 1968b; Radcliffe-Brown, 1965(1952))

& Duranti, 1992 ,p. 27; Packer, 2000). This definition of ethnomethodology is relevant
to my quest for the ways in which my participants construct their social environments.
I would suggest that the following six items delineated below describe the most
applicable aspects of ethnomethodology for the context of this study.
Ethnomethodology offers:

1. A systematic analysis of how members of a society build the events they
   participate in(Goodwin & Duranti, 1992 ,p. 27; Packer, 2000), enabling
   the observations of actors' actions and the way they construct events.
   Relative to the quest of this study this would enable an understanding of
   how participants structure discussion threads, and in so doing illuminate
   the processes underpinning these structures

2. Analysis of everyday activities as methods used by members for making
   those activities visibly-rational-and reportable for all practical
   purposes(Garfinkel, 1967), suggesting that everyday activities are
   methods, making them reportable. This aspect would enable detecting
   the patterns the participants are structuring. Visibility and reportability
   have a very practical purpose in an educational environment like the one
   studied in this study, as they facilitate research of processes, and
   formative feedback of practices.

3. Study of the mechanisms by which participants achieve and sustain
   interactions in a social encounter(L. Cohen & Manion, 1994). This
   aspect would enable understanding the mechanisms operating in online
   discussion and the ways in which they help sustain interactions.

4. Investigation of communicative activities, perceiving conversation as a
   kind of "machinery" for the construction of reality. The
   ethnomethodological "method talk" is hence, according to Gubrium &
   Holstein, a "talk about talk" (Gubrium & Holstein 1997: 8). This aspect
   depicts how interactions or communications construct the patterns
   representing the reality the participants of this study are structuring.

5. Investigation of the social realities as either "suspended" or "bundled" in
   order to investigate how they are made into structures of everyday life,
   (Gubrium & Holstein, 1997; Moser, 2000). This feature can contribute
   to the understanding of how structures emerge in everyday situations,

such as learning discussions. This is different to the perception that
structures can only be found in large institutionalised situations

6. Access to virtual social environments enabled by the
   ethnomethodological field which is not necessarily bound to specific
   geographical locations, and it does not require researchers to infiltrate a
   milieu (Gubrium & Holstein, 1997,p.52; Moser, 2000). This feature is
   very relevant to the online, virtual, non- physical context of this study.

These six points delineate the ways in which ethnomethodology approaches social
situations, establishing the ways in which individuals, rather than some a-priori
determinants, construct their environments, and through communication sustain these
environments as social structures, all of which are not bound by any specific location. In
the case of online contexts is an important realisation. Furthermore, the communicative,
interactive focus of ethnomethodology makes it a suitable theoretical framework for
studying learning processes in online learning discussion forums, where interactions are
the heart of the matter. However, the actual analysis of the interactions would call for
additional analytic frameworks and tools.

INTERACTIONS, AND RELATIONS AS A ROUTE FOR SOCIAL STUDIES-
SEARCHING FOR AN ANALYTIC METHOD

In 1973 Granovetter in his seminal essay "The Strength of Weak
Ties"(Granovetter, 1973) investigated the ways in which information is conveyed
throughout a group of people linked together through their interactions to form a
network. This orientation indicated a new route for social studies, connecting theories
of social behaviour on the one hand and social relations on the other, to evolve into a
new perspective of praxis and action(I. J. Cohen, 2000). Granovetter's investigations
indicated that the concept of social relations incorporates not just intimate bonds of
affection and acquaintances, but also a variety of types of relations that are found across
networks, communities and organisations(I. J. Cohen, 2000). Over the past two
decades, theorists have raised questions and opened new investigations of the meanings
and practices that constitute social relations. Theorists began focusing on questions of

action and praxis guided by interest in social relations. Theories of praxis focused their study around questions like 'how does human conduct constitute social life?' Some theorists such as Emirbayer(1997), argue that social life is constituted in unfolding sequences of social relations, thus agency, praxis, meaning , and purpose are subsidiary issues in the study of social relations(I. J. Cohen, 2000; Emirbayer, 1997)

Emirbayer's perception positions 'relations' at the heart of the study of social life, which seems very appropriate for the context of studying online discussion forums, where the essence of action is about sequences of social relations. Focusing on relations means no longer focusing on individuals, nor structures, but rather on what happens between them.

Relational Approach – and Structural Analysis

Rogers and Bhowmik(1971) define the relational perspective as "… a research approach in which the unit of analysis is a relationship between two or more individuals" (p. 524).

WHAT DO WE MEAN BY 'RELATIONS'?

Structural analysts such as Berkowitz(1982) break away from the conventional model of 'relations', through which the social world is viewed as an extension of sentiments, motivations, and attitudes of individual actors.

A relation in the structural analysis framework is a link between agents, which connects them to a larger relational system(Scott, 2000). In the context of online discussion threads, a relation manifests itself in the form of 'reply' or 'response' to another message. This manifestation of a link between messages is also an indication of a link between the authors of the linked messages. In other words, a person responding to a message in an online discussion forum is also creating a link with the author of the message he or she is responding to. A set of links between a number of messages, whether sent by a single or several authors establishes a relational system, or a network.

Structural analysis perceives a relational system as a social structure based on Radcliffe-Brown's model in which a structure is a dynamic interplay between relations between and among persons, or institutions on the one hand, and the positions and roles they occupy within a social system on the other (Berkowitz, 1982). Positions, roles and ability to control are all discovered by investigating the relations(Scott, 2000) The nature of a relation is established by measuring its density, or frequency, or in other cases by looking at the ability to exchange, or convey information. Each relation or link in the network can be regarded as holding a position which can be mathematically calculated to evaluate the position's influence or ability to convey information in the network, and the role the position may imply.

In the framework of structural analysis, 'relations' cannot be reduced to the properties of an individual agent. Relations are not the properties of agents but of systems of agents who are representing positions and roles rather than individuals, hence the study of social relations focuses on the investigation of the 'structure' of social action(Scott, 2000).

STUDYING STRUCTURES THROUGH SOCIAL ACTIONS

Wellman and Berkowitz(1988) argue that traditional sociologists hinge their explanations on discovering that persons with similar attributes such as gender, residence, etc. behave similarly in response to shared norms. Such analyses, which are based on inferred vocabulary of motives, can detect social structure only indirectly. By contrast, structural analysts believe that the main focus of social scientists is to study social structure and its consequences. Rather than working toward an indirect understanding of 'social structure' in the abstract, they study social structures directly and concretely. They analyse the ordered arrangements of relations that are contingent upon exchange among members of social systems. They map these structures and describe their patterns, using tools derived from mathematical graph theory, and seek to uncover the effects of these patterns on the behaviour of the individual members of these structures. Structural analysts argue that social categories are best discovered and analysed by examining relations between social actors. Rather than beginning with an a priori classification of the observed world, they begin with a set of relations or a 'social network' emerging from the data, from which they derive maps and typologies of social structures. Thus they draw inferences from wholes to parts, from structures and relations to categories and from behaviours to attitudes (Wellman & Berkowitz, 1988). An important key to understanding structural analysis is recognising that social structures can be represented as 'networks' –as sets of *nodes* (actors) and sets of *ties* (relations) depicting their interconnections, rather than the attributes of aggregated sets of individuals. This perception frees researchers from thinking of social systems as collections of individuals, and directs their investigation to the social relation, using relations as the basic unit of analysis (Wellman & Berkowitz, 1988)

WHAT ARE RELATIONS IN OLDF MADE OF

Previously in this chapter I compared the trailing of the processes in online a-synchronous discussion forums to the linking between dots on a paper, and by drawing lines between them completing a picture. In this analogy, each dot represents a message in the discussion forum, and each line connecting a dot to another dot, represents the relation between them, creating a network of dots and lines. However, the dots in this network have not appeared by themselves, but were actually produced by the people who sent the message, which in turn means that the lines connecting the dots are actually connecting people. But what are the lines comprised of? Or in other words, what are 'relations' made of?

In the context of online discussion forums observable 'relations' can only be detected through the text-based encounters between two or more persons, creating a visible link between two or more messages[17]. These encounters occur whenever one person responds to another. The nature, and style of response, and the sustainability of

---

[17]   This study has not investigated inferred links in which person A may relate to person C in a message to person B. This type of analysis could be obtained through the 'Reachability' routine of SNA however, it was not applied here.

the relation (whether it be confined to a single contact or evolve into a series of encounters), will depend on the content of the message, and the process of interpretation and meaning- making that would take place between the participants in the encounter. These processes of interpretation and meaning- making of the messages received could be seen as guided by the Documentary Method of Interpretation (DMI).*Figure 3-6* illustrates the formation of a 'Relation':

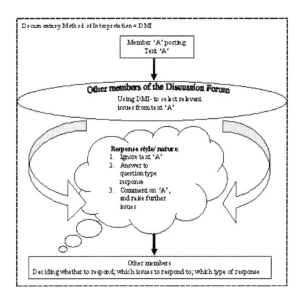

Figure 3-6 Description of a Relation

'*Figure 3-6*' describes the mental process leading to the formation of a 'relation'. This mental process links the three components identified earlier; actions and reactions creating and responding to a text (a message). Because of their unique assembly of components, linking content and people, and the application of the 'Documentary Method of Interpretation'(DMI) processes, a sequence of relations holds the potential for creating, or alternatively changing the environment or the structure within which the relations occur. Theoretically this will occur because it is the actual interpretations of the members that create the sequence of relations comprising their

social structure, or as Emirbayer(1997) suggests- sequences of social relations
constitute and unfold 'social life'. In the context of this study the 'social life' consists of
the structure of several, or a sequence of the unique 'relations', which portray not only
the 'social life' but also the *thematic life'* linking the participants and their relevant
texts into a *'socio –thematic network'. 'Figure 3-7'* demonstrates an example for a
possible sequence of 'relations' forming a *socio- thematic network.*

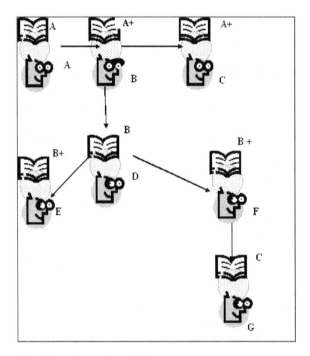

Figure 3-7 - *A Network of Relations*

'*Figure 3-7'* depicts a sequence of 'relations' through which changes in the
communication content occur, as participants apply Documentary Method of
Interpretation (DMI) to select relevant parts from within a received text(Poore, 2000),
hence producing a response that is different from the original message received. *Figure
3-7* illustrates this process by indicating a sequence in which participant 'A' posts the
text 'A', and participant 'B' responds applying DMI and SI to produce text 'A+'

representing 'B's own additions and changes to the original 'A' message. Being able to visualise this phenomenon is quite significant as it indicates a possible route for following conversation and learning in Online Learning Discussion Forums (OLDF), as it illustrates though in a simplified manner the conveyance, and at times alteration of ideas among the participants in a network.

THE 'DOCUMENTARY METHOD OF INTERPRETATION', LEARNING, AND VISUALISING RELATIONS

My research objective is to find ways of observing learning processes in OLDF. The context in which my participants operate suggests that learning occurs through people's interactions with each other, to construct knowledge. The socio-cultural theorists may have no difficulty with the idea of knowledge existing at a super personal level, but they have trouble linking this up to specific learning tasks(Bereiter, 1999). *'Figure 3-7',* may indicate a possible way of following sequences of interactions related to a specific task, hence offering some way of addressing this problem, as I demonstrate in the following section.

Following the trail of topic selection and interpretation, as exhibited in 'figure 3- 7', may shed some light on the trail of thought conveyed and shared by participants in a network of 'relations', representing participant, content, and interpretation mechanisms.

Garfinkel suggests that through DMI people select certain facts from a given situation in order to make sense of their world, arguing that this selection is an indication of what the participants see as relevant(Koschmann, Stahl, & Zemel, in press). This selection will guide the participants' response, as demonstrated in *'figure 3-7'*, showing that some participants, for example, 'B', and 'C', responded to 'A' with participant 'B' contributing something of his or her own to produce 'A+', and C linking to 'B' however, not showing any further development of the message 'A+'. Participant 'D' in *'Figure 3-7'* may have selected a different idea altogether on receiving message 'A+' from participant 'B', hence contributing message 'B'. Garfinkel(1967) would argue that these different responses are representations of the selections and interpretations the participants are making, and adhering to his DMI principles, these phenomena are standing on behalf of underlying patterns of understanding(Benson & Hughes, 1983). I would like to suggest that we may perceive these selections as portraying the topics relevant to the participants at a certain point in the sequence of 'relations'. Changes in the choice of topics will imply changes in relevancies, hence indicating changes in perceptions. This information may be of use particularly in learning contexts, however, I will not pursue this notion further in this study.

The illustration in '*figure 3-7*' depicts only a small glimpse of what a visual representation of a sequence of relations may reveal.Visualising this process across the whole of my data set may well be the solution for detecting learning in OLDF. However, conducting such an analysis would require some form of systematic trailing and visualisation mechanisms.

SUMMARY OF PART TWO

Throughout this chapter, I have acknowledged the need for discovering patterns as representations of emerging structures. Adhering to the principle of relevancy and the uniqueness of the online environment, with its seminal emphasis on relations, I searched for a methodology that would enable me to trail the origins of emerging, relation- based structures or networks of relations. My definition of a relation in the context of online discussion threads is:

1. A link manifested through a reply or response to a message
2. The link in the form of the reply/ response is triggered by the DMI process applied by the participant

3. A link is connected to the greater relational system, and its situation or position in the system indicates its ability to convey information

The unique composition of 'relation' as described earlier in this section, linking content and people through a relevancy informed selection processes guiding their responses to each other, would hopefully enable me to investigate the existence of learning in OLDF. However, in order to be able to do this, I would first need to find a way to systematically represent and visualise sequences of relations, forming networks.

Part Three

In this section I will study closely the mechanisms at work in Online Discussion Forums, so as to be able to apply the necessary methods for visualising the relations within them, in a way that would maximise the effectiveness of the visual representations in the detection of learning in OLDF.

Using a mock data- set, I will describe the development of an alternative concept for studying online discussion forums using a structural approach. The alternative concept applies 'Social Network Analysis' (SNA) and Graph Theory concepts for visualising emerging socio-thematic networks in the mock data.

Introducing Social Network Analysis (SNA)

"Graphics is the visual means of resolving logical problems" (Bertin, 1981,p.16)

A social network is a set of actors (sometimes referred to as 'points', or 'nodes' or 'agents'), that have relationships[18] (alternatively referred to as edges, or ties), with one another. Networks can have few or many actors. To understand networks one needs a complete description of a pattern of social relationships as a starting point of analysis. Social Network Analysis (SNA) employs mathematical and graphical techniques based on *Graph Theory*, which is a mathematical approach for visual representation of network matrices(Scott, 2000,p.64; Wasserman & Faust, 1994) enabling representation and description of social network in a compact and systematic way. This in turn facilitates the analysis of the relations comprising the structure of the network,

---

[18] relationships as I have noted earlier in this chapter are beyond the intimate bonds of affection(Granovetter, 1973)

highlighting the status of the actors in the network, and the nature of the network as a social structure. SNA enables the investigation of 'what goes on when people interact' as it records who talked to whom, and calculates the position of the interlocutors in terms of their ability to convey information, control the flow of information to others, and their ability to influence the individuals within the network , as well as the whole of the structure.

In other words, SNA enables two levels of investigation of social structures or networks:
1. The visualisation of the network – enabling the identification of patterns emerging
2. The mathematical calculation of the types of relations, using position and connectivity to establish the nature of the relation and the roles and positions of the actors related.

(Borgatti & Cross, 2003; Everton, 2002; Hanneman, online; Scott, 2000; Wellman & Berkowitz, 1988)[19].

Social network analysis recognises two types of networks:
One mode networks – in which people interact with other people in their group;
Two mode networks – in which people interact with another group of people, or participate in events;
(Borgatti & Everett, 1996).

At first glance 'figure 3-7', may indicate that the type of data generated in online learning discussion forums (OLDF), can be perceived as qualifying for the One - mode network definition, however, this perception would not render the full representation of the communications conveyed between the participants.

---

[19]   In this section I will only be using the visualisation feature of SNA, as this section will be using only a small mock data set to illustrate the use of the alternative tool. However, I will apply the mathematical aspects to the actual data, which I will present in the 'Findings and Analysis' chapter.

A closer look at 'figure 3-7' reveals that it not only depicts how various participants respond to each other, but also indicates instances where more than one person shows an interest in a certain topic. Although *Figure 3-7'* acknowledges these instances of mutual interest, it is unable to graphically bind them together, and can only present them as separate responses, the mutuality of which is indicated only in the related symbols annotating the messages , i.e. 'A', and 'A+', or 'B' , and 'B+'.

Identifying a mutual topic shared by a number of participants is important for the understanding of the evolvement of a discussion thread, and the meaning making processes shared by groups of participants. The sharing of a mutual topic amongst a group of participates may imply a two- mode, rather than a one-mode network. In the following sections I will attempt to unfold this notion to explain this suggestion.

HOW DO DISCUSSION FORUMS OPERATE

Usually, people refer to discussion forums as places where people can interact with other people; however, the actual way in which this happens is hardly ever mentioned outside the computer sciences and other technology oriented spheres. Attempting to describe the ways in which discussion forums operate without resorting to technological jargon, I chose to compare them to a conference event. For example: The Reflective Teacher Association decides to hold a number of conferences on the same date. Each conference is allocated ONE single hall for holding ALL its various sessions. Each session in each of the conferences is allocated a table and some chairs for members to congregate around. When the participants arrived at the venue, they discovered that sharing one hall posed some acoustics problems and people found it quite hard to conduct a conversation without disturbing all the other sessions sharing the hall.

In view of the situation, the participants decided to communicate by writing their contributions on cards and exchanging cards with their conversation partners. These rather unusual circumstances produced an incredible resource, as each conference was meticulously recorded, formulating an affluent data corpus of all the interactions including the informal ones. Each verbal interaction was recorded by writing the message on a single card. Cards from each conference were stacked separately. Each conference stack held separate files, each file holding all the cards collected from each of its sessions.

The significance of this analogy lies in the fact that the recording of the conversations was not made for any reason outside the pragmatic need to overcome bad acoustics, which may well address the problems of 'disengaged textual documents' producing Garfinkel's Gap.

In this little analogy, "The Reflective Teacher Association" stood for the online course observed; Each Conference stood for each of the Online Forums. Each Session within a conference stood for what is known as "Discussion Thread".

Once the participants populated a discussion forum, they conducted various discussions within that Forum. Each 'discussion' formulated a "Discussion Thread".

A "Discussion Thread" usually started out with all members discussing the same topic. In some threads, the participants kept to a single topic all along. In other cases this unity was broken, and somewhere along the discussion some of the participants may have taken up an alternative topic, creating a sub discussion, or a sub thread.

Sub threads may have evolved whenever an idea expressed by one participant was picked up by another, and developed as a new topic, forming a group within a group. The member whose idea triggered the sub thread is granted 'parenthood 'over the sub-group. A sub group could involve a pair of participants or more. For example: David says something, and Mary decides to pick up David's idea and develop it further, this may create a situation where Mary and David form their own sub discussion. It may be that they will continue as a pair or be joined by others. In other words, David's idea generated not only a new topic but also affected the dynamics of interactions in the group.

Understanding the way in which discussion forums operate helped me realise that attempting to follow the 'discussion threads' would have not enabled me to follow the evolvement of the thread with all its sub discussions. As I will show later in this study, this realisation of the significance of the sub discussion threads was crucial to the obtaining of the object of this study.

TRAILING SUB- DISCUSSION- THREADS AND THE EVOLVEMENT OF TWO-MODE NETWORKS

'*Figure 3-6*' in Part two of this chapter described online 'relations' as intertwined entities capable of creating or alternating structures. The application of 'the Documentary Method of Interpretation' (DMI) by the participants inform the thematic selection processes guiding the creation of each 'relation'. Trailing a sequence of 'relations' exhibited in 'figure 3-7', enables tracing the evolvement of a structure, as it depicts the trail of topics responded to by different participants, hence representing each new turn and expansion in the structure of 'relations'. However, this manner of trailing is rather unclear and is incapable of highlighting the mutuality of responses to a shared topic, hence not quite enabling the visualisation of the formation of any sub- discussion threads. Sub-threads may have evolved whenever an idea expressed by one participant was picked up by another, and developed as a new topic, forming a group within a group. These sub-threads will include at least one message and a single response to it, linking at least two people forming a point of meeting. This meeting point is created by a mutual interest and activity around it, which I suggest can be perceived as an event. Perceiving these meeting points as events meant I would approach the activities in OLDF as people participating in events, which would classify the networks created by their relations as 'Two Mode Networks', depicting a group of people participating in a series of events.

Two- mode networks also referred to as *'Affiliation Networks'*, enable the study of the dual perspectives of the actors and the events, by depicting actors as linked to one another by their affiliation with events, and at the same time depicting events as linked by the actors who are their members. Studying 'Affiliation Networks' enables modelling the relationships between actors and events as a whole system, and focusing on the ties between them(Wasserman & Faust, 1994). However, there are very few methods for studying actors and events simultaneously. One way of studying 'Affiliation networks' is to represent them as a *bipartite graph,* representing both actors and events converting two-mode networks to 1-mode adjacency matrix[20] (Borgatti, Everett, & Freeman, 2002). In a *'bipartite graph'* nodes can be partitioned into two subsets, and all lines are between pairs of nodes belonging to different subsets. An affiliation network can be represented by a *'bipartite graph'* by representing both actors and events as nodes, and assigning actors to one subset of nodes and events to the other subset. Thus each mode of the network constitutes a separate node set in the bipartite graph. The lines in the bipartite graph represent the relation "is affiliated with", (from the perspective of the actor) or "has a member" (from the perspective of the event). Since actors are affiliated with events, and events have actors as members, all lines in the bipartite graph are between nodes representing actors and nodes representing events. (Wasserman & Faust, 1994).

Representing the affiliation network as a *'bipartite graph* 'highlights the connectivity in the network, and makes the indirect chains of connection more apparent(Wasserman & Faust, 1994). In this case eliciting which members participated in which events, enables the identification of members who shared an event, or in the case of this study, a discussion topic. Furthermore, using *'bipartite'* graphs enables the processing of two-mode networks for visualisation purposes, and as I will show in the next chapter, also for calculation purposes.

---

[20]   The most common form of matrix in social networks- it has as many rows and columns as there are actors in the data set, and where entries represent the ties between actors. It represents who is next to, or adjacent to whom in the network)

The perception of the emergence of sub-threads as meeting points or events enabled me to deconstruct the processes occurring in *socio-thematic* networks, and present them as a series of three stages:

1. 'Who talked to whom?
2. Who talked to whom' and on which event?
3. Who talked to whom', on which event, and about what?

'*Figure 3-7*' in part two of this chapter illustrated quite clearly two out of the three phases: 'who talked to whom', and 'about what', and although indicating some mutual points of interest, '*figure3-7*' was unable to graphically highlight these significant meeting events. Furthermore, '*figure3- 7*' depicted a minute number of relations, enabling the trailing of the sequence of relations by using participants' names for following their involvement in the network. However, applying this system to a real data- set would be ineffective as any specific participant could be involved in several meeting events along the discussion forums, hence reappearing at different points on the sequence. Tracking by name could prove inaccurate and confusing.

'Figure 3-7'elicited two problems:

- Graphic representation of meeting points
- Systematic tracking of people and their relation to different messages at different points in the socio-thematic network

In this section I will describe the development of the alternative approach to the
analysis of Online Learning Discussion Forums (OLDF)

FOLLOWING THE FORMATION OF RELATION SEQUENCES AND HOW
THE SQL SERVER CAME TO THE RESCUE

One of the benefits of conducting an online research is the electronic
accessibility to the data, stored in the form of electronic databases. The technological
platform running the discussion forums I have observed in this study uses a SQL
(Structured Query Language) server. As commercial relational databases entered the
market and Relational Database Management Systems or RDBMSs proliferated,
Structured Query Language- SQL became the most popular language for querying and
manipulating relational databases. In fact, it became so popular that people often use the
term SQL and relational database interchangeably. A database can be understood as a
collection of related files or more specifically, tables.(DatabaseJournal, 2003) Tables in
a database are related to each other by means of a common field. Any field or
combination of fields can become a 'key'. A 'key' is a tool that unlocks access to
database tables. By knowing the key, one knows how to locate specific records, and
navigate the relationships between tables.(Gilfillan, 2002).

The 'key' feature of the server running my data-set was to become the key tool
for the development of my analysis tool.

USING SQL CODES FOR ANALYSING A DISCUSSION FORUM

The principle underpinning the SQL stated that 'by knowing a key we know how to locate specific records, and navigate the relationships between tables', which implied that I could use this principle to help me locate specific entities and follow relationships between them, but not without first solving what I would refer to as the *multiple profiles* of my participants. To solve this notion I will need to identify and classify the information available through the online discussion forums' server

The system running my data set enabled me to extract spreadsheets describing the activity in each discussion forum. The spreadsheet included an abundance of information which I would classify into two groups:

1. The human language items
2. The computer language items

The human language items included: the name of the participants; the message contributed; the subject of the message; its nature, whether it was intended as a comment, a question, a task, and so forth. It also indicated the time in which the message was posted.

The information available in this group made it easy to follow which participant contributed which messages, on what subject, and at what time, however, it gave no information about the way in which a message ventured in the discussion forum. A message is primarily a communicative tool, which means that when studying messages one must observe the ways in which a message is received. Studying online discussion forums is all about studying communication acts between people, hence focusing solely on a message, without following its reception would be missing the paramount issue of its role.

In search of a way to link between messages, I turned to the computer language group of items. Here I found three sets of key codes, automatically generated by the SQL server. Each time a message is posted to the discussion forum, the server allocates it a 'post key' code. This key is comprised of a random number and serves as the identifying code of the message it was assigned to.

When a participant posts a message which is unrelated to any previous messages, that unrelated message indicates the beginning of a new conversation or in online terminology a new 'discussion thread'. In these cases, the 'post key' code allocated to this message will be identical to the 'thread key' the key number which will identify this newly created conversation, or 'thread'. The SQL server, being a relational database, prepares for any future development and automatically assigns each message a 'parent key' , to indicate whether the message is 'parenting' any other messages. Parenting in this context refers to any messages responding to a 'parent', making the responding messages, the 'children' of the 'parenting' message. A first in a thread message will automatically be allocated the parent key code – zero, indicating that it is not a 'child' to any previous messages. The responding message to this parent will bear the same post key of its parenting message.

Table 3-1 demonstrates this progression in two separate threads:

Table 3-1: The progression of Threads

Message position	Post Key	Thread Key	Parent Key
First message in thread	1	1	0
Second message	2	1	1
Third message	3	1	1
Reply to Third message	4	1	3
Second Thread (marked 5 so as not to confuse with any of the messages in thread 1)			
First message in thread	5	5	0
Second message	6	5	5
Reply to Second message	7	5	6

The computer group items shows the way for trailing the relations between messages, however, messages do not generate by themselves, but are created and posted by people. This is a very obvious link, people create messages, and hence people are related to their messages. In computer terms this creates a problem, as one person can create more than one message. In order to establish the actor message link, actors would need to be coded differently in relation to each message they post, otherwise the

143

computer system would converge all the various messages of an actor into one. To avoid this I needed to create *multiple profiles* for each of my participants.

To achieve this I merged the actors name with the post key, so that actors had a different identity for each time they posted a message.

Using the spreadsheets generated by the server for each discussion forum, I merged the 'name', 'thread', and 'post key' columns using the formula: =A2&"-"&B2&"- "&C2. I included the thread key column so as to be able to identify the thread to which messages belonged.

The merger between messages and people meant I could systematically trail the involvement of each participant in relation to the different messages they were involved in at different points in the *socio-thematic network,* by providing them with a *multiple profile.*

In other words, in order to be able to represent events and also to be able to follow members at different points on the sequence I needed to apply two sets of SQL codes:

1. *Name + post key,* for trailing participants at different points in the network, giving each participant a 'multiple profile

2. *Parent key + post key* for graphically representing the meeting points,

Introducing the Alternative Approach- and Defining the Unit of Analysis

Manually extracting the server's generated key codes; I created *Table 3-2,* which lists on the left column the names of participants coupled with the 'thread' and 'post' keys. Combining the participant with the message coding enabled me to associate a participant with a specific message. The right column of *table 3-2* lists the 'thread key coupled with 'parent key' of the messages sent by the participant showing on the left.

Table 3-2 *Participants and 'Message Affiliation'*

Participant key codes	Message affiliation key codes
Mary- 100-100	100-0
Bob-100-344	100-100
John – 100-542	100-100
Dianne-100-678	100-344

Table 3-2 contains the information needed for discovering 'who posted', 'which message' as well as in response to whom, however, the manner in which the information is represented is not very clear, and is quite inaccessible when analysing whole discussion threads, which are much longer than the small sample shown in *table 3-2*.

Using the '*cross tab query function*' of MS ACCESS programme, I converted *table 3-2* into a binary matrix, (*Table 3-3*). Zeros (0) in the matrix indicate no entries, in other words, no posting; 'Ones' (1) indicate entries, or postings. The matrix format is better suited for visually depicting who responded to whom, by simply following columns containing more than one entry.

Table 3-3 *Participants Posting Messages*

Participant / message	100-0	100-100	100-344
Mary- 100-100	1	0	0
Bob-100-344	0	1	0
John – 100-542	0	1	0
Dianne-100-678	0	0	1

Table 3-3 shows that Bob and John responded to the same parenting messages marked 100.

Identifying the originating or parenting message and its responses was possible by following the second part of the key codes highlighted in bold fonts in '*table3- 4'*. Identical second part of the code meant people were responding to the same message, creating a meeting point or a conversational event, where participants responded to an originating message.

Table 3-4 *Conversational Events Formation*

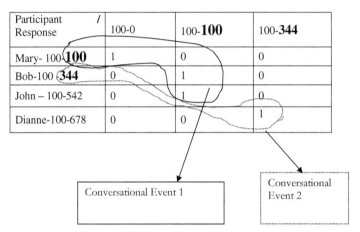

Participant / Response	100-0	100-**100**	100-**344**
Mary- 100-**100**	1	0	0
Bob-100-**344**	0	1	0
John – 100-542	0	1	0
Dianne-100-678	0	0	1

Conversational Event 1

Conversational Event 2

The concept of 'conversational events', or Event Centres, (EC) as I chose to call them, captured the notion of participants in online discussion forums, not merely as people posting messages and responding to other people, but people sharing an event with other participants. The EC is in fact the meeting point of the 'relations' I have described in figure 3-6 earlier in this chapter; it is a visual mark of a 'relation'. The EC became my *unit of analysis* for following the evolvement of ideas in conversations, in search of learning activities in OLDF.

Using spreadsheets and matrices showing SQL codes for trailing emerging socio-thematic networks can be a rather tedious and not very effective task. Although these tools allow detecting the presence of an EC, they are unable to convey any possible connections between various ECs. Furthermore, following key codes would make it difficult to identify any emerging patterns of relations that would enable the detection of groups or social structures evolving throughout the networks of interactions. What is needed is some way of visualising this type of data, comprised of two-mode socio-thematic networks.

One tool enabling visual representation of networks is a computer pack called UCINET(Borgatti, Everett, & Freeman, 2002), which is used for social network analysis (SNA), which includes a graphic software feature called NEDRAW. To visualise the matrix shown in '*table 3-4*' I used UCINET and a visualisation pack incorporated within it called Netdraw. Both packs are available for downloading from: http://www.analytictech.com/downloadnd.htm.

Copying the matrix of '*table 3-4*' into UCINET, I then used the '*bipartite*' feature in UCINET, which enables the representation of Two-Mode, or 'affiliation' networks in bipartite graphs.

In a bipartite matrix representing an affiliation network, digits represent the participation of an actor in an event, or membership in an event. (0) represents no participation or membership, (1) represent membership or participation. '*Table 3-5*' illustrates the bipartite graph of a mock data-set.

Table 3-5 *Symmetric Bipartite Matrix*

```
        1 2 3 4 5 6 7

        M B J D 1 1 1

        - - - - - - -

1 Mary- 100-100  0 0 0 0 1 0 0

2   Bob-100-344  0 0 0 0 0 1 0

3 John - 100-542  0 0 0 0 0 1 0

4 Dianne-100-678  0 0 0 0 0 0 1

5       100-0  1 0 0 0 0 0 0

6       100-100  0 1 1 0 0 0 0

7       100-344  0 0 0 1 0 0 0
```

'*Table3- 5*' shows four members, marked in rows and columns 1-4, participating in three events, marked in rows and columns 5,6,7. Following the (1) representing participation and membership, enables identifying who participated in which event, however, this is possible only once an event has been established – meaning, that at least one response has been sent to a particular message. This representation converts two- mode networks into one mode, so that mathematical calculation could be applied (Everton, 2002; Scott, 2000; Wasserman & Faust, 1994).

Once converted into one mode networks, I exported the data into Netdraw pack, choosing the network feature under 'file >UCINET data set> networks'. UCINET and Netdraw are both SNA tools; however, there is still no tool available for processing EC, as this is the newly developed concept. Therefore the final stages of processing my data had to be done manually. Netdraw produced the ECs in clusters scattered on a page, not being able to identify any links between them.
'*Figure 3-8*' depicts the way in which Netdraw produces the network.

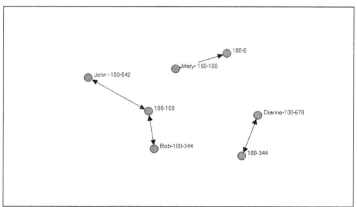

Figure 3-8 *Netdraw Results Unsorted*

To construct the visual representations of the EC I had to manually link messages with their responses. To be able to achieve this I needed to consult the SQL coding. An EC is comprised of an initiating and at least one responding message. All messages responding to this initiating message will bear its post key as their parent key; hence the coding of the EC itself will show the parent key of all its responding messages which is the post key of its initiating message. Linking between EC is done by relating messages showing a post key identical to the parent key of the EC.

To identify the first response, so crucial to the creation of an EC, I needed to manually make the connections, matching post keys to parent keys- for example Diane parent key 344, responding to Bob post key 344. *Figure 3-9* depicts the manually sorted network

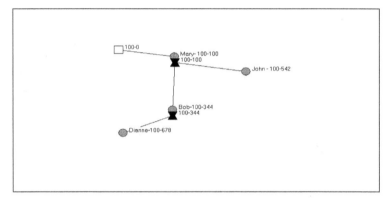

Figure 3-9 *A Network of Event Centres*

'*Figure3- 9*' marks participants in grey circles and conversational events in black shapes. The white square identifies the initial message at the start of the discussion
'*Figure 3-9*' is a graphic representation of the matrices depicting the conversational events shown in '*table3-5*'.

'*Figure 3-9*' depicts not only the event centres (EC), but also the relations between them, forming a network of EC, recreating the evolvement of the conversations all through the discussion thread, depicting the development of discussion and sub discussion occurring along the way.
Identifying the conversation events completed the *third stage* I have identified earlier in this chapter, revealing 'who talked to whom' and 'on which occasion'.

Using UCINET and Netdraw, with the help of some manual intervention, I was able to visualise my data, to discover emerging patterns and structures[21]. At this point I have not applied any mathematical calculations to the relations in the emerging networks. I will refer to these in the next chapter.

CONVERSATIONAL EVENTS – OR 'THE EVENT CENTRE (EC) CONCEPT'

The concept emerging from this process perceives the activities in online discussion forums as interactions between people, communicating with other people in different conversational events, which I chose to name, Event Centres (EC). An Event Centre (EC) is formed when one or more participants respond to a message posted on the discussion thread. The various EC, and the participants contributing to them, form networks of people connected by events.

Addressing the third stage—'who talked to whom', on which occasion, and about what', the EC approach enables the visualisation of the participants of each EC with the relevant messages and responses associated with it. *Figure 3-10* below, indicates the participants in each EC linking participants to the messages they contributed in the particular EC. (Full content of messages appearing in the referred appendices 1-4).

---

[21] See Appendix 5 for detailed procedures

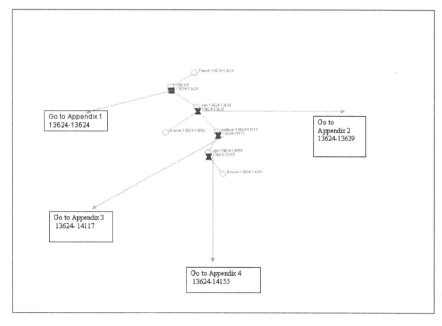

Figure 3-10 *Socio-Thematic Network*

A Web view of this concept is available on: http://etalk.bravehost.com. This Web view demonstrates the EC approach, which at this point in time I manually constructed. Further technological development needs to be done for the EC to become accessible and ready for practical use by e-tutors or researchers interested in processes occurring in online discussion forums.

SUMMARY

Studying online discussion forums is not about reading through individual messages, but rather trailing conversations as they evolved and progressed. Conversations are about communication, which in turn suggests that in studying them one must acknowledge their communicative and relational features, involving actors, texts, and relating to others. These communicative, relational features collaboratively create emerging contexts or environments, and may construct new understanding and knowledge.

In attempting to study the relational features of the online conversations occurring in my data- set, I have deconstructed the notion of 'relation' as described in *'figure 3-6'* in this chapter. Figure 3-6 illustrates the process occurring when people communicate, as they act, and react while engaging with a text. Using notions expressed in Garfinkel's Documentary Method of Interpretation (DMI), I was able to reconstruct the notion of 'relation' as comprised of a combination of actions through which people select relevant topics to help them make sense of their world and construct meaning, creating a contextual bond between a person, their actions, and the contexts they participate in.

To corroborate my participants' choice of topics, I used the SQL code system to help me trail sequences of 'relations'. Applying the SQL coding, contributed objective data, confirming the sequences and links made by the participants applying the SI and DMI to their communicative actions. The sequences identified through the SQL coding allowed for a further enhancement of the alternative analytic approach I have introduced in this chapter, as the mathematic SQL codes enabled applying Social Network Analysis (SNA) techniques. SNA enabled the visualisation of sequences of relations, offering visual maps of 'who talked to whom'; on which occasion, and about what' for the observation and identification of emerging topics of interest shared, and discussed by more than one individual. These mutual meeting points – or the Event centres (EC), comprised my unit of analysis, which is a graphic representation of the choices and interpretations people make in responding to each other, hence illustrating the formation of socio-thematic networks.

Using the EC approach, I am able to visualise and map the occurrences in online conversations, depicting each sub discussion, breaking the constraint of following the discussion thread as the structure of analysis, and constructing a visual reflection of the way in which conversations in the discussion forum progressed. Because of the inherent link between actors and their messages, the visual reflection provided by the EC approach has the potential to depict the evolvement of the conversation by eliciting each twist and turn in the progression of ideas, as they are presented by the participants.

The graphic structure depicting the development in the conversation as they unfold through the 'relations' created and networked by the participants, is a representation of the underpinning understandings and its progression as they emerge throughout the network. Each EC represents a sub network of relations depicting the perceptions, relevancies and choice making made by a number of individuals, ranging from dyads to small groups, hence revealing supra- individual understandings at different points throughout the network.

Using the EC as my unit of analysis has provided me with an insight beyond the 'Individual', opening a way to understanding meaning -making processes occurring between communicating individuals. The EC are visible marking points, visualising the 'relations' described in *figure 3-6* in this chapter. The mental processes occurring in the minds of the participants, inform the choice of *'who'*, and *'what'* to interact with illustrated by the EC, and the links between various EC. In other words, the EC is a visual symbol, marking the meeting point of the 'mental relations'. An EC is NOT the sum of its members, but a visual mark, delineating the occurrence of the *relation,* the mental process occurring when people communicate in three interlinked components; actions and reactions creating and responding to a text (a message).

Following the trail of EC along the whole of the network allows constructing the mental routes taken by the participants in their meaning -making journey. Hence following this trail holds the potential to point to changes in perceptions, which as I have defined earlier as manifestations of 'learning'.

In the next chapter I will demonstrate the implementation of the EC approach across the actual data-set collected in this study.

4. THE TEST DRIVE- APPLYING THE ALTERNATIVE EC ANALYTIC
APPROACH

Introduction and Organisation of Chapter

In the previous chapters I suggested that the research arena of online discussion
forums is gradually shifting its focus of investigation from the content of 'stand alone'
messages conveyed by an individual contributor, to encompassing entire conversations
comprised of sequences of related messages, evolving into an environment of meanings
and content. However, the previous chapters have also identified a need for research
tools that would enable the implementation of the conceptual shift and facilitate the
study of relations between people and interrelated messages in online discussion
forums.

Searching for a tool that would enable the study of relations and interrelated
messages rather than focusing on messages as 'stand alone' entities, I developed the
Event Centre (EC) approach described in chapter three. The EC approach enables the
investigation of a number of messages alongside their relevant contributors. The
approach enables the visualisation and analysis of messages and contributors linked
through a sequence of *relations* creating a mutual meeting point of shared interest, and
in so doing generating a centre of interactions I called Event Centres. The emergence of
an EC is corroborated using the ethnomethodological tools, the Documentary Method
of Interpretation (DMI), alongside computer network server generated data- the SQL
(Structured Query Language) codes.

The EC approach was developed out of an emerging need identified not only
through the literature reviewed for this study, but also through the experimentation I
described in chapter three in the 'preliminary attempts' section, in which I applied
various available analytic tools to the data-set of this study, only to realise their
shortcomings.
In chapter three I described the development process of the EC approach and introduced
its application on a small and containable mock data -set, enabling a clear exposition of

the tool itself. In this chapter, I venture one step further and apply the EC to a real data – the set collected for the purpose of this study. This chapter is a first trial, a '*test drive*' of the EC approach, and in many instances is providing a mere introduction to possible routes for future research.

In applying the EC approach to the actual data-set, I hope to address the issues I have raised in 'Part Two' of chapter three, presented in the two following questions:

1. In what ways do the patterns obtained by the EC approach contribute to our ability to observe and analyse the learning related dynamics, and social structures emerging in Online Learning Discussion Forums (OLDF)?
2. How can the patterns obtained by the EC approach begin to illuminate ways in which they operate relative to meaning making and learning processes in OLDF?

In this chapter I attempt to address the second part of the research objective I have identified in chapter three, and search for conversational patterns underpinning learning dynamics. Here I hope to be able to suggest possible connections between the structural analytic view obtained by the EC approach and the investigation of collaborative learning and social construction of knowledge. To achieve these aims, I investigate the visual patterns emerging from the application of the EC approach, alongside the mathematical observations emanating from the structures revealed. The analysis approaches applied to the data are primarily reliant on Structural and Quantitative Content Analysis (QCA) approaches. In some instances I ventured on to pursue in depth excursions into the data, in attempting to demonstrate in further detail the indications and suggestions implied in the empiric data, and corroborate indicative structural and quantitative observations by applying qualitative methods of analysis. However, the magnitude of the data and limitations of time and resources prevented me from pursuing these excursions across the whole of the data-set; however, these provide preliminary indications and possible routes for further studies.

I structured the chapter in two main sections:

- **Part One**: *Representations of online Relations as indicators of Teaching/Learning dynamics.*

I begin this section with an investigation of what constitutes the patterns, and in what ways would they contribute to the understanding of learning dynamics in online discussion forums. I then proceed to investigate possible manifestations of roles as emerging from the structures of the patterns as representations of sequences of relations in the online discussions forums. I hope that the discovery of roles would facilitate preliminary investigation of the notion suggesting that online environments are conducive to socio-constructivist collaborative learning. By applying the EC approach I am hoping to obtain mathematical and visual representations of learning dynamics which would point to the discovery of roles and relation supporting such learning dynamics.

- **Part Two**: *Visual representations for trailing meaning making and learning processes*:

In this section I investigate the ability of the visual representation to facilitate the trailing of meaning- making processes as indicators of possible progression of learning. Pursuing this notion in an online discussion forum entails investigating the ability of the graphic illustrations to recreate and illustrate the original order of the messages, and in so doing facilitate the identification of any meaning making processes.

In this section I explore the notion of reconstructing conversations beyond the thread and the linear features offered by the prevalent computer communication systems. Here I demonstrate the visual, contextual and thematic reconstruction of the order of the messages enabled by the EC approach. Applying the server key codes, combined with the DMI framework, the EC facilitates the trailing of the meaning making processes[22]. I hope that the reconstruction of the meaning making processes will elicit the dynamics of the progression of learning, hence enabling the discovery of underpinning teaching/learning approaches. This discovery process will possibly open the way for observing socio constructivist and collaborative notions of learning in online discussion forums.

---

[22] Extensively discussed in pp 37-43 in chapter 3

THE VIRTUAL ENVIRONMENT – OR THE TECHNOLOGICAL CONTEXT OF THE STUDY

The course I observed in this study utilised a Learning Management System (LMS), which was developed in New Zealand. The aim of the developers of the system was to create a collaborative, socio-constructivist online learning environment, or in their exact words: "where discussion and sharing of ideas and documents can occur"(Chirnside, 2002). To accomplish their aspirations, the developers structured the discussion forums tools in a way that would facilitate two complementing forms of representations of the discussions; a 'threaded' form, showing the entire thread, depicting clusters of messages bundled together under a computerised identification of a shared topic. The system is able to identify the shared topics by following the messages 'subject line', which is a built- in component in the message template. The additional message representation is the 'linear' forms, in which all posts relating to a thread are piled' up in chronological order(White, 2004). Systems like the ones I observed, offering the two forms of presentation are referred to as 'hybrid' platforms.

The Learning Management System (LMS) observed here allows for two types of a- synchronous discussion forums – *'public'* forums, and *'private'* forums. The 'open' forums are accessible to all participants in the course; the *'private'* forums are only accessible to designated participants.

WHO ARE MY PARTICIPANTS, AND WHAT DO THEY DO?

In this study I observed the discussion forum activity of nineteen educators, who came from all sectors of the educational system:

1. Five of them are early childhood educators;
2. Two, are primary school teachers;
3. Two, are primary school principals;

4. Four, are secondary school teachers;

5. Six are tertiary education lecturers.

The course I observed was a 'Reflective Practice', Distance Learning Masters course, which lasted one academic year.

Participants in the course were required to partake in 'class activities', which in this case meant logging on to the course website set up on the Learning Management System (LMS) described earlier. To meet the course requirements, participants were required to log on to the Website once a week and respond to questions as well as take part in the discussions.

THE SETTING OF THE CLASSROOM FOR 'CLASS ACTIVITIES'

The course I observed in this study was set up as a distance course incorporating some online components, rather than being exclusively online.

The course materials included videocassette, hard- copy printed materials, and books. However, participating in the online component of the course was to play an important role in this course as explained by the course co-ordinator in the welcoming video sent out to the distance learners:

> We expect you to be using StudentNet[23], it's an important part of the course...
> and it's not anything like the biggest part of the course, we expect you to be
> involved in reading and in work where you'll be thinking about your practice,
> this [the course Website]is a place for our communication".... I think it's
> important to emphasise that it's not all electronic, that there is a tremendous
> amount of reading, and to be able to discuss what you have learned over the Net,
> and to be able to communicate with each member of the group and with us as
> tutors ....we thought what we would do in really 'good classrooms' ......we
> sometimes put people in groups, ask them to do a small task, and your group

---

[23] StudentNet is the name of LMS used in the course observed

agrees on that and then you report to the whole group,,, so you get close contact
with some, and hear how others have done the same tasks , a different way,,,,,,
so we are really relying on that communication to build it as being something
that's not just you to us, but you to community……. So we are really, really
keen that will,,,, something that you all take part in and that we build a learning
community. Yes, social interactions all from a distance, we get to know one
another, we meet in a block time, you'll be interacting with one another
throughout the duration of the course ….. Comspace, where we do most of our
conversations that are more informal,. …… The course is very dependent on the
social interaction, discussion, and debate between the course members….. we
base our modification on what research is saying about learning, and what are
colleagues in the course are commenting on your work, because if you
remember, the course is predicated on the fact that we have a lot of social
interactions and interacting with each other on what we write…….. (Welcome
pack video)

The course co-ordinator, Elaine, aspired to build a 'learning community'. The
LMS used in the course observed was to provide a social sphere, - "*yes social
interactions*", but not only for 'informal' interactions but also for '*discussion and
debate*'. The image Elaine had for the interactions on the course Website was that of a
real-life classroom, where conversations move naturally between learning contents and
less formal topics of conversation. Nevertheless this vision did not stop Elaine from
attempting to structure the online conversations by allocating different 'discussion
forums' to different roles, for example – "*Comspace, where we do most of our
conversations that are more informal*" .

'Formal' conversations were to take place in the 'learning; allocated spaces,
where participants were expected to debate and formalise a position. Formal
conversations were to follow guidelines such as those shown in the example below:

- *In your investigations, ensure that you use a critical analysis to
  identify questions pertaining to Vygotsky's work that contains
  unexplained assumptions and contradictions with your
  developing position on learning or indeed any other theorist.*

- *The meaningfulness/importance of these terms to Vygotsky's position and your critical analysis of identified assumptions and contradictions now need to be discussed with colleagues from your discussion group. This discussion will need to take place over the StudentNet. It is expected that all members will participate fully in the discussion*

THE PEDAGOGY UNDERPINNING THE 'CLASS ACTIVITIES'

The notion of *collaboration* is apparent throughout the course philosophy: The course outline states that:

> *"Through this course teachers will develops skills and knowledge to enable them to relate their personal theories and practices to those of other educators and to published theories of teaching and learning".*

This statement acknowledges the importance of individuals relating their own beliefs not only to published works, but also to the knowledge of others.

Collaboration is embedded into the praxis of the course on two levels:

1) Institutional level:

The college provided a material incentive for students to buddy up in giving fees incentives for any students who brings along a friend to enrol in the course: *".... you probably realise, we actively encouraged people to join this course in pairs so that you are not working alone - **and there are fees incentives** [my emphasis] to make this attractive".*

2) Course requirements level:

The course encourages, and in fact structures collaboration, as participants are required to buddy up for the completion of tasks, as indicated in the second module of the course:

By the end of this second module, you should be talking regularly with your GROUP and also with your BUDDY who is someone in a different group. Some of you

enrolled in the course with a buddy – those who do not have buddies should pair up
before the end of this module. I will help if necessary – but perhaps you can sort this
by using the "find a buddy" thread within our RP Module 2 forum.
(Overview of module 2)

Furthermore, Elaine requires students to work with buddies in a task she posts in
the discussion forum of the second study module of the course:

Posted by:*Elaine on 01-03-02 at 17:34*

Subject: *Buddies - who is your buddy?*   *Formal Task*

We expect that you will be working with a buddy during this course. ….

………..so the next thing to do is for you folk to sort out a buddy for yourselves. Can you
matchmake among yourselves? You are all able to email each other - and you could use
this thread to advertise yourself if you like :-) This is very safe place to sell yourself!!!
Everyone will have a buddy - if we have an odd number of members there will be one
threesome.

Limitations - buddies should be in different groups - if you are in the same group now
then we will make sure that does not happen in the longer term - this is so that when
you share ideas you are bringing different conversations together.

Buddies are basically your first port of call if you want to check out something you do
not understand - or if you want to seek reassurance about something you are going to
post into a more public space.

Have fun sorting yourselves and for existing buddies - reporting on yourselves.

Elaine

                                  Post No. 1765, Thread No. 1765, Parent No. 0

Collaborative activities are allocated a time frame within the course activities as
Elaine notes in an interview I conducted with her during the first days of the course:
"*Collaborating with the buddy should take about one hour a week and this will be*
referred to as 'class time', which can be done over the net" (Elaine- Mary interview
4.2.02).

Kendall (1999), suggests that in researching online discussion forums, the researcher should take the role of 'participant observer'(Kendall, 1999). Kendall's approach has its merits, as it allows the researcher to gain first hand experience obtained through immersion in the dynamics and processes studied. However, the circumstance of this study, where the discussions were a part of a study course, meant that for me to assume the role of a 'participant observer' would entail choosing between the position of either a learner or a teacher (lecturer). These circumstances could be said to have evolved from two points:

- The discussion forums observed were contextualised as 'classrooms', and as such entail a hierarchical structure of 'teachers and learners' (as much as collaborative learning environments aspire for non-hierarchical situations, learning situations will always imply a dissimilarity or inequality of positions and a distinction between the 'more and the less', the more experienced participant, and the less experienced one)

- The technological features of the LMS used in the course observed allowing for two types of users:
  - o Member level- allocated to students. This level allows for accessing, reading, and contributing to discussion forums
  - o Lecturer level – allocated to lecturers. This level allows for accessing, reading, contributing and monitoring all activities, including viewing statistical data. In other words, lecturers are able to monitor students' activities using two options, one, by simply accessing the various discussion forums and reading the messages posted, or through the automated monitoring system which allows the lecturer to extract statistics of students' activities.

Choosing either position, would have constrained my perspective, either to that of the learner, or that of the teacher. Furthermore, assuming the role of the learner would have denied me access to the monitoring data statistics, a feature which was important for my analysis as it provided me with an empirical perspective of the activities in the discussion forums. Weighing my options, and at the same time negotiating my role with Elaine, the course coordinator, we agreed that we would ask the students for their consent to my monitoring their actions, so that I could be allocated 'lecturer level' access. Furthermore, in order to prevent any misunderstandings about my role, I would refrain from actively participating in any of the course related discussion forums, so that students would not mistake me for a 'real' lecturer, monitoring their performance as learners. However, to enable me some first hand interactions and experience with the students, Elaine and I agreed that I would host specially assigned forums, where no teaching would occur, and no compulsory participation would be required, hence diminishing any teacher/learners hierarchies. To set our mutual solution in motion, Elaine sent an all course message to introduce my role as a researcher observing the activities on the courses discussion forums, and accessing the statistics of students' involvement generated by the LMS, or in Elaine's exact words:

> Hi, All
> .... Given Mary Allan access to all groups and to the
> statistics of your involvement" (Elaine, in - **Notes from module 4 intro page**
> 19-04-2002)

Elaine also introduced my specially allocated discussion forums inviting students to participate on a voluntary basis:

> "Mary's teacup forum"
> A place to talk with Mary Allan about her research into communities of
> learning. She might ask you questions - you might ask her questions. It is totally
> voluntary, of course. (Elaine, introducing the first discussion forum I hosted)

"Mary's cocktail time forum"
A place where Mary can lead our conversations (or be led - as the case may be)"
(Elaine, introducing the other discussion forum I hosed)

The first forum I hosted - Mary's Teacup, was launched on the 27th of March (about 2 months after the beginning of the course), and ended its activities on the 25th of August. This forum was primarily a place for me, and the students to talk about online learning communities, and the ways in which each of us experienced and perceived these cyber spaces. The conversations with the students enabled me some observation into their thoughts and feelings about the online situation they were experiencing.

Interacting with the students at this level was exciting as it allowed me a glimpse into the students' point of view. It also enabled me to experience the technologically framed environment used in this study, from a 'lecturer' point of view.

The second forum I hosted was called 'Mary's Cocktail Party'. This forum was launched towards the end of the course, and ended its activities one month after the closing of the course. Elaine conditioned the participation in Mary's Cocktail party, requiring completion of course requirements prior to being granted access to the forum. This forum was used for creating a space that would assimilate in some ways group interviews, and in others, facilitate receiving feedback and reflections from the students about their impressions of the online environment experienced in the course.

DATA COLLECTION PROCEDURES

As I have noted in the methodology chapter, my primary data source were the observations I conducted on the online interactions occurring throughout the course, however, I deployed other data colleting strategies for obtaining additional perspectives to the phenomena I have observed.

The non – observational data collecting strategies included:

- Distributing questionnaires on two occasions (mid, and end of course)
- Conducting three interviews with the course coordinator
- Maintaining an ongoing e-mail contact with the course coordinator. Elaine and I used the e-mail contact to update and alert each other about various occurrences, behaviours, and dynamics. We also used this for mutual consultations about ways of addressing these various occurrences

Observing online activities entailed accessing the course website, where course participants conducted their Online Text-Based Asynchronous discussions. In accordance to my agreement with Elaine, I participated only within the forums I hosted, in which participation was voluntary.

ORGANISATION, AND SPAN OF THE DATA

The course coordinator first set up five discussion forums launched as segregated, accessible to assigned members only groups. Allocation to the groups was decided according to the order of their enrolment to the course. Once all members were logged on, the course coordinator regrouped the members according to their geographical locations, setting up regional groups. At the same time, as these groups were activated, the course coordinator set- up course related groups and forums. These were linked to the various course modules.

The regional groups were abandoned for lack of activity, for the reasons I have attempted to describe in the methodology chapter. To replace these, Elaine, set up professional sector groups which were open to all. These also ran in parallel to course module groups. In addition to those, Elaine set special groups to accommodate people who wanted unique talking spaces. These were set as private segregated groups, viewed only by designated members.

Elaine, has accomplished what every online moderator aspires to, an abundance of online contributions.

'Table 4-1' depicts all the online activities performed on the course's website.

Table 4-1 Total activities

Type of activity	Totals
Number of postings to the total Forums	1104
Number of postings to all 'Discussion Threads' exceeding 3 posts	846

This proliferation of contributions to the Online Learning Discussion Forums (OLDF), denotes that Elaine, has obviously succeeded in enticing the participants' enthusiasm to participate vigorously in the discussion forums in an almost frenzy of interactions over rather a significant period of almost 11 months.

This abundance provided me with an excellent ground for studying OLDF, however, when I attempted to study this abundance I was faced with

- A maze of online activities across numerous contexts
- No apparent detectable time-frame for the myriad of activities
- Extremely elusive and at times hard to detect structure

I have described these phenomena in details in chapter three, when I attempted to illuminate my quest for analytic tools that would enable the observations of such a maze of interactions, enabling the trailing of learning in OLDF.

DEFINING THE SCOPE OF DATA

Over the duration of the observed course, my research participants generated 1104 text contributions throughout 32 online discussion forums, encompassing 299 discussion threads, out of which 131 threads showed three and above contributions. Simmel in his seminal work "Quantitative Aspects of the Group"(1950), argues that a super-personal life or a collective action can only occur in a formation of three and above participants(Coser, 1977; Simmel, 1950). Furthermore, Hare Borgatta, & Bales (1966) suggest that points connected by more than a single straight line are connected by the third element, which offers a different side to each of the other two. Based on these two arguments, I chose to focus on the 131 threads ignoring the shorter threads.

This part is comprised of two main sections:

Section one describes the application of the EC approach to the data, and then proceeds to analyse the visual patterns as signifiers of learning dynamics, and processes occurring in the online discussion forums. The section unfolds the various stages, and techniques used for identifying indications of learning processes in the visual representations.

Section two, investigates the emergence of roles as possible indications of learning dynamics and their suggestive nature as to teaching/ learning approaches and practices applied in the discussion forums.

PART ONE SECTION ONE: VISUALISING DISCUSSION THREADS

Applying the EC visualisation approach to my data, I was now able to process the 131 discussion threads, to produce 131 networks of Event Centres (EC), similar to the one exemplified in *'figure 3-9'* in the methodology chapter.

Attempting to focus on my unit of analysis, the EC, I chose to follow the links spawned from one EC to the next. To achieve visual clarity of these links, I blurred the graphics representing all other activities not directly related to the EC, highlighting only the ones linking one EC to another.

Looking at the 131 EC focused networks; I was able to detect some reoccurring graphic representations, indicating similar patterns of emerging dynamics across a number of processed threads. I have grouped these reoccurring representations into six categories, showing in *Figures 4-1*, to *4-6*.

Category 1 reveals uni-focal dynamics, resulting in a single Event Centre (EC) consisting of the initial EC. This pattern emerges when all participants respond to the initial EC, creating a star- like shape, of all responses directed to one single point, while at the same time the information conveyed by the initial message initiating the EC is disseminated equally to all members of the network. This type of dissemination dynamics is referred to in Social Network Analysis (SNA), as the 'Star'.

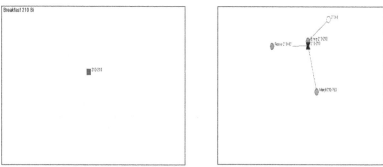

Figure 4-1: The uni-Focal, or The 'Star'
(The shape of the star is visible only when members are revealed as shown on the right)[24]

Category 2, reveals Duo- focal dynamics generated by two EC; one is the initial EC (marked in a square shape), spawning a response, and further discussion resulting in a second EC. This pattern emerges when one or more participants engage in responding to a response made to the initial EC so that a second EC emerges.

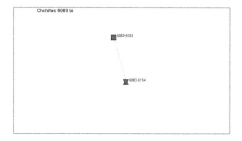

Figure 4-2 Category 2: The Duo- Focal

The third, Category 3a, depicts three and above EC, linked in a chain- like format, hence I called this category the 'Chain'. The sequence of three or more EC

---

[24] Members were blurred to enable clearer view of the patterns

enabled me to observe a flow of responses, each activated by a previous message, incrementally compiling contributions, and unfolding multiple perspectives. This compilation, as Hare and others(Hare, Borgatta, & Bales, 1966) suggested, is not possible in a dual EC format where a single line connects a mere two centres.

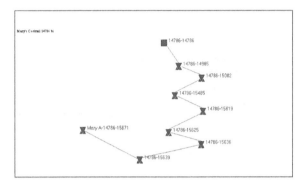

Figure 4-3 Category 3a: The Chain

The fourth, Category 3b, depicts multi- chains, where a primary chain (marked within the dotted area in 'figure 4-4') spawns from the initiating EC (marked as a square), and additional chains branching out of it at various points. These additional chains are comprised of three and above EC, triggered by a message originating in the initial chain, and triggering a sub sequence of conversation.

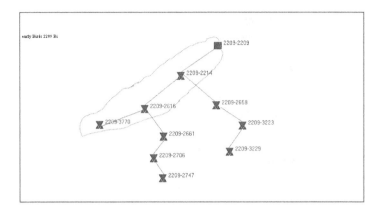

Figure 4-4 Category 3b: The Multi chain

The fifth, Category 4a: the 'Branch', depicts two separate responses, branching out from the initiating message (marked as a square), and at times evolving into a short (up to 2 EC) sequence of independent conversations.

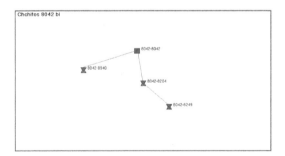

Figure 4-5 Category 4a: The Branch

Finally the sixth, Category 4b: the 'Branch and Chain', depicts chains entailing three and above EC evolving from each of the branches creating two, or at times several chains. The count of the branching out chains is exclusive of the initial EC (marked in a square), as in this case, it is initiating both chains, and cannot be included twice in the count. Furthermore, where chains branch out from within an existing formation (either a branch or a primary chain), I found it important to ascertain the development of an impendent conversation and hence begin the count of three beyond the activating messages to ascertain Simmel's triad formation, I described earlier in this chapter.

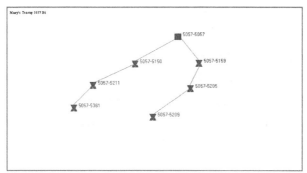

Figure 4- 6 Category 4b: The Branch and Chain

The Multi chain (3b) category differs from the Branch and Chain (4b), because the 3b pattern, illustrates a situation where a primary discussion, emanating from the initial EC, and unfolding a whole sequence of conversation, spawns further conversation chains, activated at certain points of the primary conversations. These further conversations depicted in the sub-chains evolve whenever a certain message triggered a separate or additional discussion, or topic branching out from the initial topic discussed on the primary chain. The Branch and Chain (4b), on the other hand illustrates two or more chains emanating directly from the initiating EC.

Classifying the Networks Working with Patterns

Having identified the six categories I proceeded to classify all my 131 EC networks according to these categories. To carry out the categorisation, I invited two uninvolved colleagues to join me. Each coder viewed the 131 networks set on a slide show. While viewing the slide show, coders were required to tick an X in the appropriate spaces in a 'coding table' comprised of 6 columns and 131 rows. Each column represented a category; each row represented an EC network. *'Table 4- 2'* below illustrates a sample of the 'coding table'

Table 4-2 - Coding Table

EC Network	Category 1	Category 2	Category 3a	Category 3b	Category 4a	Category 4b
Comspace13041		X				
Chchities 6083		X				
Chchities 8042			X			
CP Paradigm			X			

I then compared each of separate 'coding tables' filled out by the two coders and me, to arrive at the final categorisation of the whole of the 131 threads. Differences between the coders occurred on **six** out of the 131 threads showing 4.5% inconsistencies. Coding differed around categories 3a, 3b, and 4a, 4b, which as could be perceived in figures 4-3, to 4-6, represent a similar chain like pattern. Whenever an inconsistency in the coding occurred, I chose the coding chosen by two out of the three participating votes.

Establishing definable reoccurring patterns, could prove valuable as I suggested in the methodology chapter, where I cited Mooney and Singer pointing out the value of being able to show regularity in social phenomena(Mooney & Singer, 1988), which in turn would enable generalisation of observed phenomena(I. J. Cohen, 2000)

Using the six categories of patterns representing the dynamics of the evolvement of EC networks for classifying the 131 not only enabled me to work with six generic patterns instead of 131 specific networks representing particular situations, making my data more manageable, but it also provided me with an overall view which enabled me to identify reoccurring, generalisable features emerging from the EC networks. Although in the course of this chapter, I will at times refer to specific threads in my data; these would serve as representatives of the category to which they belong.

The six categories of patterns represent structures comprised of sequences, or networks of 'relations' , which, as I have shown in chapter three, are in themselves representations of the choices and interpretations made by the participants applying the Documentary Method of Interpretation (DMI), and the Symbolic interaction in the Online Learning Discussion Forum (OLDF) in their pursuit of meaning. To demonstrate how these relations operate I will focus on the aspects of the relations which can be made visible, hence I will focus on the DMI as a choice mechanism, a praxis which in a network context as is the case in this study can be clearly describable and made visual. The DMI is the process through which participants choose the topic and so doing are also choosing the person or persons they will communicate with, hence creating visible links. The act of choice in a network environment where people choose which message to respond to, hence picking their conversation partners is a visualisation of the interpretation process occurring in the minds of the participants, hence making their mental processes visible

To demonstrate this phenomenon, I selected an excerpt from the data depicting a section of a discussion thread through which I hope to demonstrate Garfinkel's DMI process, as used in my data.

Example of DMI usage

In her first message to the thread Debbie introduces one of the course topics, Social Constructionism, and attempts to relate the ideas of this topic to her professional practice context- the parents in her centre [my note- Debbie is an Early Childhood teacher]Next, Debbie attempts to put her thoughts into "assumptions"
In the final part of her message, Debbie describes her observation of the behaviour of the parents in her centre. Below is Debbie's original message:

Posted by: Debbie on *09-10-02* at 18:05

Subject : DEBBIE's DISCUSSION ON Hegemonic Assumptions

Formal Task

. Social constructionism: This topic interests me greatly, and is a theory that could help explain the particular 'patterns of actions' that I act out in my proffessional life, and how they may differ from the 'patterns of actions' I act out in my personal life.

Social constructionism talks about us being a product of social encounters and relationships and that we create ourselves through these social encounters.

This takes me to my next thought...

The parents in my centre...and some hegemonic assumptions that both they (as parents) and us (as teachers) may well be having.

I am also wondering if social constructionism plays a part in these assumptions and whether either us (as teachers) or them (as parents) really want anything to change anyway!

We might be quite comfortable with these assumptions, however, I think that this is what makes them hegemonic, because over time they become embedded, and to quote Brookfield (pg 14-15)
"these assumptions that they think are in the best interest, but have actually been designed by more powerful 'others'"

So, my assumptions are in regard to our social encounters and relationships with our parents;
a. Our assumptions of them.
b. their assumptions of us, and
c. Societies assumptions of the relationship between centre/school and parents.

1. Parents don't really want to be stopped by teachers for social encounters, they just want to pick their children up and go home.

2. Parents don't want to know all the details about their child's learning that occurred

that day, they just basically want to know that their child has been happy and settled.

3. The teachers have all the expertise, therefore it's not the parents place to question the teachers actions - the teacher must be right!

4. A good e.c.e centre or school should be meeting the 'needs' of all parents.

So there you are, what do you think about these assumptions, how much of a reality are they in your learning environment, and what (if anything) prevents change from occurring within these assumptions?

Cheers, Debbie.

Post No. 13934, Thread No. 13934, Parent No. 0

In response to Debbie's message Jennifer (a Secondary teacher), Joyce and Elaine reply the following:

Posted by: Jennifer
on *09-10-02* at 19:09
Subject: secondary system   Answer

Answering these questions Debbie has really emphasised to me how different our sectors are.

"1. Parents don't really want to be stopped by teachers for social encounters, they just want to pick their children up and go home. "

We have a lot of whanau connections where parents are involved in the school community. In a town of thirty thousand you know a lot of families anyway. However, teenagers would generally be mortified if their parents went anywhere near their classrooms. I like to think I have open and positive communication with parents but there are definitely many situations I am glad to be removed from. I have seen some very towy customers.

175

"2. Parents don't want to know all the details about their child's learning that occurred that day, they jusy basically want to know that their child has been happy and settled. "

Many parents do and many parents don't. Neat when they do as they can do so much to support their child's learning from home.

"3. The teachers have all the expertise, therefore it's not the parents place to question the teachers actions - the teacher must be right! "

Not always....parents with bad school experiences give the DP a right grilling. Uggg I would hate to be in her shoes.

Students who complain at our school go to the Dean. The Dean mediates quite often. They quite often empathise with the student's viewpoint and have the option to confront their colleague or move the kid.

"4. A good e.c.e centre or school should be meeting the 'needs' of all parents."

However, primarily the needs of their children.

Cheers
Jenny

Post No. 13939, Thread No. 13934, Parent No. 13934

Jennifer responds conveying her observations from her sector. Joyce is a Kindergarten teacher.

                                                Hi Debbie

In kindergarten, the setting is different to yours I suspect in that we have 3 teachers to 45 morning session children and then 35 afternoon session children. The ratios are quite different to what you have in childcare - at least 1 teacher to 8 children. You are also more likely to have children for the whole day rather than different sessional morning and afternoon children - although I realise that some children do come for part of any day.

>1. Parents don't really want to
>be stopped by teachers for
>social encounters, they just
>want to pick their children up
>and go home.

Is this is talking about time constraints? Are parents too busy to want to find out about their child's day? In my setting, do I as a teacher make it easy for parents to approach me at the beginning or end of the session? At the end of session, I am possibly reading stories to children at one of the last mats (two mats) where the children gather together to hear a story before going home with their adult, or I am washing paint pots in the sink etc. So, is it easy for them to approach me? At the beginning of the session, I try to sit with children at desk top activities so that I am available when the children come in with their parents. Again, how easy is it for parents to approach me if I am seen to be busy working with children?

>2. Parents don't want to know
>all the details about their
>child's learning that occurred
>that day, they jusy basically
>want to know that their child
>has been happy and settled.

Some parents don't ask about their child's day, some do. Again, is this because of rushing in the door to collect the child? Is this because I am reading stories and I am assumed to be too busy to answer questions about their child?

>3. The teachers have all the
>expertise, therefore it's not
>the parents place to question
>the teachers actions - the
>teacher must be right!

At college I was taught and believe that parents are children's first teachers. I try to convey that fact to parents in my work by talking with them about the work they have already done with their children or what they can do with their children at home.

>4. A good e.c.e centre or school
>should be meeting the 'needs' of
>all parents.

If they don't communicate those needs, how will I know what the needs are? We have held parent education evenings and had very poor responses to those meetings. Is it lethargy on the part of parents or is it some other factor which prevents parents from coming? Did we advertise or talk with parents enough about the upcoming evening? Is it because parents don't feel confident enough to come to meetings or because they won't do that because they assume we are the teachers, so we know what's "best" for the children?

>So there you are, what do you
>think about these assumptions,
>how much of a reality are they
>in your learning environment,
>and what (if anything) prevents
>change from occurring within

>these assumptions?

Recently at kindergarten, an Asian mother took her child to a school visit. The child is staying at kindergarten till the end of term, rather than go to school at age 5 in about 2 weeks. The child is considered not yet ready for facing the challenges of school, socially or developmentally. As a teaching team, we feel she would be better prepared for school by staying at kindergarten for another term.

The parent came to kindergarten and said that the primary teacher told her the child had to go to school at age 5. The parent wants to keep the child at kindergarten for another term, but she is afraid of the primary teacher's statement that the child must go at age 5. Who is the expert here? Presumably we all want what is best for the child.

I think your assumptions are alive and well Debbie in my situation. I have tried to talk with the team about changing the role of the person who cleans the paint pots at session end, to one where that teacher reports to parents about accidents children sometimes have. My suggestion wasn't taken on board because the other two staff members felt that accidents are best reported by the teacher involved with helping the child. I think I will have another go at trying to have the paint pot cleaner role changed slightly, from the point of view that this person will be available to discuss with parents their child's day. Again, though I am reminded that as teachers we are on different duties, like inside and outside teacher. I may not see a child all morning if I am outside and that child works inside all day, so how can I report to the parent about that child's day if I haven't seen the child?

So I make another assumption that there are impossible time and lack of knowledge (about particular children's happenings during a day) constraints all round?

A lot of ramblings Debbie.
Over and out
Joyce.

Post No. 13951, Thread No. 13934, Parent No. 13934

Joyce shares her observations in her kindergarten, again the discussion focuses on the differences between different sectors.

Posted by: Elaine on *09-10-02* at 22:33

Subject: Hegemonic Assumptions   Request for clarification

                                                Hi, Debbie

I followed your reasoning until I reached your assumptions.

How do you distinguish between those assumptions and broad generalisations? Things that stereotype your parents? Or essentialise them - classify them in some way that trivialises them? Are these assumptions that you have become aware of and are working on changing?

I could not quite see the point of them - sorry - I am actually mystified - I might just be a bit vague tonight! Help.

I wonder why we are looking for assumptions - so that we can a share them? So that we can identify them - and wonder about how they affect our practice? I see from Joyce's submission that this is a very helpful discussion. But I wonder - what status have assumptions for you?

Cheers

Elaine

             Post No. 13957, Thread No. 13934, Parent No. 13934

Elaine – shifting the conversation back to Debbie's "assumptions" stated in her initiating messages at the beginning of the thread. Next, Debbie responds to Elaine and a chain evolves.

Posted by: Debbie on *10-10-02* at 16:51

Subject: Hegemonic Assumptions   Comment

Hi Elaine

I guess what's happening for me, is that I have started another process in reflection upon our practice in our centre, in regards to social constructivism - how this is starting to positively impact on the children, the teachers, but I wonder where the parents are sitting in this scenario (for want of a better word).

So, I am looking at my assumptions around this area. I realise that it's nearing the end of the course and we are being guided to look at critical pedagogy (and this is where I must still be having some confusion - please comment on this).

My thoughts were before I can look at the 'power-play' of critical pedagogy in regards to the interactions with our parents with our programme, I need to look at my assumptions that underpin that power play.

I would like some comment, because I am thinking that there must be some bigger picture that I am just not getting, and I think it's perhaps got something to do with the dynamics (?) of critical pedagogy.

Cheers, Debbie.

Post No. 14001, Thread No. 13934, Parent No. 1395

Posted by: Elaine on *11-10-02* at 19:54

Subject: Hegemonic Assumptions

Answer

HI, Debbie

    but

        >I wonder where the parents are

        >sitting in this scenario (for

>want of a better word).

That makes sense.

>So, I am looking at my
>assumptions around this area.

Cool

I
>realise that it's nearing the
>end of the course and we are
>being guided to look at critical
>pedagogy (and this is where I
>must still be having some
>confusion - please comment on
>this).

Please clarify - what is your confusion?

>My thoughts were before I can
>look at the 'power-play' of
>critical pedagogy in regards to
>the interactions with our
>parents with our programme, I
>need to look at my assumptions
>that underpin that power play.
>
>I would like some comment,
>because I am thinking that there
>must be some bigger picture that
>I am just not getting, and I
>think it's perhaps got something

>to do with the dynamics (?) of
>critical pedagogy.

Perhaps you are making it harder than was intended - you have read three articles and synthesised these - I am expecting to see that people would refer to these articles within their discussions.

I was talking with Meryl today about this - perhaps you might like to comment, Meryl? That conversation has helped me to see where your problem might lie. Suppose that one of your articles was bell hooks and her talk about engaged pedagogy. You might bring into the conversation, within your thread, a question that raises for you - eg - how engaged are your parents in learning about how their children are progressing and what it means for a child to learn - and what insights might that idea give you as an ECE teacher - and what might others think. OR if you had read Freire about the banking notion of schooling - you might wonder about what knowledge about learning your parents have 'banked' in the past and how your contact with parents might be based on banking (where you give them the info that you think they ought to have in their banks - or whether it is based upon a more liberatory pedagogy - where you and they are seeking to support each other in addressing your common problems.)

Remember that others will not have read YOUR critical pedagogy articles - so a little bit of context will be needed so that others will understand what you are talking about -or you could point people toward your submission in the critical pedagogy abstracts area (I have not been there - so I have no idea what is there).

Does that help?

Thanks for the question

E

A visual representation of this segment of the thread reveals a 'star 'shape beginning, evolving later into a chain[25] as shown in figure 4.7.

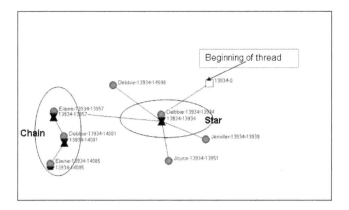

Figure 4-7 Various Patterns

The "star" segment illustrates how several participants respond to Debbie's initial message, contributing their own comments and observations of parents' behaviour in their own work contexts in the various educational sectors each of them work in. The thread changes its dynamics from Elaine's point of entry to the discussion, and flows on in a chain of three entries: Elaine- Debbie-Elaine

At the start of the thread, when participants first responded to Debbie's initiating message, they responded to the aspect of parents' behaviour in a way they felt relevant to them and the context they experience. Both Jennifer and Joyce contributed their own

---

[25] The star segment depicts two messages sent by Debbie; however, her second message was posted much later, and entails the concluding remarks and reflections of Debbie about the course. This concluding message has no relation to any of the other messages in the thread, which may provide some explanation for its odd positioning, however, no explanation was made available.

observation of parents' behaviour, depicting the contexts of the educational sectors they work in.

These responses are in alignment with Garfinkel's notion arguing that the application of the Documentary Method of Interpretation (DMI) is guided by the respondent's constant search for elements from the context for pursuing their own interpretive process(Garfinkel, 1967).

On Elaine's entrance to the discussion, she enables Debbie to use current events as resources to interpret past actions and to discover and give them new signification, which is another aspect facilitated by applying the DMI(Coulon, 1995,p.36) :
Below is an excerpt of Debbie's response to Elaine (post key 14001):

> I have started another process in reflection upon our practice in our centre, in regard to social constructivism ..... but I wonder where the parents are sitting...... I am thinking that there must be some bigger picture that I am just not getting, and I think it's perhaps got something to do with the dynamics (?) of critical pedagogy

The excerpt clearly shows the three phases of this aspect of the DMI:
1. "Reflection" – signifying past
2. "Social constructivism" – current events - attempting to apply course issue to practice
3. "Critical pedagogy"- new signification

The visual pattern of this excerpt illuminates the ways in which different participants interpreted the actions of others as "standing on behalf of a presupposed underlying pattern"(Benson & Hughes, 1983,p.90; Coulon, 1995,p.32). All but Elaine assumed that Debbie is expecting them to respond to her questions, Elaine, however, interpreted Debbie's questions as an invitation to a discussion, spawning a chain like conversation with Debbie.

This excerpt is only but a glimpse into the application of DMI by my participants; however, it provides an insight into the processes occurring in the online discussion forums, and the ways in which participants construct their reality out of their interactions and in so doing are also constructing the network and the dynamics in which it operates. Similar to the students in Garfinkel's experiment, my participants are choosing what is relevant to them through their interpretation of other people's messages in the discussion thread. In the special circumstances of an online discussion forum, choosing which message to respond to automatically creates a link between the authors of the message and response, hence creating a network of 'meeting points' – the EC, and relations, the links between them, made visible through the use of the visualization feature of the EC approach.

The analysis of DMI processes visualised by the EC could contribute to the understanding of learning processes in online discussion forums in two modes:

- As portraying the topics relevant to the participants at a certain point in the sequence of 'relations. Changes in the choice of topics may imply changes in relevancies, hence indicating changes in perceptions, or as Bohr refers to it "widening of conceptual frameworks"(Bohr, 1987(1958)), which can be perceived as contributing in some way to processes of learning. However, ascertaining such a link would require an investigation which is beyond the resources available to me as a researcher in this study.
- Establishing links between certain discussion topics and the dynamics of interactions portrayed in the various categories of patterns.

To study the topics elected and discussed by my participants in each of the EC, I applied Quantitative Content Analysis (QCA) techniques, which entails segmenting communication content into units, assigning each unit to a category, and providing tallies for each category(Rourke & Anderson, 2004).

MAPPING THE TOPICS OF THE ONLINE DISCUSSIONS

In order to identify any emerging discussion topics I read through the whole of the 846 messages posted throughout the 131 threads comprising my data set, however not as standalone messages, but as bundled into EC. Choosing the EC as my unit of analysis meant that I could not resort to content analysis of individual messages, but rather would have to deal with the content of the EC as a whole. In other words, I would have to conceptualise the total content conveyed throughout the various messages in an EC as a collective thematic unit. Therefore in attempting to identify topics of discussions I had to take a birds- eye view of the content in a given EC rather than a detailed look of every sentence entailed in the various messages comprising the EC. This approach allowed me to avoid weighting, or quantifying sentences, or any other verbal utterances relating to any discussion topics, but rather attribute the whole of the EC to an identified topic of discussion.   The content conveyed in the EC revealed two key discussion topics:

- *Course related discussions*, exhibiting: references to course readings or theories discussed in the course; tasks related activities; instructions and requirements related activities
- *Socio emotional discussions,* exhibiting: expressing personal perspectives, personal experience, empathy; or posting personal messages; humour

My next step was to categorise each EC in the 131 threads comprising my data set as belonging to either one of the two topics I have identified.

To enable categorisation of the EC I devised a set of criteria for each topic:
Course Related Topics Criteria
- Task, or task related activity (reflective practice personal linked to theory)
- Exchanging, debating, ideas readings, other people's reflections (considered here tasks) raised in the course
- Comments about course related issues, readings tasks, and ideas.
- Instructions for tasks, course work, use of the technology involved in the course
- Housekeeping messages

- Advice to other members
- Sharing personal work experience (part of the reflective activity required in the course)
- sharing personal views, opinions, linking ones circumstances to other educators, and theories

Socio Emotional Topics Criteria
- Expression of feelings
- sharing personal issues, situations, circumstances
- expressing personal views, opinions referring only to ones' self
- Expressions of support, and inclusion
- Humour
- Arranging for social meetings
- Thanking members

To validate my categorisation, I needed to corroborate my interpretations with those of others, however, it was quite obvious that I could not expect people to analyse the whole of my data-set, therefore I needed a way of making my data-set accessible to others. To achieve this, I chose a random sample of EC and classified them according to the criteria shown above. In the process of analysing this sample I discovered that in some cases a single EC entailed elements belonging to both categories, hence I added a third category called the 'Mix'. I then asked a group of three academics to review my classification. Each reviewer was given a copy of the sample EC categorised, identifying the criteria I used for my classification. The sample included the three classifications: course related, socio – emotional, and the 'mix'[26]. The feedback from the three reviewers verified my interpretation of the criteria.

Having validated my categorisation, I proceeded to categorise all the EC throughout my data-set. The classification involved two tiers, as each EC was categorised according to the topic of discussion it related to, and classified under the visual pattern category relevant to which they belonged.

---

[26] Please access Appendix 7 for review of the sample categorisation

'*Figure 4-8* below shows the different ratios of the discussion topics in each of the six categories:

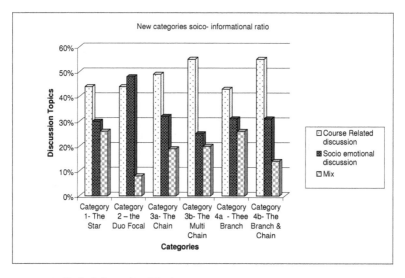

Figure 4-8 : Socio Informational Ratio

The graph in 'figure 4-8' shows that category 1, 2, 3a, and 4a show an average of 45% 'course related' discussions, while categories 3b and 4b show an increase of 10% with a soaring 55% of course related discussions. To explore the significance of the 'Mix', I searched for a broad overview that would highlight any emerging significance. Looking at the six categories I could detect two distinguishable dynamics:

- Centralised – revolving around a centre point
- None centralised- spreading in a chain like manner

I regrouped the six categories according to the dynamics they displayed, and formed three Dynamic Driven Groups:

- The 'Orbitors': comprised of the 'Star' (Category 1) and the 'Duo Focal', (Category 2), representing centralised dynamics
- The 'Simple Chains': comprised of the 'Chain' (Category 3a), and the 'Branch' (Category 4a), representing single chains

- The 'Complex chains': comprised of the 'Multi chain' (Category 3b), and the 'Branch and Chain' (Category 4b).

'Figure 4-9' reveals the broad overview of the distribution of the discussion topics across the three dynamic driven groups, as indicated by the number of EC related to each topic.

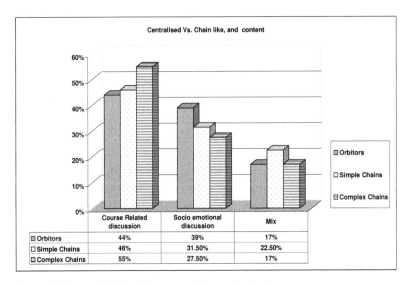

Figure 4-9 : Dynamic Driven Groups and Discussion Topics

Orbitors N=105

Simple chains N=202

Complex chains N=138

Figure4- 9 shows:
- High levels of course related topics in the complex chains group
- High levels of socio emotional topics in the Orbitors group
- High levels of 'mix' in the simple chains group

This observation only reveals that the mix category has some significance; however, it is beyond the scope of this study to pursue this significance.

The distribution of topics across the various categories of patterns provides the building blocks for identifying and describing different dynamics. These findings imply that different topics may generate or evolve in certain dynamics represented by the different patterns, however, this is only a preliminary observation and further study is needed to verify this notion.

PART ONE SECTION TWO –PATTERNS AS NETWORKS OF INFORMATION

Patterns as information conveying structures

The findings illustrated in figures 4-8 and 4-9 indicate a possible relationship between patterns representing structures, and the type and quantity of information flowing within them. To pursue this issue I turned once more to Social Network Analysis.

Patterns representing structures outline the routes and paths through which information can be conveyed. Social Network Analysis (SNA) techniques not only enable visualising these routes as I have shown earlier, but are also able to mathematically analyse how information is distributed throughout different patterns of a network, i.e. the star, the circle and line I have discussed in the literature review chapter. One of SNA mathematical techniques calculates the potential of an actor (in the case of this study the EC[27]) in a network to influence the flow of information within the network by measuring its connectivity and levels of involvement as indicated by the location of the EC on the network. This routine is called Centrality, and it calculates the number of links, or ties an EC has to measure its connectivity, or in SNA terminology, Centrality. The more links and ties an EC has, the greater Centrality it holds. The level

---

[27] I am able to interchange between the two as the EC represents the meeting points of the *mental relations*, representing the mental processes of communicating members in the network as the 'participants' or actors operating, hence an EC is actually representing active actors.

of Centrality conveys the ability to disseminate, or alternatively control the
dissemination of information through a network. In other words, centrality can be seen
as defining *roles* in a network. Defining roles is important for understanding and
discerning the emergence of social structures which according to Radcliffe-
Brown(1965(1952)), and Bourdieu(1992) are comprised of roles and positions. This
notion is of particular importance for the study of collaborative learning often
associated with online discussion forums.

Centrality can be measured in various modes, the simplest of which is *Degree
Centrality*, which measures the centrality of an EC by calculating its direct
links(Wasserman & Faust, 1994). However, this type of centrality measure is rather
limited and is cannot represent the complexity of situations arising in online discussion
forums in which the conversational situations may present a myriad of direct and
indirect connections comprising the conversation as it evolves throughout the network.
An expanded mode of centrality measure, the *Flow Betweenness Centrality* extends the
approach of centrality to include all possible pathways available for connecting various
EC. For example, EC 'A' may be directly connected to EC 'C' however; 'A' can also be
indirectly connected to 'C'' by way of 'B'. 'Figure 4-10' shows the two paths possible
for connecting A and C:

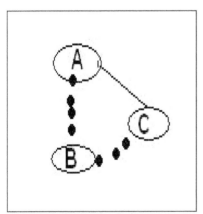

Figure 4-10 : Connecting Pathways

In searching for a relation between patterns and information flow, a third mode of centrality routine, the 'Information Centrality' seems an appropriate measure to explore. *Information Centrality* routine perceives *information* as "the level of ability to transmit, to communicate", and measures the centrality that uses all paths available for an EC to link to anther (Stephenson & Zelen, 1989).

Stephenson and Zelen(1989), argue that it is probable to assume that information can flow through indirect paths for various reasons. I would like to argue that in this study information may at times take indirect routes within a discussion thread because of the inherent nature of the EC as representing mental meaning- making processes, which can sometime follow odd routes and paths in search of meaning; hence I included the Information Centrality mode in my centrality measurement models. According to Information centrality measuring the centrality of EC 'C' described in 'figure 4-10' calculates the *combined path* that is all the paths linked to EC 'C', which in this case include, A>B, and B>C, and A>C(Stephenson & Zelen, 1989; Wasserman & Faust, 1994,p.193). Information centrality measures show that the combined path would have more information than the direct path (A>C) alone(Stephenson & Zelen, 1989). This observation is of particular importance in the context of this study in which I am searching for relations between patterns, illustrating paths or relations, and information flow as I will show later in the study.

The Centrality of the EC measured in this study is equivalent to that of participant, or Actor *Centrality,* as they are often called in the SNA literature. Actor, or EC centrality can be expanded to measure '*Group Centrality*', which measures the average centrality across all the ECs in the network(Wasserman & Faust, 1994,p.192-8), in this context representing a whole pattern or discussion thread. I applied Group Centrality measures to the 131 threads comprising my data. For pursuing my search for a link between pattern and information flow, I measured the group centrality of all the threads according to their pattern categories, so as to be able to discern connections between pattern represented by the category and the information levels it shows. *Table 4-3* ranks each of the six the categories' levels of centrality in a descending order.

Table 4-3- Categories and Levels of Centrality

Category	Flow Betweenness Centrality	Level of Group Information Centrality
1- The Star	4.7	9.1
2- The Duo Focal	4.4	0.46
3a – The Chain	4.2	0.71
3b – The multi Chain	1.9	0.16
4a -The Branch	3.9	0.81
4b – The Branch and Chain	3.2	0.36

Table 4- 3 distinctly shows that Category 1 'The Star', holds the highest levels of 'Centrality' in both centrality measures while category 3b, the 'Multi chain', holds the lowest levels of centrality, with category 4b, the 'Branch and chain', holding second place from the bottom of the scale.

Category 1- the Star, exhibiting the highest levels of centrality implies its potential for being the most 'efficient' pattern for disseminating information. The Star category links all responses to one single point, the initial message initiating the EC, hence, equally disseminating the information entailed in that single point to all members of the network.

Category 3b, the 'multi chain' on the other hand exhibits the lowest levels of centrality, which in the SNA context would imply its least effectiveness in conveying information. The multi chain seems to convey various chunks of information to different parts, or fragments of the network. The information dissemination process observable in the multi chain seems to suggest that different parts of the network may be receiving different information, and that it may be that not all participants receive the same content or amount of information.

Centrality measures enabled me to detect the dynamics occurring in each pattern and measure the potential quantity of information available to each EC and its potential to relay this information. Juxtaposing the SNA 'centrality' measures of information dissemination next to the QCA measures of levels of course related topics reveals an interesting situation in which the 'effective' information dissemination category showing high levels of centrality, reveals relatively low levels of course related topics, and vice versa. The QCA analysis identified categories 3b, the 'Multi chain' and 4b the 'Branch and chain' as conveying high levels of course related discussions, however these categories scored poorly on the SNA 'Centrality' measures. 'Table 4- 4' illustrates the differences.

Table 4-4-Centrality versus QCA

Category	Centrality (Flow-Betweeness)	Qualitative Content Analysis QCA
1 – the Star	4.7	44% course related
2 – Duo focal	4.4	44% course related
3a- Chain	4.2	49% course related
3b – Multi Chain	1.9	55% course related
4a – the Branch	3.9	43% course related
4b- the Chain+ Branch	3.2	55% course related

'Table 4-4', highlights a significant observation, in which the lower levels of centrality, seem to attract higher levels of course related discussions. Centrality measures imply status of control, power, and in a way authority. The person sending the message creating the single EC in the 'Star' category draws power and authority from the position the message holds in the network, and although this may have been created by the response of the other participants, it is still a position of power and authority. The 'Star' pattern showing high centrality measures indicates the dynamics in which the information is conveyed, in this case, illustrating centralised dynamics where all activities relate directly and only to a single EC. Participants respond to a single EC, hence rendering that EC a central position in the network, directing all transfer of information. On the other hand, the position of the EC at the centre of all interactions renders itself a position of power and authority. In contrast to the high levels of the Star pattern, categories 3b, and 4b, show low levels of centrality indicating less hierarchical dynamics, with no distinguishable source of power or authority. The dynamics described in each case indicates roles in terms of power, authority, and the potential for contribution to the dynamics.

The 'Star' type of dynamics grants the EC high levels of power, control, and authority. At the other end of the spectrum, the Multi chain (category 3b), and, the Branch and chain, (category 4b) show what Ioannides(2003) describes as decentralised dynamics, where no single EC can be identified as having more control or authority than others. In the 'multi chain'(3b) and the 'branch and chain'(4b) the dynamics seem to flow among dyads of members and EC, granting all almost equal opportunities for communication and access to information, although some participants in the network may hold a somewhat higher level of centrality than others. For example, the pattern illustrated in *Figure 4-11* depicts a primary chain stemming from the initial message, and two sub- chains branching out of the primary chain. The EC marked in the *arrow*, hold a higher level of 'centrality' than the EC marked in the *circle*. These observations help identify roles of participants and they way these roles construct the social structure represented in the network.

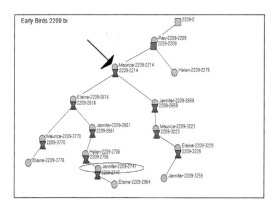

Figure 4-11 : Multi Chain: Category 3b

For measuring the levels of centrality of the marked EC in *figure 4-11*, I chose the Flow Betweenness routine, which measures the levels of intermediary of an EC connecting two other EC to ensure maximum flow of transaction between them(Degenne & Forse, 1999,p.138-9). The EC marked in the 'arrow' measured 0.285 level of Flow-Betweenness centrality, and the EC marked in a 'circle', measured 0.0 level of Flow-Betweenness centrality.

The observations above may lead to two routes of interpretations:

- The discovery of different centrality measure at different points in the network may have significant ramifications for the study of the different stages and progression of learning processes in online discussion forums. However, deeper investigation beyond the scope of this study is needed, for a thorough investigation of this observation.

- Projecting the observation of different measures of centrality in deferent categories of patterns to the context of learning, can be perceived as illustrating the different concepts of learning as perceived by two of the overarching approaches to teaching –on the one hand the *transmitive* approach, in which information and knowledge are perceived as entities to be disseminated from a central point of authority, and on the other hand, the, *socio constructivist* approach advocating peer interaction and collaboration, rather than authoritative dissemination of information.

THOUGHTS ABOUT PATTERNS AS STRUCTURES OF PERCEPTIONS OF TEACHING AND LEARNING

The transmitive approach would probably appreciate the potential entailed in centrality measures for predicting 'effective' learning situations, in which information can be 'efficiently' disseminated. The transmitive approach perceives knowledge as an entity to be disseminated in a 'sage in the box' type dynamics, in which information emanates from a single source of authority(Sherry, 1996). It would be within reason to suggest that this approach would view 'category one'- the Star pattern, as the preferred mode of teaching/learning. Categories 3b, and 4b, on the other hand, would appeal to the teaching paradigm perceiving learning as a two- way communication process where learners engage in dialogue among themselves, the e-tutor and the learning material. This paradigm perceives social interactions as supporting the social construction of knowledge(Sherry, 1996). The dynamics observed in the *multi chain* (3b), and the *branch and chain* (4b) would possibly indicate some evidence of social interactions and the conveyance of different chunks of information in different parts of the network, potentially indicating an emerging knowledge constructing process, in which members participating in different EC positioned in different parts of the network may be involved in different parts or stages of the process.

THE MORE THE MERRIER- PROLIFERATION OF EC AND LEARNING

The inversed results obtained through the QCA, and the Centrality measurements, described in table 4-4, represent yet another significant phenomenon for the study of learning processes. Observing these inverted results, I was able to detect that the more EC are in a network (a representation of a discussion thread), the less centrality it shows. Although centrality does not convey the content discussed in the EC, the fact that the high levels of course related discussion appear in the patterns showing higher numbers of EC per network, suggests that the number of the EC may affect the levels of course related discussions. This observation further implies a possible link between the number of EC and the content discussed in the network. 'Figure 4-12' shows the average number of EC in each of the categories.

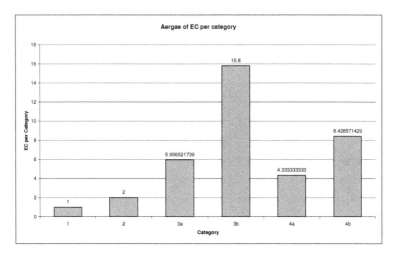

Figure 4-12 : Average EC per Category

Category 1 shows the lowest average number of EC per network, and 3b shows the highest, showing an average of 15.8. Interestingly, it rates the lowest in the centrality measures, but shares the high level of 55% together with category 4b in the QCA measures. Indeed category 4b comes second in the average of EC (8.4), as well as in the Centrality levels. It is possible to deduct from these findings that the more EC in a network, the more 'course related' discussion it will hold.

In an attempt to further investigate the thematic aspect of this phenomenon, I chose to conduct a limited excursion into the content of the networks by analysing a small sample of four threads from 'category one' representing the *Orbitors* group, and four threads from patterns 3a- and 4a representing the *Simple chains*. I chose to sample the Simple chains as this category seems to represent the most prevalent pattern as shown in the 'table 4-5'.

Table 4-5 – Distribution of EC per Pattern

Category	Total of EC in category	Course Related EC	Socio Emotional EC	Mix EC
Orbitors	105	46	40	19
Simple Chains	202	95	64	43
Complex Chains	138	76	38	24

N=445

Reading through the sample threads, I was able to identify certain reoccurring activities, listed in 'table 4-6':

Table 4-6 – Reoccurring Activities in the Dynamic Driven Groups

Activity classification	Activities appearing in both the 'Orbitors' and the 'chainies' groups
Informative issues	• Theoretical materials and course reading
	• Informative comment
	• Adding information to ideas raised previously
	• Commenting on ideas raised previously
	• Fulfilling/responding to a task
	• Instructions
Personal /social issues	• Personal experience/feeling
	• Humour
	• Personal message/ response to specific member

	▪ Personal Perspective
	▪ Personal Opinion
	▪ Comments involving another person or member's ideas
	▪ Personal comment about ones' self
	▪ Empathy
Questions	▪ Theoretical/ philosophical Questions
	▪ Questions to the group
	▪ Questions to particular members
	▪ Extending question
Collaborating	▪ Story/anecdote
	▪ Sharing course related issues
	▪ sharing reflective thinking

To investigate whether any differences emerge between the two Dynamic Driven Groups, I juxtaposed the sample threads from the *Orbitors* and the *Simple chains*. The tables below show the juxtaposition of the *Orbitors* group versus the *Simple chains*. The juxtaposition revealed that although most of the activities appeared in both samples, some were unique to the simple chains sample, and were apparent in the 'Questions' and 'Collaboration' classifications as the tables '4-7', and '4-8' illustrate.

Table 4-7- Types of Questions

Questions	Orbitors	Simple Chains
Theoretical/ philosophical questions	45%	50%
Questions to particular members	22%	17%
Questions to the group	33%	0%
Extending question	0%	33%

Table 4-8 – Collaborative Activities

Questions	Orbitors	Simple Chains
Sharing course related issues	1%	50%
Sharing reflective thinking	1%	25%
Story/ Anecdote	1%	25%

'*Table 4-7*' shows a significant difference relating to the 'extending question', standing on 0% in the Orbitors, and on 33% in the Simple chains.

'*Table 4-8*', shows a significant difference in relation to 'Collaboration'. The 'Orbitors' sample show levels of 1% in all the 'Collaboration' activities, whereas the 'Simple chains show significant levels of activity in all the three different identified collaboration activities.

This limited yet indicative sample implies a more collaborative mode of actions in the 'Simple Chains' group, and in doing that is indirectly corroborating the findings of the SNA 'Information centrality' routine, where the Chain patterns showed less centralised dynamics and suggested low levels of control and authority within the network, indicating distributed rather than centralised dynamics. In learning contexts, this kind of dynamics is usually associated with socio-constructivism, in which peer learning is encouraged, and 'teacher' authoritative position is exchanged for a facilitating role. The Simple Chains also showed significant levels of extending questions usually associated with socio- constructivist learning.

Although the observations described in this section are based on a small and limited sample, they are indicative and suggest possible further investigation into the possible relations between patterns, centrality and teaching/learning approaches

'WHERE IS THE LEARNING'- FROM THE MOUTHS OF PARTICIPANTS

Although my findings so far seem to find the chain related patterns as showing higher levels of course related discussions, implying that these would be the preferable patterns for teaching; accepting the assumption that these patterns proclaim the existence of peer collaboration facilitating constructivist learning is a matter yet to be investigated. It may well be that the chain like shape suggests some form of an on-going movement, or a conveyance of ideas among collaborating peers, alas it may simply indicate a simple 'question- answer' exchange. The only way to verify the nature of the chain related, or in short *Chainies*, was to investigate how my participants felt about their actions, as well as actually observe their actions.

For this investigation I used one of the discussion forums I hosted, 'Mary's Cocktail Party' as a type of an interviewing lounge. Through this 'lounge', I was able to tap into my participants' thoughts and feelings about their experiences of the online discussion forums.

When asked to comment on the "online interactions and experiences triggered by this course and its affect on your interactions with colleagues online as well as off line", one respondent stated that: "True sustained conversation normally tends to happen between two people" (Thread 14787, post 15680)

When asked to address the question of "can meaningful conversations be carried out by a whole bunch of people? Or is it a more intimate phenomenon"? One response read: "I know for myself during the course the most meaningful conversations that I have were usually on a one-to –one basis (Even if they were only for a short period)" (Thread 15735 post 15756).

These two excerpts from the discussion forum show that the participants perceive the one-on –one context of conversation as more conducive to 'true sustained' and 'most meaningful' conversations. This perception of the one-on-one conversation represented in the 'chainies' pattern, signifies the notion the participants hold about one-on-one conversations, implying that it was not the 'question-answer' mode of conversation the participants conducted in those chain pattern conversations, but rather the 'most meaningful ' ones took place there.

Observing participants' actions in an online discussion forum is usually perceived as a search for 'what did they say'? However, I will focus on 'how', rather than 'what' my participants said in those 'chainies' patterns. To study whether my hypothesis arguing that the chainies are used for on-going conveyance of ideas I analysed one discussion thread belonging to the 3a category – the basic chain pattern. In this thread, my participants discussed the role of 'critical researcher' criticising his/her surrounding provoking reactions. The term 'boundaries' was raised in the first response in the thread. In the following excerpt, I shall follow the different terms used by different participants for 'boundaries' as it evolves throughout the discussion thread[28]:

Message 1:
Jenny refers to 'boundaries' of the 'critical researcher' by describing different modes of actions by different actors in the role of a 'critical researcher': – "………*lob-in a grenade and watch-'em scramble Maurice! And then we have I-like my job and want to keep it chicken Jenny"* (Schools 12017 post -12017 parent –0)

Message 2:
> Another metaphor for boundaries- *'heat shields'* - identifying differences – boundaries as *'heat shields'* or having *a moat and a drawbridge. drawbridge , extending the idea of boundaries – as not letting people in , as opposed to letting them in on your own conditions- using the moat and drawbridge.*

Message 3:
> Boundaries as *'walls'*, or boundaries as *bridges that connect*

Message 4:
> *Boundaries, as 'mending walls'. Going on to expand the idea to 'good fences make good neighbours'.*

Message 5:

---

[28] Please access 'Appendix 6' for full thread

'Bridge' as seen 'from a slightly different perspectives' - 'walls and bridges '–' thick walls like a castle and let nobody in or I can draw the draw bridge to allow my boundaries to connect and let people in'.

The discussion continues to another issue, the notion of *collaborating* over the course LMS. This issue was raised in the second message already, but it was in the context of boundaries, testing the 'boundaries', putting your thoughts out there for everyone to see on the Net. The first five messages focused on trying to define, describe, different perceptions of 'boundaries'. Once people felt they have exhausted the issue they moved on to discuss the use of boundaries, in the meaning of 'opening up'- which was mentioned by Debbie in message 3, where she links to *'supporting colleagues'*, and *'collaborative work'*.

In message four, Maurice links to the issue of *collaboration challenging* Debbie's boundaries of comfort zone.

Maurice and Debbie continue the debate about boundaries on the LMS adding aspects as they go along, as can be observed in the following excerpt:

Message 2:

'I'd be brave,,,, Put some thoughts out here in the Net'.

Message 3

Opening up- support group circles, supporting colleagues,

Message 4

Working together as a Net community, comparing to face to face interaction, deep collaboration?

Message 5:

The medium falls short encouraging deep collaboration

Message 6

.... even distribution of involvement,

Message 7

The dialogue is important ; the forum as a collaborative place, dialogue extends train of thought help reflect think critically pose questions

Message 8

The dialogue is the critical component in the Net

From here onwards the discussion drifts to other topics

Message 9 –12 social exchanges I not related to the issue discussed in this excerpt

Message 13

Bringing in a discussion about course   materials- reflection – the main issue of the course

Message 14, 15

Continuing the discussion about course materials - reflection

Message 16 – postponing the discussion to the face-to-face meeting

Looking at the way in which the participants treated topics, it is possible to observe how the thread unfolds the evolvement of rational discussion around the issue of 'collaboration', first, by discussing the whole question of 'putting ones thoughts for everyone to see', and how does it reflect on our *boundaries*. Next, the discussion revolved around collaboration, and the context of collaborating online. Only when these issues have been discussed, the discussion enters into the actual course materials.

The excerpts from this discussion thread show the progression of ideas from one EC to the next. The resources available to me as an only researcher in this study prevented me from expanding this kind of analysis to other threads, as this is a very time consuming task. However, the single example I have shown here, demonstrates the conveyance of ideas across several EC. This single example cannot eliminate the possibility that 'Chainies' will be used for 'question- answer' forms of conversation, however, it does demonstrate the potential of this type of patterns to act as 'conveyer belts (chains)' of ideas.

QUASI SUMMARY-TOWARDS THE DEEP END OF THE EC APPROACH

Earlier in this section I mentioned the ability of Centrality measurements to indicate the dynamics of the diffusion of information. These measurements showed that the less EC there are in a discussion thread, the more centralised it will be, suggesting a single source of information. Whereas a large number of EC means that the number of sources of information equals to the number of EC in the network. This multiplicity of sources of information and lack of apparent centre of authority may suggest a chaotic situation where participants contribute messages with no apparent logic or reason.

However, reading the messages of these multiple EC networks patterns, I have already established that this is not the case, and in fact quite the contrary; these are the high course related levels patterns, and furthermore they are showing high levels of collaboration and extending questions suggesting socio constructivist learning.

It is becoming apparent that the Multiple EC Networks or 'Chainies' are the patterns holding more EC, less centralised authority, implying socio –constructivist dynamics and higher levels of course related discussions, making these category patterns an interesting arena for the investigation of the role of interactions, or 'relations' in Online Learning Discussion Forums (OLDF).

In chapter three I described a 'relation' as a representation of sorting and selecting of topics for meaning making. Could the order in which messages were posted to the discussion forums exhibit this notion, and if so what is the contribution of the EC approach to this process? I will attempt to address this notion in the next section.

Part Two – Visual Representations for Trailing Meaning Making Processes

In the methodology chapter, I described the development of the EC concept, using a small mock data set. However, applying this concept to the real live data set, presented challenges, the most important of which was to ascertain the significance of the EC in representing the meaning making processes, exhibited by my research participants.

Being able to follow such processes required genuine reconstruction of the conversations, and the meticulous representation of its evolvement and dynamics.
In this section, I will explore the prevailing routes available for reconstructing online conversations, followed by the new realisations introduced by the application of the EC approach.

Before embarking on the meaning-making quest, I conducted a comprehensive search encompassing all the 846 messages in my data set, to ensure that no messages were sent randomly, or misplaced. Throughout the whole of the data, I detected three instances in which participants mistakenly submitted the same message twice. This could have occurred due to some technological malfunction. However, in all three instances, responses were made only to the message submitted first.

THE IMPORTANCE OF THE SORT ORDER AND CONVERSATION ADJACENCY

My first acquaintance with the content of the discussion forums was when the course was still in progress and I observed the various forums. Back in those days, I used to log on to the course website regularly, read the new messages in all the forums, and respond to the ones posted in the forums I hosted. At that stage, I was not yet aware of the importance of the order in which the messages appeared on my computer screen, nor was I aware of any possible limitations in the way in which the system organised the messages for me to view. Back then, I was primarily concerned with the content of the messages. I was constantly looking out for interesting topics that flared up the discussion, and got people involved, thinking that this would help me identify and follow any occurring knowledge enhancement processes. My initial approach to understanding what the content emerging in the discussion forums were conveying resembled the prevalent approaches adopted by e- moderators, as well as researchers of discussion forums, focusing on the content of individual messages for studying group learning (Creese, 2003; Salmon, 2000). This approach predominantly treats discussion forums at the level of content conveyed through messages posted, using 'content analysis' techniques to extract information relating to occurrences in discussion forums. Being acquainted with the content of the separate messages in online discussion forums, does not provide a view, nor the comprehension of the conversations occurring. A message- by- message view does not reveal the relations between messages, hence preventing what Rorty so clearly phrased as: "seeing conversation as the ultimate context within which knowledge is to be understood"(Rorty, 1979,p.389)

Attempting to study learning, or as I have previously in this chapter referred to it as 'changes in perceptions', I needed to seek for a way of following the order in which messages were contributed to the OLDF in their construction of the conversations.

THE MYSTERIOUS REPRESENTATION OF THE ORDER OF MESSAGES

Discussion forums function as self-transcribing platforms.(Levin, Haesun, & Riel, 1990), automatically recording all messages. However, I wondered how helpful and informative this self-transcribing mechanism would prove when attempting to follow the flow of the conversations in a way that would facilitate the trailing of the meaning making processes informed by the deployment of Documentary Method of Interpretation (DMI) by my participants.

Initially, I assumed that the automatically allocated numeric key code assigned by the server to each and every message contributed would automatically allow the recreation and representation of the order in which my research participants posted their messages, hence making the trailing of meaning making process an innate and simple task to follow. However, when I attempted to follow the content of these self-transcribed conversations, by simply printing out the messages the way they appear on the computer screen, I discovered, to my surprise, that the flow of conversation seem to be disrupted at some points, and the stream of messages failed to portray comprehendible meaning. Being able to follow the order in which messages were contributed, is the key to following the meaning making process, hence reproducing the exact sort order is of great significance to the study.

The system running the discussion forums I observed provides the three modes of representation of messages posted frequently found in prevalent LMSs: **Screen shots-** presenting the messages in the exact order they appear on the website, as shown in 'figure 4-13'.

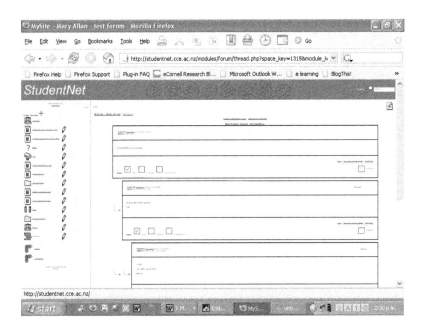

Figure 4-13 : Screen- Shot of Messages in a Discussion Forum

Save/print- presenting messages in a printer friendly format – omitting website features irrelevant for printed pages, as shown in 'figure 4-14'.

New thread: Subject = hi from Mary

Posted by: Mary Allan on *07-05-04* at 12:36
Subject: hi from Mary

hi there this is my message

Reply - Reply with original quoted - Edit/Delete
Post No. 37890, Thread No. 37890, Parent No. 0
Status: ☐ Read ☐ Follow up ☐ Monitor replies ☐ Print/Save

Posted by: Mary Allan on *10-12-04* at 18:08 Answer
Subject: Re: hi from Mary - Bob

thanks Mary that was nice

Figure 4-14: Printer Friendly Discussion Thread

Spreadsheet- presenting the messages in a spreadsheet format, as shown in 'figure 4-15'.

Thread No.	Post No.	Parent No.	Nature of Post	Subject	Message	Date added
37890	46869	37890	Answer	Re: hi from Mary - Bob	thanks Mary that was nice Bob	10/12/2004 18:08
37890	46870	37890	Comment	Re: hi from Mary - John	Hi MAry i think this is just great John	10/12/2004 18:09
37890	46871	46869	Agree	Re: Re: ih From Mary- Dianne	Hi Bob I am with you on that Dianne	10/12/2004 18:10

Figure 4-15 : Spreadsheet Representation of a Discussion Thread

I assumed that in view of the fact that the system recorded messages automatically, it would present an identical sort order throughout all three modes; however, when comparing the three modes, I discovered that this was not the case. 'Table 4-9' displays this phenomenon in a single randomly chosen example, representing discussion thread '13934':

Table 4-9 –Three Modes of Representation

	Save/Print	Spreadsheet
13934-0	13934-0	13934-0
13939-13934	14598-13934	13957-13934
13951-13934	13957-13934	13939-13934
13957-13934	14001-13957	13951-13934
14001-13957	14085-14001	14598-13934
14085-14001	14148-14085	14001-13957
14087-14085	14237-14148	14085-14001
14241-14087	14400-14237	14087-14085
14259-14241	14087-14085	14148-14085
14148-14085	14241-14087	14241-14087
14237-14148	14259-14241	14237-14148
14400-14237	13951-13934	14400-14237
14598-13934	13939-13934	14259-14241

Having exhausted the route of 'key codes' as a possible sorting criterion, I turned to investigate the chronological order in which messages were represented, by following the date of posting, using the same thread as before. 'Table 4-10' illustrates this attempt using the same thread I used in the key code example- thread 13934:

Table 4-10- Chronological Sort Order

9th Oct at 18.05pm
9th Oct at 19.09pm
9th Oct at 20.57pm
9th Oct at 22.33pm
10th Oct at 16.51pm
11th Oct at 19.54pm
11th Oct at 21.25pm
14th Oct at 17.51pm
14th Oct at 22.39pm
BUT then
13th Oct at 16.22pm
14th Oct at 17.11pm
and then back to timely order
17th Oct at 12.40am
21st Oct at 19.10pm

'Table 4-10' presents some peculiar chronological irregularities in the order of the messages. For some unexplainable reason, a message sent on the 13th of October appears as following two messages posted on the 14th of October. The only solution to this riddle could have been an intervention by the moderator reorganisation of the order of the discussion. A moderator's intervention could be understood if the content of the message clearly showed that it was initially placed in the wrong place by the sender, or that the content could communicate better if it were repositioned differently in the sequence.

To confirm this assumption I followed the content of the message preceding and the one following the oddly positioned message in thread 13934:

Thread 13934 odd positioning of message

(Messages post key -14259; 14148; 14237)

Preceding message:

Posted by: Merian on 14-10-02 at 22:39

Subject: Learning takes 5 years

Comment

Hi Elaine,

It has taken me four years to have some of the readings that I read in my very first paper in Dip Ed Man to actually mean something. All that background reading is starting to click in. I know that as I go on in my journey of learning this will continue to happen. Just think it takes a child about five years to learn to read. All that background in learning and developing and Bingo round five or six they can read. Amazing!

Cheers,

Merian

Post No. 14259, Thread No. 13934, Parent No. 14241

Oddly positioned message

Posted by: Maurice on 13-10-02 at 16:22

Subject: Hegemonic Assumptions

Request for clarification

Hi Elaine

>... *you have read three articles and*

>*synthesised these - I am expecting to see that people*

>*would refer to these articles within their discussions.*

mmm, well ... that bead was one which fell off my string some time ago ... and other beads are there now - so "my" discussion related to other readings (though inevitably, those which I'd written the abstracts of still had a place in my background

---

213

consciousness ... and now I'm just going to write the synthesis - which will be benefitting from the distance since I wrote the abstracts!

>... or you could point people toward your

>submission in the critical pedagogy abstracts area

>(I have not been there - so I have no idea what is there).

frankly, I'm shocked at such a confession!! ... now I don't know what to think! ;-)

:-) Maurice

Post No. 14148, Thread No. 13934, Parent No. 14085

Following message

Posted by: Elaine on *14-10-02* at 17:11

Subject: Hegemonic Assumptions   Question

>>... or you could point

>people toward your

>>submission in the critical

>pedagogy abstracts area

>>(I have not been there - so I

>have no idea what is

>there).

>frankly, I'm shocked at such a

>confession!! ... now I don't

>know what to think! ;-)

Tough - that's your problem!

But why are you shocked? - no don't bother to tell me - that is your business - why on earth should I interfere in Ian's territory? I am running the discussion section of this course. I am expecting to see how your reading of critical pedagogy is showing through in your final discussions. If I read what you have written elsewhere then I will become confused about what I read where - it is that simple.

Cheers

E

Post key 14237

To ascertain the irregularity of chronological order of messages, I observed other threads, and found that this was a reoccurring phenomenon and the same erratic order appeared at some points of the thread in the other examples I observed[29].

At this point I decided to put aside any aspirations of understanding how the system organises the messages and simply attempt to print them out and read them, so as to attempt and make sense of a sequence of the conversation in a thread. I printed out a segment of the messages of the thread (13934) I have analysed for sort order, using save/print mode, as shown below:

Thread 13934, illustrating a 'save /print' mode:

Subject: DEBBIE's DISCUSSION ON Hegemonic Assumptions
Posted by: Debbie on *09-10-02* at 18.05
Formal Task

1. Social constructionism: This topic interests me greatly, and is a theory that could help explain the particular 'patterns of actions' that I act out in my proffessional life, and how they may differ from the 'patterns of actions' I act out in my personal life.
Social constructionism talks about us being a product of social encounters and relationships and that we create ourselves through these social encounters.
This takes me to my next thought...
The parents in my centre...and some hegemonic assumptions that both they (as parents) and us (as teachers) may well be having.
I am also wondering if social constructionism plays a part in these assumptions and whether either us (as teachers) or them (as parents) really want anything to change anyway!
We might be quite comfortable with these assumptions, however, I think that this is what makes them hegemonic, because over time they become embedded, and to quote Brookfield (pg 14-15)
"these assumptions that they think are in the best interest, but have actually been designed by more powerful 'others'"
So, my assumptions are in regard to our social encounters and relationships with our parents;

---

[29] Erratic sort order in the additional examples can be observed in appendix 8

a. Our assumptions of them.

b. their assumptions of us, and

c. Societies assumptions of the relationship between centre/school and parents.

1. Parents don't really want to be stopped by teachers for social encounters, they just want to pick their children up and go home.

2. Parents don't want to know all the details about their child's learning that occurred that day, they just basically want to know that their child has been happy and settled.

3. The teachers have all the expertise, therefore it's not the parents place to question the teachers actions - the teacher must be right!

4. A good e.c.e centre or school should be meeting the 'needs' of all parents.

So there you are, what do you think about these assumptions, how much of a reality are they in your learning environment, and what (if anything) prevents change from occurring within these assumptions?

Cheers, Debbie.

.

Subject: confused !

Posted by: Debbie on *21-10-02* at 19.10

Comment

I have been reading the last few discussions and find the whole thing totally confusing, but hey! that's me! I was under the assumption (there's that word again) that we were meant to be leading discussions, which I feel I did half O.K.

What I am aware of for me is the need to start to 'put closure' around my comments on studentnet.

I never know whether I'm commenting in the right forum, but I have always found this one less daunting to comment in.

I've found this to be an extremely empowering paper and I am hoping that the confidence I have gained through this paper will see me through the more rigid TL801 I'll need to do next year.

In some ways I think we have shared on a far more personal level then if we had been in a classroom together.

I found this form of communication to be very non-threatening. I could submit to a conversation when I wished, somehow not being able to read the facial expressions has helped me go that little bit further with my comments.

I also recognised that when I was wanting feedback to a comment I would normally verbally invite a response in some way or other.

What I do know is that my practice with my colleagues and the children has taken on a completely different direction this year. It seems to involve for me gentle reflection on my practice continually.

I found I no longer work within pre-determined outcomes, rather I allow my thinking to remain open to whatever may reveal itself.

For the children we work with it means that our curriculum is now very much focused on their present interest and needs.

Am I concerned that I am not planning for them. No, I have now become comfortable with the fact that our children can plan for themselves, and my job is to document and record these plans and work with the children with them.

How's everyone else feeling about this course finishing?
Cheer, Debbie.

The first message in the example above is indeed the initial message; however, the message represented, as the response to the initial message, seems out of context.

The chronological sequence, or date of submission the message appearing here as second to the initial message, was actually the last to have been submitted, as showing , in the **screen shot representation** of thread 13934 in 'figure 4-16'.

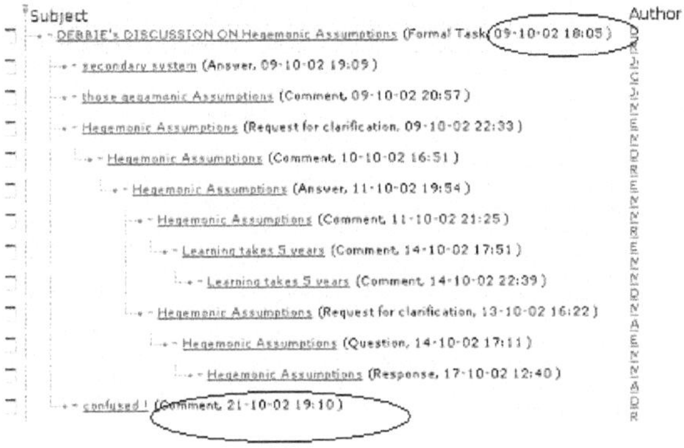

Figure 4-16 Thread Screen Shot Chronology

Both messages were posted by the same participant, however they do not seem to have any contextual sequence, on the contrary, the second message implies that other messages should have preceded it as it begins by saying:

"I have been reading the last few discussions and find the whole thing totally confusing....." (thread 13934). The content quite definitely does not relate to the first message, seen as preceding this message.

This small example shows the confusion a reader may be confronted when reading through messages. The technology of the discussion forums self transcribes every message posted to any of its threads, however, the discrepancies in the sort order of the messages indicated an emerging need for an alternative concept or tool for observing the order of messages.

The self-transcribing feature of discussion forums can be applied with no further manipulation for investigating individual messages, however, as the investigations I have conducted earlier indicated, recording individual messages entails a different perception to the one needed when attempting to recreate whole sequences of conversations.

This notion became clear to me as my analysis attempts offered me a second encounter with the online messages. The first time I read the messages was when the course was still running. Back then when I was observing the activities of my research participants, the messages seem to make sense, they seem to be in comprehensible order. However, I now realise that back then I was focusing on a message-by-message concept, where as now I was looking for something more than sporadic reading of messages as they came in, this time I was looking for a way to follow a process.

THE EC FOR REVEALING CONVERSATION FLOW

Investigating the visual representations of the discussion threads provided by the EC approach, I was able to detect and understand the reason for the confusing sort order of the messages in the available modes of representations I explored earlier. The visual patterns provided by the EC approach portrayed the discussion forms as networks of sometimes intertwining relations, not as the linear thread like entities represented by the available methods. Discussion threads, like conversations, move between different topics, and lateral points move the conversation to new topics(Holzschlag, 2001), creating non linear structures, and producing multiple chains or spawning branches. Trying to follow such structures using linear and representing tools like key codes or chronological order, proved limited, constraining our understanding of the conversations observed.

The EC produced visual networks revealing branches and multi chains, illustrating complex and elaborate structures rather than simple thread like configurations. The key feature of the EC lies in its ability to discern and represent points where the discussion 'branched out' to start a sub-thread of conversation. I called this key feature, the *'Pivot EC'*. The 'pivot EC' is a representation linking more than one response which marks specific contributions spawning multiple trails of conversations, creating sub discussions, groups within groups, and conversations within conversations. In other words, the 'Pivot EC' marks incidents in which the multiple responses to a messages generated multiple threads or chains, or split the conversation into sub threads or branches similar to the one showing in 'figure 4-17' .

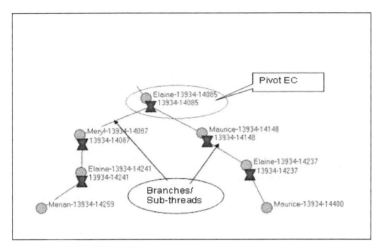

Figure 4-17 : Pivot EC and Branches

Returning to the mysteriously misplaced messages, and the disrupted chronological order of posting dates, I now revisited the three messages I analysed before, in the example titled " *Thread 13934 odd positioning of message"*- (Messages post key -14259; 14148; 14237), and observed their content through the eyes of pivot EC, as shown in 'figure 4-18'.

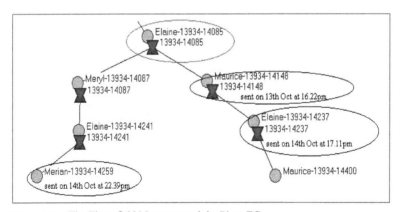

Figure 4-18 : The Three Odd Messages and the Pivot EC

Through the 'pivot EC' view, the three oddly placed messages suddenly made sense. The illustration in 'figure 4-18' explains the order in which the messages should be read. According to this illustration, the message sent on the 14th of October at 22.39pm, did not precede the message sent on the 13th of October as was suggested in the '**Thread 13934 odd positioning of messages**' as well as the chronological order described in '*Table 4-10*', but rather related directly to the pivot EC message, sent on the 11th of October.

The scope of this study does not allow me to verify whether all chronologically displaced messages appear at pivot points. However, it is quite clear that following any linear guided order will result in a single sequence of messages with no indication of the emergence of sub threads, representing sub conversations, hence failing to portray that certain messages actually belong to different chains in the network. The 'pivot EC' view enabled me to look into meaning making, as it is being created and developed throughout a discussion thread.

THE PIVOT EC IN ACTION: AN EXPLORATORY VENTURE INTO THE POTENTIAL OF PIVOT EC VIEW

In this section I present small exploratory ventures, which I used as preliminary indication of the possible investigative routes enabled by the Pivot EC view. These are limited explorations, and further studies are needed in order to verify findings. However, I suggest that these exploratory ventures provide important indications and signal potential features and application entailed in the pivot EC, to be further explored in future studies.

Looking through the 'Pivot EC' view not only offered a non-linear outlook, but also indicated the potential of certain message to hold multiple meanings, as its position within the network could be interpreted in more than one-way. 'Figure 4-19' highlights the pivot EC, and 'figure 4-20' illustrates four possible chains in which the pivot EC can play different roles.

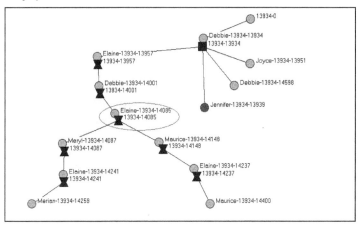

Figure 4-19 : The Pivot EC 13934

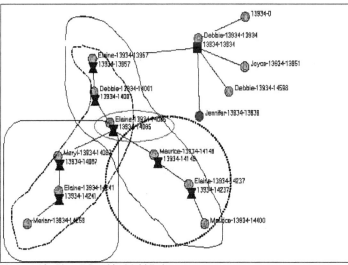

Figure 4-20 : Pivot EC and its Multi Roles

222

The pivot EC 13934-14085 can take four different positions filling different roles:

- As part of the major sequence, positioning 14085 within the sequence of the chain beginning with 13957- ending in 14400;
- Positioning 14085 as a trigger of a sub chain beginning with itself – 14085 and ending in 14259
- Positioning 14085 as a branching message dividing the thread into two sub-threads both beginning with 14085 and splitting into branch 14148 – 14400, and branch 14087 – 14259
- Positioning 14085 in the middle of a sub chain begging with 13957, and ending with 14259

This is just an example of how the EC approach enables new options for sorting messages, in a non-linear form, facilitating the investigation of multi sequences of messages, to discover meaning making processes. In the next page I explored this example a little further and investigated the content of the EC it encompasses.

As a starting point for investigating the four different sequences I have identified in 'figure 4-20', I analysed the pivot EC, and found it held three themes. I gave each theme a title to allow clear reference whenever it appeared in other messages on the sequence:

- The Three-article Theme
- Meryl's Theme
- Critical Pedagogy (CP) Abstracts Theme

Next, I attempted to find thematic relations within each of the four sequences.

Messages following 14085 proceeding to 14148 (positioning 14085 either in the sequence or as branching the thread into divided chains taking the 14148 sequence) Showed the following engagement in the identified themes:

14148- The Three-article Theme

14148- The Critical Pedagogy (CP) Abstracts Theme

14237 - The Critical Pedagogy (CP) Abstracts Theme

In 14148 the author spurs a new theme triggered by a personal note posted at the end of 14085 -"I have not been there- so I have no idea what is there". The author of 14148 responds ..." I am shocked….. "

14237, and 14400 focus on this remark.

Positioning 14085 as triggering a sub-chain – 14085- 14259

14087- Meryl's Theme. This message is also referring to an earlier message (14001 positioned just before 14085) and themes mentioned in it. The author of message 14087 added a personal note at the end of the messages spawning a new theme – 'The Five Year Theme'.

The next two messages 14241 and 14259, take up 'The Five Year Theme'.

(Interesting to note that in both chains a personal note added at the end of a message, as a incidental, or a mere joke, i.e.1:

4087 "PS- Elaine and I joked- give me 5-10 year to come to terms with CP"; and 14085 " I have not been there-so I have no idea what is there", spawned a lot of interest from others)

The two branching out chains do not seem to have anything in common.

14087	14148
Meryl's theme + the Five year theme	The Three article theme + the Shock theme

The chain starting with 13957 and ending in 14259, positions the pivot EC 14085 in the middle. The two messages preceding the pivot seem to be leading into it. After the pivot this sequence is identical to the sub-chain – 14085- 14259

The different sequences showed thematic relation and exhibited meaningful successions demonstrating yet another route of investigation made available by the Pivot EC view.

To further support the findings of the thematic relationships, I proceeded to find relationships between messages using *echoic, or reference response(Levin, Haesun, &*

Riel, 1990; Shimojima, Skoiso, Swerts, & Katagiri, 1998). I define *reference response* as terms, sentences or phrases quoted in a responding message, not necessarily done by using the 'reply with original quote' available on many systems including the LMS used by my research participants.

The quotes I am referring to in this study are incorporated into the content of the responding messages. By following these quotes, I hope to be able to further support my assumption that the EC concept is significantly important for ascertaining the order of messages hence helping reconstructing the flow of the conversations. Achieving this would suggest that the EC can be regarded as a sustainable concept for pursuing meaning making and advancement of ideas which is significantly important in the application of discussion forums as learning environments.

The examples showing *reference responses* in 'table 4-11, are taken again from thread 13934.

Table 4-11 - Reference Responses

Please note!!! The numbers represent the message's number and the number of the message it is responding to

	Original message main points	Responding message content relation
Elaine-13934-14085 / 13934-14085 / Meryl-13934-14087 / 13934-14087 / Maurice-13934-14148 / 13934-14148 (image saved as: 13934-14085 junction.gif)	**14085- responding to14001 –** "it's nearing the end of the course…."	**14087-14085-** ".. you mentioned coming to the end of the course…"
	14085- responding to14001 – "I was talking with Meryl today …"	**14087-14085-** "Elaine commented – I was talking to Meryl today…"
	14085- responding to14001- …"you have read three articles and synthesised these- I am expecting…."	**14148-14085-** …"you have read three articles and synthesised these- I am expecting…."

Meryl-13934-14087 13934-14087 Elaine-13934-14241 13934-14241 Merian-13934-14259 (image saved as 13934-14087 junction .gif)	ORIGINAL MESSAGE MAIN POINTS	Responding message content relation
	14087- responding to14085 - "Elaine and I(meryl) joked , -give me 5-10 years to come to terms with CP (Critical Pedagogy)	**14241-14087-** " Yes, Meryl and I (Elaine) talked about it taking 5 years to grasp and idea and learn to run with it" (Critical Pedagogy).
	14241- responding to14087- Yes, Meryl and I (Elaine) talked about it taking 5 years to grasp and idea and learn to run with it"	**14259-14241** – no direct quote but a lot of paraphrasing around the notion of five years for grasping – "it has taken me four years to have some of the readings…"

Maurice-13934-14148 13934-14148 Elaine-13934-14237 13934-14237 Maurice-13934-14400	message main points	Responding message content relation
	Responding to14085- (linking to the first the head of the subdivision) 'm shocked at such a confession… now I don't to think!"	**14237-14148- direct quote:** "Frankly, I'm shocked at such a confession… now I don't know what to think!"
	Responding to14148 –" Tough—that's your	**14400-14237-** –" Tough— that's your problem"

226

The excerpts in 'table 4-11' show consistent *reference responses* across the whole thread, exhibiting referral connections across messages, linking EC and following pivot sort order, to maintain flowing and comprehendible *reference responses*.

I would like to argue that ascertaining this 'referral' linkages support the notion that the EC help recreate the online conversations, and the meaning making processes guided by application of Document Method of Interpretation (DMI). Following the *reference response* across sequences of EC and more importantly, across pivot EC to discover a flawless continuance of references suggests that the sort order created with the help of the EC and the pivot EC have helped establish the choice order, (the DMI), and the meaning making processes exhibited by my research participants through the network of 'relations' they have established in the discussion thread.

SUMMARY

In this chapter, I set out to investigate whether the EC concept would indeed provide information otherwise not clearly observable, about the occurrences and dynamics in online learning discussion forums (OLDF).

Visualising the discussion threads comprising my data- set, I was able to detect 6 emerging patterns, which could be viewed as depicting two overarching types of dynamics, highly centralised and hierarchical – the "Orbitors" and the more dispersed, collaboration oriented patterns, the "Chainies". I suggested that these dynamics imply two different perceptions of knowledge, and learning; the 'Orbitors' representing the knowledge dissemination and retrieval model, predominantly identified with the 'transmitive' model of teaching, and the 'Chainies' representing the knowledge sharing and negotiating model, identified with the socio constructivist, collaborative approach to teaching. I then proceeded to look for a way of identifying the roles of different EC across a network. In this case I defined 'roles, as 'the potential or ability to convey, or

227

control the information flow in the network. Using SNA *centrality* measures I was able to identify the 'roles of EC, and their potential to convey, or control the dissemination of information and elicit the overall dynamics of the thread. Having identified 'roles' of EC across a network, and overall dynamics of a thread , I projected these centrality informed role definitions as tools enabling the discernment of the teaching/ learning dynamics taking place in the thread.

In the second part of this chapter I looked at the ability of the EC approach to recapture the evolvement of conversation and the meaning processes it entailed. The EC approach with the aid of the 'Pivot EC view, enabled the trailing of' branching out' conversations, breaking the constraints limiting other analysis approach using the discussion thread as the structure of analysis.

The findings described in this chapter provide a first glimpse into the type of analysis enabled by the EC approach. Many more studies are needed for confirming my preliminary explorations, and assumptions about the ability of the emerging visual patterns created by the participants applying DMI, and corroborated by SQL key codes to provide a comprehensive view of the occurrences in online discussion forums in a way that would allow evaluation of their contribution to learning. However, the study opened up new ways of investigations and indicates several routes for further studies.

5. VISUALISATION IS GREAT- BUT.....DISCUSSING THE OUTSET OF THE STUDY

Introduction

All throughout this study I attempted to share my emerging thoughts, and convey the evolvement of the ideas forming this study. Using this style of writing served as a testimony of my conceptual deliberations, teasing, investigating and sifting of ideas, theories, approaches and methods. On reaching the designated space of 'discussion' traditionally allocated to the fifth chapter of a dissertation, I would like to invite my readers to yet another journey, in which I attempt to revisit the theoretical frameworks I have chosen to apply throughout the study, and explore aspects which lead to concepts venturing beyond the scope of this work.

Prelude

I opened this study with a scenario in which I fantasized on how space people might perceive planet earth's classrooms. In the scenario I envisaged that the space people on reporting to their leader, said:

> Some pictures [taken from outer space] showed rooms full of learners all facing in the direction of one person who seemed to be speaking to them. Others showed rooms in which learners are sitting in small groups, facing each other and seem to be conversing….."

In summarising their report, the space people concluded that:

> …….in some classrooms on planet earth, learners are made to follow the words of a leader, and in others they seem to engage with the words of each other.

From their bird's eye view of classrooms, the space people deduced that seating arrangements demarcate social spaces, revealing social interactions and dynamics.

This scenario suggests looking at the ways in which people relate to each other, not by investigating 'what' they said, but rather on 'how' they said it, focusing on the dynamics of the social interactions occurring in the classroom rather than the content conveyed or the specific individuals involved. Furthermore, the scenario implies that the different ways in which people related to each other created different social contexts, as some were "following" while others were "engaging". The focus of this study is concerned with investigating the ways in which people relate to each other and the social dynamics and structures these relations may create.

I chose to begin this chapter with a short review of the way in which I approached the investigation of the notion of relation, followed by a description of the ways in which I addressed the research questions. Finally, I revisit and challenge some of the concepts emerging from the theoretical framework I have applied throughout the study.

Observing 'Relations'

In conversational contexts, like the ones occurring in online discussion forums, a relation in its crudest form, is a linguistic connection between two or more participants, however, the motivation for a participant to initiate or respond to another is triggered by mental processes. Observing mental processes including those related to learning is problematic in the sense that we cannot actually see them, hence we rely on either actions or artefacts underpinned or produced by mental processes.

Garfinkel's(1967), Documentary Method of Interpretation (DMI), inspired my thinking about a possible way of making mental processes visible. In the context of this study I referred to the DMI as a choice mechanism that illustrates the interpretive processes occurring in a participant's mind, making them visible and describable. Through the perspective of the DMI, the act of choice can be perceived as an externalisation of an internal –mental process of interpretation, making it accessible to observation. Garfinkel (1967) argues that the DMI is a method in which a person selects from the surrounding environment the parts which seem relevant to them for their sense making progression. This notion suggests that the DMI identifies 'action' in the form of selecting or choosing, and 'artefact' in some form of a document either verbal or written or as further action/s, revealing the meaning the person has constructed.

The selections people make when participating in discussion threads are indicated by the messages they choose to respond to, hence revealing their sense making progression, however, there is an even more exciting feature entailed in this selection method. Messages in online discussion forums are representations of their author, thus choosing to relate to a certain message automatically creates a link between the person choosing the message and its author, which means that messages and participants are interchangeable. Realising this interchangeability notion is of great importance for the study of collaborative social constructivist environments, as the choices performed through the application of the DMI enables the observation of the sense making progression of individuals, while at the same time charting the creation of links between people. Furthermore, this means that the choices of topic of discussion people make depicts their own interest, while at the same time depicting their choice of conversation partners. These processes chart the exchange of content in the form of ideas, questions, and negotiations, which opens the way for going beyond the individual mental processes to explore the supra individual. In other words, by choosing 'what to talk about' through the application of the DMI, participants are choosing 'who to talk to', hence the mental, becomes the social.

The reciprocity between the individual mind and the social has been discussed by social theorists of learning such as Vygotsky(1978), Bandura(1989), Lave and Wenger(1991), to name but a few . This notion encompasses a wide field of inquiry, and although this study touches on related issues such as the social construction of knowledge and collaborative learning, for reasons of scope it does not venture beyond the point of offering an alternative way of observing the phenomenon.

Identifying the choice mechanism as the action triggering the creation of social contexts through the use of language mediated communication between people was the first step, to continue the investigation I returned to the interpretation of the seating arrangements of classrooms on planet earth attained through the birds' eye view of my scenario. I hoped that this view would provide me with a fresh outlook for studying the dynamics and social structures created when people communicate. In order to assimilate the birds eye view of the scenario in the online context of this study, I needed to find a way of mimicking seating arrangements in a cyber classroom, so as to be able to observe the dynamics occurring in the online discussion forums. In a way this meant reversing the out of space scenario, by looking at a '*trio puzzle*' of 'who talked to whom, on which occasion, and about what' for detecting the dynamics and the social spaces in which they occurred.

Completing the 'trio puzzle' enabled by the Event Centre (EC) approach described throughout chapters three and four in this study, provided me with a birds eye view, similar to that observed by my scenario characters, depicting the interactions occurring in a learning context, only this time in cyber space. Whether the interpretation of the out of the space people about learners on earth either "*following a single leader,* in this study represented by the 'Orbitors' pattern of interactions, *or alternatively following their own initiatives*" here represented by the 'Chainies', is accurate or not remains to be investigated. The important achievement obtained by the EC approach is that it made the virtual classroom 'seating arrangement' visible, and the dynamics it generates observable and open to investigation. The EC approach revealed a number of significant issues:

1. The visualisation of sequences of choice making
2. An identification of mutual interest topics alongside the participants involved
3. An identification of multi participant conversations
4. An identification of every new development in the progression of ideas, as the choices made by the participants revealed the emerging new links and new EC. This feature enabled going beyond the limiting frame of the discussion thread as it is presented by the prevalent technology supporting discussion forums

Furthermore, the application of the EC approach, utilising computer network key codes for the identification of choices participants made throughout each discussion thread provided an empiric stance to the representation of the mental processes externalised by the choice actions. Additionally, in making choice processes visible, it made the process of the construction of the network visible as well. This is crucial for beginning to understand collaborative learning and social construction of knowledge, as it depicts the emerging of links or relations between people, charting mutual interests hence identifying 'birds of feather' among participants. Furthermore, the EC approach contributes to our understanding of the ways in which groups evolve, and how collaborative processes emerge. It also charts the trail through which ideas are exchanged, processed, and forwarded throughout the network charting routes of knowledge construction.

The visual Representation and Beyond

Focusing on visual representations may seem a limited or at least an odd way of investigating mental processes such as learning, however, Bertin(1981) suggested that we use vision for thinking and *"Graphics is the visual means of resolving logical problems"* (p.16). Using graphics for clarifying complex problems is something we have all experienced in a variety of contexts from the most ordinary and mundane to the conceptually sophisticated. Visualising something is usually done for making something otherwise invisible or undetectable, visible, therefore making the issue under investigation either clearer or adding to the understanding and realisation of aspects unknown prior to the visualisation. Achieving a visualisation of a concept demands the deconstruction of its most intricate details and the reconstruction of these details in a way that will exhibit the understanding of their interrelations. Visualising abstract concepts like the ones I am addressing in this study requires acknowledging even the most mundane detail, in search of an understanding of the intricacies of the problem at hand.

The most basic details concerning this study were to identify 'who talked to whom, on which occasion, and about what'. Having to acknowledge this basic notion enabled me to understand the essence of learning in online discussion forums as comprised of a network of relations between people, participating in events of conversation. This realisation may seem insignificant in itself; however, it opened up the way for significant realisations about the study of learning in online discussion forums, as it revealed aspects which were undetectable before.

To explore some of these realisations I framed the study within the following research questions:

1. In what ways do the patterns obtained by the EC approach contribute to our ability to observe and analyse the learning related dynamics, and social structures emerging in Online Learning Discussion Forums (OLDF)?

2. How can the patterns obtained by the EC approach begin to illuminate ways in which they operate relative to meaning making and learning processes in OLDF?

In the next couple of sections I explore the ways in which I was able to address the conceptual issues raised by the two questions throughout the study, however, since these have already been discussed in previous chapters, what these two sections offer is a crystallisation of the key notions discussed in the study, while highlighting the links between my excursions into the implementation of the EC approach and the theoretical frameworks I have applied.

VISUAL PATTERNS FOR UNDERSTANDING LEARNING

Visualising the *trio puzzle* of 'who talked to whom, on which occasion, and about what' facilitated identifying the patterns of actions created by the participants' choice- making guided by the application of the DMI, which among its other virtues is said to be "standing on behalf of a presupposed underlying pattern"(Benson & Hughes, 1983,p.90; Coulon, 1995,p.32). In the frame of this study, the visual patterns identified, illuminated "presupposed underlying patterns" depicting perceptions of meaning making, such as for example a *Question >Answer* model of interaction, or alternatively an exchanging, debating and negotiating process. The DMI example in

Chapter four, illustrates a situation in which all but Elaine assumed that Debbie expected them to respond to her questions. Elaine, on the other hand, interpreted Debbie's questions as an invitation to a discussion, spawning an intensive exchange of messages with Debbie. The different types of responses generated different dynamics as could be observed in the excerpt exhibited in Chapter Four, in which the Question>Answer dynamic shaped the 'star' at the beginning of the thread, and the debate with Elaine triggering a 'chain'. The dynamics illustrated by the 'star' and the 'chain' are visual models used by SNA, for identifying roles of actors in a network. In a 'star' model, the person (or their representing message) in the centre outranks the others, and is usually perceived as the most powerful in the network. In a learning situation this position is usually allocated to the 'teacher'. In the excerpt of chapter four, Debbie, as a student, has been allocated the temporary role of an online teacher as she was asked to lead this discussion thread. The visual pattern suggested that the others perceived her role in the traditional classroom concept of the 'authoritative teacher' asking the learners to respond to her questions. Interestingly, in the excerpt presented in Chapter Four, it is the teacher (Elaine) who triggered a negotiating/ debating situation rather than assuming the traditional authoritative position. The participants in this excerpt demonstrated their "presupposed underlying pattern" about a learning situation in which "*a teacher asks, and you as a learner are expected to answer*", which implied their underlying pattern of the relationships they associate with the social structure of a learning context.

The DMI then not only generated the dynamics, but also illuminated the 'roles' of participants either as students responding to an authoritative figure (teacher), or as collaborators in a negotiation process. The question is are these roles guided by the contexts and structures existing in the minds of the participants, or alternatively in the environment they are participating in, or are emerging mental processes guiding their choice of roles and shaping the social structures they are participating in, making the notion of 'roles' a dynamic and changeable entity, and consequently creating dynamic and changing social structures. Entailed in these questions are two notions, one looking at 'roles; as intertwined with the notion of social structures, and the other is the exploring the origin of social structures. I shall return to these notions later on in this chapter, however, at this point I can conclude that the patterns obtained by the EC approach charted choice making processes, which illustrated perceptions of meaning-making manifested in the dynamics visualised presented in the patterns. In the next section I further investigate the meaning making processes emerging through the patterns.

VISUAL PATTERNS AND MEANING MAKING PROCESSES

Discussion forums are part of the technological infrastructure potentially seen as facilitating collaborative learning environments capable of amplifying intellectual discourse and fostering social construction of knowledge (Harasim, 1990a; Moore & Anderson, 2003). Murakami, Nagao, & Takeda(2001) argue that discussion forums' messages contain the knowledge exhibited by the participants in the discussion. If we are to follow the constructivist approach to knowledge construction, we need to be able to follow the order of the messages, in order to observe any changes in the knowledge indicating learning processes. In other words, attempting to investigate whether knowledge construction took place in the online learning discussion forums observed is extremely reliant on our ability to trace the order in which messages were contributed, as this is the key for following meaning making processes.

Contrary to what we would assume, simply printing out the messages the way they appear on the computer screen, does not convey an undisrupted flow of conversation, and the stream of messages failed to portray comprehendible meaning. Most participants in discussion forums reading their way through individual messages would not notice these disruptions in the flow of the conversations, however, e-lecturers and e-researchers, interested in the whole process occurring through the interactions would need a way of following the bigger picture beyond individual messages and their immediate responses. Being able to follow the order in which messages were contributed is the key to following meaning making processes, therefore being able to reproduce the exact order in which messages were posted is of great significance.

The visualisation of the socio-thematic networks enabled by the EC facilitated the reconstruction of the flow of the messages, following each twist, turn, and branching out of the conversation throughout the discussion thread.

In chapter four I described the ambiguity of the order of messages as presented by the system running the discussion forums observed. This ambiguity is a result of the inability of the prevalent systems to construct non -linear, multi participant conversations. The current formats of organising online discussion forums apply either the *Linear* model in which posts appear in chronological sequence, one after another, within a topic, or the *Threaded* model in which posts follow a branching "tree" structure, and replies can be appended to particular posts(White, 2004).

The EC approach enabled a non- linear representation of the conversation as it conceptualised them not as a sum of messages to be recorded according to some predetermined system like for example, dates of posting or subject line themes, but rather as networks whose construction is driven by the choices made by its participants, as reflected through the server's key codes. This feature is of great importance because it enables the construction of an empirically based network, the structure of which can be triangulated by following the content it conveyed.

The data excerpts I exhibited in chapter four demonstrated how the sort order provided by the EC conveyed a coherent sequence of conversation. The network concept of the EC approach revealed pivot points in which the conversation branched out or subdivided. These pivot points or 'Pivot EC' as I called them, marked the instance of branching out, of splitting, of developing new directions in the conversation. Being able to pinpoint this instance is important for following any emerging knowledge constructing processes, as the visual representation of the Pivot EC provides important landmarks for any content focused investigation.

However, the present study stops short of the interpretation of the processes and only provides the tool which focuses on 'how' processes occur, so as to pave ways into the study of the 'what' is happening in online learning discussion forums. The focus on the 'how' implies a *praxis* approach, which is entailed in the ethnomethodological stance I chose as my theoretical framework. In the next sections I discuss the conceptual issues emerging from the ethnomethodological stance I adopted.

At the outset of this study, the extra terrestrial scenario formulated the realm of this study as focusing on the visible and reportable actions, situating it well within praxis theories, and in particular the Ethnomethodological stance. In searching for a way of studying 'how' language mediated communication between people creates social contexts, I distinctly pronounced a praxis approach, looking at the enactment of social conduct rather than what Cohen(2000) describes as the Weberian Action Theory approach looking at the subjective meaning that the individual attaches to his or her behaviour. One could argue that the DMI could be considered as a subjective interpretivist action; however, the focus presented in this study was on the action of choice guided by the DMI, hence focusing on the enactment triggered by the DMI, rather than the conscious aspects motivating it.

Having applied my conceptualisations in attempting to understand the actions of my research participants has brought me to the point where I feel the need for expanding the horizon of the investigation to include issues stretching beyond the observable activities. At this point I feel a need to revisit the notion of the enactment in relation to conscious and unconscious aspects underpinning actions. Furthermore, there arises the question of the ability of the DMI, here presented as a choice mechanism, to contribute to our understanding of cognitive processes occurring in the minds of the participants, and consequently the grounding of our understanding of the supra individual cognitive system portrayed by Dillenbourg, Baker, Blaye, and O'malley, (1996). This inquiry may have implications regarding some of the notions I have raised in the literature chapter regarding the ability to provide Laurillard's (1993) 'customised learning'(p.153), and support the negotiation of meaning for the construction of knowledge addressed by Kanuka and Anderson (1998).

The DMI in the context of this study underpinned the enactment of social actions, given that by choosing which message to respond to, participants were indirectly choosing who to talk to, and hence they were engaging in social interactions making their choice of content a social action. Sequences of such choices created social networks or structures.

The notion of participants constructing social structures is acknowledged by anthropologists such as Radcliffe –Brown(1965(1952)), Nadel(1957) and Garfinkel(1967; , 2002). However their perception of 'structure' is different from that of Parson, structuralism, post-structuralism, and postmodernism, all of which in some ways share the Parson's Plenum – perceiving structure as a space filled with matter sort of way, and as in some form "constraining" individual behaviour (Garfinkel, 2002)

Radcliffe-Brown(1965(1952)) and Nadel(1957) perceive social structures as entities in which participants are not perceived as individual persons but rather as occupying positions or roles. Adopting this perception defines 'structure' as an abstraction of relational features, which can be transposed irrespective of the concrete data manifesting it. It can be alternatively said that the parts composing any structure can vary widely in their concrete character without changing the identity of the structure(Nadel, 1957). The notion of decontextualisation is shared by Garfinkel and ethnomethodologists in general, who make no assumptions about contextuality, instead they seek to investigate how social practices reflexively depend upon whatever context has been produced in a social encounter and whatever new bits of context are generated by every subsequent move in the encounter(I. J. Cohen, 2000). Ethnomethodology views context as emerging 'here and now'(Coulon, 1995,p.2), suggesting a disregarding posture towards any context or contexts existing beyond the observed social activity. Ethnomethodology can be said to perform what phenomenology regards as 'Bracketing'(Orleans, 2000), conducting a 'reduction' in the terms under which the item assessed is operating in consciousness. The reduction process exposes the essentials of the investigated item while at the same time ascertaining its meanings independent of all particular occasions of its use. Furthermore, Benson and Hughes(1983) argue for the indexicality of ethnomethodology, claiming that "natural language as a whole is profoundly indexical in that for members, the meaning of their everyday talk is dependent on the context in which the talk occurs; an idea which is embedded in the Documentary Method of Interpretation(DMI)"(p.101). Here again, having explored my data I feel inclined to query this non- contextual approach, and the affects it may have on our understanding of the ways in which people relate, interact and operate within social structures. These decontextualisation notions raise questions about the ability of the ethnomethodological framework to consider possible influences rooted in contexts surrounding the investigated phenomena or its participants. For example the particular context surrounding this study can be said to include the specific technological infrastructure, which could have affected the manner in which participants related to the online environment shaping their contributions accordingly. Decontextualising the investigation may have failed to consider these aspects. Furthermore, the specific title of the course observed "Critical Reflection" may have contributed to the creation of a unique intellectual environment, and may have attracted a unique group of people, both of these aspects may have had some implications for the ways in which participant interacted, however, these aspects were not included in the investigation hence their possible affects are not known to us. Finally, the outline of the course clearly stated a requirement of a minimum participation frequency in the online discussion forums, making the contribution compulsory rather than voluntary, which in turn could have affected the way participants acted in relation to contribution to the forums.

Not a summary, merely an opening

Conceptualising cyber relations as visualised social meeting places offered an exciting and innovative outlook on the meaning of online discussion forums. The study opens the way for looking at these cyber based entities as rich social spaces created, and modified by the relationships between people communicating and contributing to each other and to the social space as a whole. The visual focus embraced throughout the study enabled a much needed view of the processes creating and sustaining the social spaces and the contexts they aim to achieve. However, the viability of inferring cognitive processes from visual representations is yet to be examined. Adopting the ethnomethodological notion of 'here and now', enabled focusing on the phenomenon at hand, as 'untainted' by external issues concerning the technological environment, the course context, or the participants' personal attributes, and real life contexts. However, the study stops short of reviewing the cost of the decontextualised stance from within which it operated.

6. THE GOOD, THE BAD, AND WHAT'S NEXT

Introduction

In investigating the theoretical concepts underpinning online discussion forums in learning contexts, I hoped to gain an understanding that would inform my attempts to develop a practical solution that would address some of the issues entailed in the study of Online Learning Discussion Forums (OLDF).

In the discussion chapter I reviewed the understandings gained through the theoretical concepts addressed throughout this work. Building on these understandings, I now turn to investigate ways in which the theories may support the practice. In this chapter I focus on the practical implications enabled by the EC approach.

After a brief review of the problem identified in the field, the study proceeds to outline the conceptual shift proposed here, followed by a brief review of ways in which the theory may help address the issues entailed in the study of online discussion forums. The chapter then proceeds to review the ways in which the EC may contribute in addressing the research problem, reviewing the strengths and limitations of the proposed solution and the possible routes of further research. In the final sections of this chapter I express some personal realisations as they crystallised in my mind through the writing of this work.

The Problem At Hand

Harasim(1990a), conceptualised e-learning as a collaborative environment capable of amplifying intellectual discourse and fostering the social construction of knowledge(Harasim, 1990a; Moore & Anderson, 2003). Online discussion forums as "discussion media" technology are expected to facilitate and support these notions.

The research literature in the field attempted to study online discussion forums as collaborative socio constructivist environments. However, review of the literature revealed that until recently it was said to lack a unifying and established theoretical framework, agreed objects of study, methodological consensus, or agreement about the concept of collaboration, or unit of analysis(Lipponen, 2002).Furthermore, a substantial portion of the research was comprised of practice based reports, hence deemed anecdotal rather than empirical(Romiszowski & Mason, 2004; Warschauer, 1997).

Methodologies used in the studies reviewed seem to struggle with the issues related to collaboration and social construction of knowledge, and remain entrenched in the three entities:

1. The individual learner
2. The group, or the social context
3. The content and the linguistic/ semiotic aspects

Theorists like for example Vygotsky, acknowledging the interrelationship between the three entities give no indication of how we may study and understand these relations, so seminal to understanding collaborative social constructivist processes.

The abundance of data available through the self archiving systems of computer networks recording all the messages in online discussion forums does not seem to attract large numbers of research studies. Reasons for this scarcity of research are said to arise from lack of procedures, and proven research paradigms(Marra, Moore, & Klimczak, 2004; Roberts, 2004; Rourke & Anderson, 2004).

This study suggests a conceptual shift in the investigation, moving away from the study of individuals, groups or content, to studying relations between individuals communicating with others and engaging in content, communicated and archived on the computer network's server.

In focusing on the relations between communicating individuals and the content they convey to each other, the study acknowledges an important link between content conveyed and social interactions so seminal to the investigation and understanding of social learning contexts in which content conveyed among learners can be seen as the building blocks of meaning making processes, and the social construction of knowledge. The study addresses this link through the two research questions(RQ), in which RQ1 attempts to scaffold our understanding of the link by looking at the social dynamics and the teaching/learning approaches they may imply, in an attempt to find ways of visually identifying dynamics conducive to social constructivist, collaborative learning. RQ2 opens an investigation of the affect the social dynamics have on the construction of knowledge, suggesting that by following meaning making processes we learn 'who' interacted, and 'how' interaction evolved to create the route or "riverbed" through which meaning was processed and knowledge was constructed. However, I must note that at this point this investigation is still in infancy stages.

In this study I described the development and preliminary implementations of an analytical framework for studying online discussion forums, called the EC approach. The approach enables the visualisation of sequences of mental processes expressed through the choices participants exert throughout their activities in the Online Learning Discussion Forums (OLDF) observed. The primary concept of the EC approach portrays the activities occurring in online discussion threads as interactions guided by the participants' DMI choices of conversational themes and partners. The approach perceives points of interactions in which people engage with each others' ideas as centres of events, or Event Centres (EC). For facilitating the trailing of long sequences of DMI guided choices, the EC approach utilises the coding mechanism of the network server running the discussion forums. Employing the network codes helps corroborate the accuracy of the DMI choices, by verifying the 'trio puzzle' ('who talked to whom on which occasion and about what'). Using the network codes enabled the visualisation of the DMI guided choices to reveal the "presupposed underlying patterns" forming the participants' perceptions of meaning making models, and the social structures they associate with learning contexts.

What Does the Study of Collaborative and Social Constructivist Learning Entail – Putting Theories to Practice

Researching collaboration and social construction of knowledge entails, a conceptual shift venturing outside the single message and the individual contributors, moving away from the individual message, or participant, to the network of messages and participants, which in turn raises issues relating to the relationship between individuals and the structures in which they operate. This notion was discussed within the framework of Structuration in which theorists Bourdieu(1977; , 1992) and Giddens(1976; , 1984) offer a new perspective for the study of collaborative learning and the emergence of learning related social structures, as it depicts social learning processes as something 'becoming' through constant movement. In the context of online discussions, this notion could be detected through the conveyance of an idea from one participant to another or the movement of a participant from one relation to another, creating a trail of interactions, and in so doing constructing the structure and facilitating the further conveyance of ideas and the ongoing of interactions and further movement. Hence, 'becoming' may develop into a 'perpetuum mobile' of movement and evolvement of the individual, the interactions, and consequently the structure.

In online discussion forums these processes of 'becoming' can be identified only through the following of messages posted to the discussion, as it is the messages that demarcated the position of the person, the actor, and his or her position relative to the network, which can be seen as an illustration or a map charting the progression of ideas.

Structural analysts have focused on relative positions or roles held by specific individuals, groups or organisations in channelling flows of information throughout a social structure. Structural sociologists, such as Berkowitz(1988) recognise that because of their location within systems, some elements, or in this case authors of messages, will be better able to control this flow of effects than others. In Structural Analysis terms this is referred to as *Centrality*.

To describe the movement and relativity of positions or roles, they can be said to be:

- Artefacts of processes
- Dynamic, not static and changing. Changes can be observed through the messages, and since these are related to authors, different messages, positioned at different positions in the network indicate a different position and hence different role for the author of the message. This in turn may imply evolvement in the author's understandings. However, it may be that some overarching roles specific individuals seem to hold can be identified through the 'centrality' measurement of SNA.

According to Structural Analysis the changeability of roles facilitated by different positions in the network, define changes in the ability to channel information throughout a network, which in turn means that any person can play different roles in different situations, hence overriding the notion of social stratification and social classes traditionally associated with social structures. The interchangeability between persons and message means that a person can be in a powerful position in relation to one posting, and in a less powerful position in relation to another posting. The EC approach moved this study beyond looking at messages as standalone entities, but rather as parts of an EC which is an entity comprised of a minimum of two messages, a message and response. The EC is referred to as an 'event', hence a person's position in the network is observable through the artefacts /messages the person is contributing to various 'Event Centres', or positions in the network. A person's role is redefined according to the position the EC in which their message appears in the network.

Roles contribute to the structural organisation of problem solving institutions of a social structure. Hence, artefacts (messages) representing processes are representing roles carried by individuals. Hence, individuals are affecting the structure they operate in. 'Figure 6-1' illustrates this process.

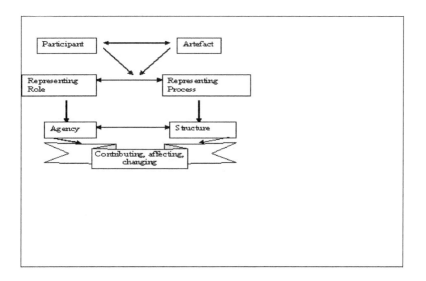

Figure 6-1 Interchangeability of Interactions

The interrelation between structure and agency demonstrated through the EC network approach introduced in this study, sheds a new light on the study of collaborative learning, shifting our focus from studying how individuals act in their social environments, and in that I refer to 'social structures', to looking at how collaboration between individuals creates structures and reshapes them as the participating individuals progress.

Bourdieu and Wacquant(1992) suggest that structures are created by individuals operating in a network of roles . Bourdiu's concepts of '*habitus* and *field*' were of particular interest in this study as the notion of *field* is perceived by Bourdieu (and Wacquant 1992) as a social network. Moving away from the perception of individuals to the perception of a social network in a learning context, shifts our focus from the individual mind to the supra individual processes. In attempting to address this notion I chose to conceptualise a way of investigating, or at least charting, cognitive processes which have to do with the individual reaching for their social environment. Using the documentary Method of Interpretation (DMI) as practiced by the participants through their choice of who and what to respond to, I was able to begin to explore a possible approach to the investigating supra individual processes.

In view of the interrelation between the participants of a network and the structures they create, I searched for a way of investigating the supra individual processes while at the same time observing the ways in which social networks emerged. I hoped that this approach would enable a glimpse of how social constructivist collaborative learning emerges. In this study I chose to create graphic images of the occurrences in the hope that these would make the processes observable and open to investigation.

Choosing the visual approach entailed an attempt to respond to the lack of empirical studies of collaborative and constructivist online learning environments as expressed by the literature review. To be able to visualise abstract notions such as cognitive and social processes I needed to identify an artefact that would represent the processes occurring. Defining the artefact meant finding a unit of analysis that would embody supra individual features while at the same time enable the observation of network structuring. Using the concept of the EC as comprised of two or more messages linked together provided an entity representing the choice processes of interacting individuals choosing what to respond to, and in so doing, possibly revealing their own state of understanding, and preference of topic, while relating it to that of the person they are interacting with, hence implying a glimpse of a supra individual situation. The observations of the network structure, was enabled by applying the interchangeability principle discussed in this study in which messages are perceived as representations of their authors, which in turn enabled tracing the emergence of networks of both authors and messages. Authors choosing to relate to a specific message created a link between their own message and the one they related to, while at the same time created a link between themselves and the author of the message. To corroborate the processes of choice and the creation of the different EC, I used the computer network key codes recording messages contributed to the online discussion forums.

The computer network's server triple numeric codes comprised an important part of the EC approach, as it ascertains not only dyadic relation of message>responses but allows the identification of all the relating messages responding, not only on the basis of

247

lexical or semantic cohesion similar to the method Sack(2000) used in his 'conversation map' tool, but on the basis of participants' choice of placement of the response, guided by their application of the DMI. The EC approach enables a three tier framework for verifying the structure of the networks emerging.

- The DMI applied by the participants
- The computer network server's key codes following the trio puzzle
- The content of the conversations

Furthermore, the numeric key codes used for identifying the structures, enabled adopting Social Network Analysis (SNA) techniques. The visual patterns generated with the help of SNA graphic tools are mathematically based, hence enabling mathematical measures to identify centrality of members in the network, to denote the various roles emerging. However, as mentioned earlier in this study, my perception of mathematics is that of an abstraction tool, hence, the mathematically based patterns are an abstraction of situations rather than a description of reality. Therefore, the abstracting of a situation enables the patterns observable to be applied to other contexts than the one specifically observed here.

Preliminary Observations of Visualised Collaborative and Social Constructivist Learning - Putting the EC Approach to the Test

Applying the EC approach enabled the creation of visual models which I would suggest contributes to our understanding of the processes occurring in online discussion forums. The EC approach provided a visual representation of the activity accruing in each discussion thread within the forums, enabling the observations of occurring processes , and most importantly, charting their route of evolvement, an aspect invisible to us through the prevalent discussion forums technologies. The ongoing aspect can be observed through changes in the pattern emerging at different parts of a discussion thread. For example the illustration in 'figure 6-2' shows a threads starting off in a 'star shape and evolving into a chain and later a branch.

248

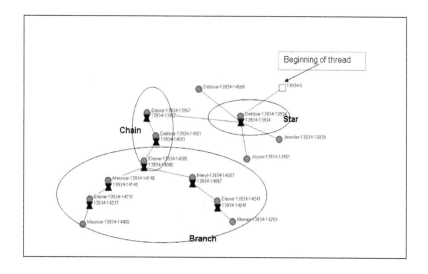

Figure 6-2 Changing Dynamics

The different shapes emerging throughout the thread could imply different learning dynamics occurring at different points in the learning process. Each of the visual shapes could imply a different perspective of learning, either as teacher centred or alternatively learner centred. However at this point these can be regarded as preliminary observations and interpretations in need of further investigation.

The ability of the EC to chart the emergence of processes facilitated the study of the order in which messages were contributed and most important, the order in which they were linked to each other. This feature is of great importance for the identification of pivot points and the branching out of routes of conversations, further clarifying the structure of the conversations to reveal the routes through which meaning was socially constructed. Furthermore, being able to chart the emergence of processes facilitated the study of the inner structure of networks revealing key players in the meaning making processes and networked activities.

These preliminary observations facilitated by the EC approach may be of use in the field of online learning research, but they could also have practical implications for e- e- educators.

The two sections charting the significance of the EC can be seen to relate to each of the two research questions (RQ), the first section – *visual dynamics* can be associated with RQ1- "In what ways do the patterns obtained by the EC approach contribute to our ability to observe and analyse the learning related dynamics, and social structures emerging in Online Learning Discussion Forums (OLDF)?" and the second section the *dynamics and content* can be seen to address RQ2- "How can the patterns obtained by the EC approach begin to illuminate ways in which they operate relative to meaning making and learning processes in OLDF?"

VISUAL DYNAMICS

The idea underlying the EC concept simply suggests that people participating in online discussion forums, or more specifically, discussion threads, are in fact taking part in various conversational events, which linked together, comprise a network of EC comprising the discussion thread. Each of these conversational events may involve constant or varying groups of participants

This conceptualising enabled me to refer to the data as 'relational'[30], and study relation created structures to inform the investigation of members' behaviours as indicators of attitudes (Wellman & Berkowitz, 1988). Adopting the relational approach enabled me to apply Social Network Analysis (SNA) techniques, facilitating the visualisation of the behaviour of my participants and the detection of emerging patterns of behaviours, and the learning perceptions they may imply.

Visualising the *trio puzzle* of 'who talked to whom' etc. facilitated identifying reoccurring patterns of actions, which implied that the way my participants

---

[30]   Relational approach or relationalism perceives social structure as a system of relations and differences rather than a set of attributes or 'essences'(De Nooy, 2003).An elaborate discussion of this term is found in the literature review chapter, describing relational data and structural analysis.

communicated was not entirely random, and their behaviour can be said to produce patterns of behaviour which could reveal the dynamics and the formation of roles.

Although the actual visualisation of the interactions was achieved by applying computer network server's key codes, their origin lies in the mental processes externalised the Documentary Method of Interpretation (DMI). The visual patterns are in fact manifestations of the mental processes, corroborated by the server's key codes. Combining the key codes data alongside the DMI, resulted in combining empiric, computer generated data alongside participants driven findings, to present a double tier analytic framework which may allow for further investigation of the meaning of interactions.

The key codes approach provides an empiric framework validating the structures (represented by the visual patterns), created by the participants' choices guided by the DMI, hence supporting the validity of the reconstruction of the emerging social relations and meaning making sequences. Although the interpretation of various aspects of the discussion thread will need further investigation involving for example study of the semantic structure of the messages, nevertheless, it is important to note that the DMI processes generated patterns which were made visible with the help of the visualisation features of the EC, and hence highlighted probable instances in which future researchers can begin looking for collaborative and social constructivist learning.

The EC provides a means for producing models of dynamics occurring in Online Learning Discussion Forums (OLDF). These visual models can provide an investigative framework which allows us to compare, contrast, and discern different implications emerging from each model. These implications may contribute to our ability to identify different dynamics implying different learning processes. For example the 'Orbitors' model showing dynamics directed at a single EC may indicate a transmitive model of learning in which a central source of authority is recognised as the source of teaching, alternatively a the 'chainies' model comprised of sequences of small groups interacting, may indicate a collaborative approach.

DYNAMICS AND CONTENT

The main aim in the development of the EC approach was to discover a tool which could combine social interactions and the content they convey, using the first hand data of the self-transcribing conversations to produce accurate representation of the learning processes in OLDF.

The ability to combine interactions and content is of great importance in the context of OLDF in which collaborative and social constructivist learning are expected to occur, because these modes of learning imply an intrinsic link between social dynamics and social construction of knowledge, for without the social interactions generating the social dynamics there is hardly going to be any learning processes in the manner in which social learning theories perceives it.

The EC approach enables the observations of more than pairs of participants responding to the same message, enabling the observation of 'multi participants. This feature is of great contribution to our understanding of social processes.

The EC approach conceptualises a group of related messages as an event – the Event Centre'(EC), which can indicate exactly which topic was discussed by a specific group. By collating all these separate 'event' centres together, it is possible to detect details concerning the learning processes occurring in relation to for example, which topics were discussed in which stage of the course, or the level of study, and by which learners. Because of the special network setting constructed through the EC approach it is possible to observe the routes in which learners chose to progress in terms of choosing their learning buddies represented through their messages. Choice of a learning buddy may entail more than social implications, to include cognitive aspects affecting the learning processes of individuals and the group as a whole. However, these are only suggested routes for applying the EC, and further research is needed to ascertain any of the suggestions.

The EC could serve as a helpful tool to be used by e-researchers as an analysis tool, and by e-teachers for providing relevant feedback, supporting meaning making and knowledge construction processes.

WHAT'S INNOVATIVE ABOUT THE EC APPROACH?

- It uses interactions for learning about patterns and structures of inner dynamics of the discussion.
- It treats messages as representations of their authors hence making an inherent link between content and persons (and their actions)
- It uses first hand data- unlike most studies relying on questionnaires and interviews which are in danger of falling into Garfinkel's Gap
- It conceptualises the activities in discussion forums as that of people participating in events.
- Using relations as the focus of analysis, and a relational entity like the EC(who talked to whom) as the unit of analysis, breaking away from the focus on the individual, the structure, or the content, to look at these three entities as related and interlaced
- Perceiving online discussion as socio-thematic networks highlighting the link between the linguistic processes and the social processes, a link so central to socio constructivist learning

The Practical Implications of the EC Approach

The EC approach enables visual representation of the dynamics of interactions across whole discussion threads. This feature can provide e-educators or moderators a swift and current update on the happening in the discussions. In chapter four I indicated that different visual patterns revealed different topics of discussion, showing that for example 'complex chains' showed higher percentages of course related discussions.

Implied in this is the fact that the EC links dynamics to content, which in a practical teaching /learning situation an e educator can obtain a general idea of the processes just by looking at a pattern of dynamics. This is by no means a suggestion that the EC approach will free e-educators from reading discussion thread messages altogether, as I do not believe that any automated system can replace humans, however, the EC approach can provide a 'road map' of the occurrences in the discussion thread.

The EC approach breaks the 'discussion thread' barrier, and in so doing enables investigating the branching out and the emerging of sub conversations. This features enables identification and mapping of topics discussed throughout a discussion thread.

The EC allows two levels of investigation:
- An in depth view of the discussion forum looking beyond the structure of 'discussion thread' to investigate micro situations in the form of local conversation events,
- An overview of the thread in general as provided by its visual representation offering a macro outlook of the relations between the micro events

The study is by no means an attempt to suggest a one size fit all strategy of "what makes a good discussion group or a learning situation". All it is offering is a tool that would allows periodic snapshots into the discussion group, by producing patterns of communication. These patterns could indicate gatekeepers,' weak tie' members, moving among many cliques, style of communication and dissemination of information. These snapshots can prove valuable for e –educators as they enable them to decide which action to take. They would also prove useful for e-researchers as they can provide an informed or processed sample of messages for further more detailed analysis of the content conveyed throughout discussion threads.

The dynamics of interactions visualised by the EC approach can be used for analysing styles of moderation and the affect it has on the dynamics in a discussion thread. For example if at some stages the e –educator would like to get everybody's response to a single issue, or on other occasions to facilitate the evolvement of a discussion. In each case the visual patterns would enable observing whether the desired dynamics have occurred.

PRACTICAL FEATURES ENTAILED IN THE EC APPROACH FOR E-EDUCATORS

- Periodic processing and analysis of large amounts of information generated by the interactions occurring throughout discussion threads
- Help manage e-educators' workload, particularly in situations where a single e- tutor is responsible for several learning groups.
- Keeping track of the occurrences in the discussion so as to support the learning process at various points and stages of the process
- Enabling e-educators to provide learners with relevant informed feedback which could be used for enhancing learning in online discussion forums, and enabled formative assessment

PRACTICAL FEATURES ENTAILED IN THE EC APPROACH FOR E-RESEARCHERS

- Studying collaboration – going beyond the single message to study interactions
- An analytic tool providing empiric information enabling corroboration with qualitative interpretivist findings
- Unveiling the structure of conversations in their original form – serving as a tool enabling the unfreezing conversation flows.
- Visualising choices of topic and people making mental processes of choice visible
- Making visible the DMI guided choices, consequently facilitating the tracing of social construction of knowledge because choosing 'what to respond to', is also choosing 'who to do it with'. This notion enables investigating mental processes constructing the supra individual leading to the construction of social entities
- Introducing the principle of interchangeability of actors and artefacts, another perspective looking at the blurring of the structure agent boundaries.

TECHNOLOGY BASED LIMITATIONS

My study was conducted on a 'hybrid' system, enabling 'threaded' and 'linear' presentation of the discussion forums. This could have had an impact on the way in which participants interacted; forming the high correlation between the key- codes based structure, and the coherent representation of the content of the conversation. However, this level of correlation may not be the same in other discussion forum systems using either linear or threaded methods, as the hybrid model may have affected the placing of the messages, whereas other systems may show weaker or no correlation between the structure and the coherence of the conversation.

In this study, the EC approach was implied for the first time and applied to a single Learning Management System (LMS). Further testing of the approach is needed across various LMS to ascertain similar findings across a range of technological infrastructures and diverse LMS.

At the closing point of this study, the EC approach is not yet available for implementation, as the preparation procedures necessary for processing raw data before it can be analysed are not yet automated, and at the present point require tedious and time consuming actions. However, the numeric foundations embedded in computer key codes serve as a sound starting point for programming the approach and facilitating a fully automated tool capable of processing large data sets.

METHODOLOGY- BASED LIMITATIONS

Key Codes and Content The EC concept inherited the limitation of SNA to convey the content, or nature of the relations The server's key links used for establishing interactions between participants do not convey any of the content conveyed in the interactions, and although the concept leading this study argues that the server's codes are only a reflection of the DMI processes, the visual patterns representing the network of relations do not convey their content. Furthermore, the inability to convey content means that it is not possible to verify any content links between messages, however, reading through the 846 messages comprising my data I would argue that messages linked through the key codes were content related, hence I was able to hyperlink patterns linking the content of EC to their position in the network, as shown in http://etalk.bravehost.com

Social Network Analysis Measures and Content SNA Centrality measures enable to detect the dynamics occurring in each pattern and measure the potential quantity of information available to each EC and its potential to relay this information. However, it does not disclose the nature of the information conveyed, nor its quality. Furthermore, the notion of measuring the ability and effectiveness of conveying information by calculating the quantity of links is questionable in terms of what these links contribute to the quality, content progression of the information dissemination, and the effectiveness of the inclusion of various participants in the informing processes occurring throughout the network

Empiric Observation In this study I limited the scope of interactions to include only those indicated by the server's key codes, in other words, the study focused on the empirically observable. However, it is possible to include other measurements enabled by the SNA. For example the *Reachability* routine which enables predicting possible relations between participants who are indirectly interacting with a member in the group by referring to them in a message sent to another participant. For example:
'A' sending a message to 'B' and in that message refers to something said or concerning C. The simple bipartite routine I used in this study conveys only the connection between 'A', and 'B', depicting 'C' as unrelated,

A_____ B   C

whereas a Reachability routine would have indicated the probable connection between the three. Although there is no actual message connecting C to A or B, the referral by A made in the message to B establishes a relation between A and C. 'B' by
receiving A's message about C can be seen to relate to C, therefore the three are linked as the illustration below shows. (Dotted lines indicate the inferred rather than direct relation)

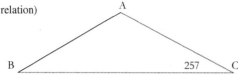

257

Focusing On the Event following Ethnomethodological notions the study focuses on the 'here and now'(Coulon, 1995), on the event observed, and in doing so is in danger of decontextualising the participants, looking only at their online activities disregarding their offline contexts.

Focusing On the Observable This study focused on the active participants the ones contributing to the discussion forums, however, further research and additional tools are needed for studying the silent learners the 'lurkers' the ones who would rather read through other people's messages than be out there responding or initiating discussions

Versatility of Participants The population of study in this case was comprised of educators sharing an interest in reflective practices, which may have contributed to their perception of the role of discussions and interacting with others for learning purposes. It may be that different populations may have different notions about the role of discussion forums hence; there is a need for further testing of the EC approach across a variety of populations in diverse contexts of work or learning.

ANALYSIS BASED LIMITATIONS

Addressing issues of 'Roles' – the Role of the Teacher In introducing the Orbitors and the Chainies models, the study suggests the possible existence of different models of teaching and learning. For example, it may be that the role of the 'catalyst' teacher associated with the 'cognitive- constructivist' model (Henri, 1992) may be identified in cases where the Orbitor model appears. Alternatively the Chainies model may imply the application of the 'social constructivist' model where the teacher takes the role of the 'facilitator' diverting the conversation towards the learners, and enabling the construction of knowledge through social interactions (D. H. Jonassen, 1991; Vygotsky, 1978). However, an analysis of the data suggests a blurring of the boundaries between roles, showing that in some cases a single discussion thread may reveal both models being practiced by the same "teacher' in a single conversation[31]. In this study I attempted to illustrate roles as emerging rather than pre-assigned, and that different roles can be performed by the same teacher responding to altering circumstances. This perspective suggests viewing teachers as 'responders' responding to situations rather than performing pre-defined roles. The study suggests that the visual representation of the Chainies and the Orbitors may well illustrate situations in which different types of responses were practiced, implying that the visual patterns illuminate an aspect of the DMI through which different participants interpreted the actions of others as "standing on behalf of a presupposed underlying pattern"(Benson & Hughes, 1983,p.90; Coulon, 1995,p.32). The excerpts from the data show but a glimpse into the application of DMI by my participants although providing an insight into the processes occurring in the online discussion forums, and the ways in which participants construct their reality out of their interactions. In so doing, the participants are also constructing the network and the dynamics in which it operates which in turn may construct and mould various emerging 'roles' or 'responses'. However, the stage of development in which the EC approach is available at the time of writing this work does not allow for a closer investigation of the circumstances surrounding the emergence of these different 'Responses', and further analysis of a wide variety of circumstances is needed for ascertaining the assumption suggesting that the role of the teacher in this study is seen as multifaceted, and alternating in the ways in which different functions are applied or activated at different emerging contexts.

Levels of learning The study suggests that when addressing notions relating to levels of learning in online contexts there is a need for revisiting our linear, often time related approach to defining levels indicating processes of learning. The online environment and in particular a- synchronous discussion forums like the ones observed in this study highlights the problem of following processes evolving in this non, or should I say, alternative temporal environment. In off line contexts we tend to frame progress in terms of elapsing time between beginning and end or from one phase to the next. As I have shown in excerpt of the data[32] in the online context conversations seem to progress along content and contexts created by messages and their linked responses, or in other words, the progression of ideas and understandings is propelled by people sending and

---

[31] See figure 4-7 on p.186 here

[32] See p. 206 here

responding to each other's messages. This study focused on identifying, illustrating, and observing this movement or progression by following the different dynamics generated by the activities of sending and responding to messages. Applying the EC approach the study has shown different models of dynamics. It may be that different phases of a learning process materialises in different dynamics. It is the assumption of this study that such differences may exist however, the study focuses on mapping the dynamics in the belief that these would enable the study of all things associated with learning, however, further investigation across a variety of contexts and contents is needed in order to ascertain this approach to the detection of processes or levels of learning in online a-synchronous contexts.

Types of knowledge- Reproduction or transformation Although the study stops short of addressing any cognitive issues, it does insinuate cognitive activity by applying the use of the DMI as a choice making mechanism and presents visual representations of the choice processes performed by the participants. The study suggests that sequences of choice making reflect some cognitive processes. An illustration of a sequence of choice making is available on p. 132 figure 3-7[33]. The cognitive processes can be followed in the ways in which ideas, and terminologies are discussed and negotiated, one example is illustrated in the excerpt showing the evolvement of the term 'boundaries' found on page 206 in the work. However, whether these reflect knowledge transforming operations or stored memory is hard to tell. However, I can assume, and I stress this is only an assumption, that because the context observed in this study resembles a conversation rather than a carefully pre-prepared text, I would cautiously suggest that what we see here is a knowledge transforming operation. Further investigation into the matter is needed if we are to ascertain or reject my cautious assumption.

---

[33] *'Figure 3-7'* depicts a sequence of 'relations' through which changes in the communication content occurs, as participants apply Documentary Method of Interpretation (DMI) to select relevant parts from within a received text(Poore, 2000), hence producing a response that is different from the original message received. Figure 7 illustrates this process by indicating a sequence in which participant 'A' posts the text 'A', and participant 'B' responds applying DMI and SI to produce text 'A+' representing 'B's own additions and changes to the original 'A' message. Being able to visualise this phenomenon is quite significant as it indicates a possible route for following conversation and learning in Online Learning Discussion Forums (OLDF), as it illustrates though in a simplified manner the conveyance, and at times alteration of ideas among the participants in a network.

The History of the participants Turkle in her book *'Life on Screen: Identity in the Age of the Internet'* (1995) suggests that the Internet is changing our psychological lives and our evolving ideas about minds, bodies, and machines. Turkle suggests that there is an-ongoing evolvement process through which a new sense of identity-as de-centred and multiple is emerging, creating a dramatic shift in our notions of self, and the other(Turkle, 1995).

For me Turkle's observations seem to align with my own questions of the relevancy of the traditional real-life social environment and its social groups and identities when applied to the online environment[34]. If the Internet is to enable social equality (as it indeed set out to be) then should we insist on linking offline identities to the online? Responding to this question as interesting and important as it may be is beyond the scope of this study, and I would suggest that further investigation of this notion would be of great contribution to the field.

R o u t e s   f o r   F u r t h e r   P u r s u i t

The preliminary application of the EC approach introduced in this study offered a preliminary glimpse of the many routes of studies opened up by this alternative approach to the study of online discussion forums in the context of learning. I would like to suggest that the EC approach is one type of a flashlight that can be used for illuminating what is still concealed from us in the study of the supra individual, and further investigations are needed for studying collaborative and social constructivist learning from a social and communicational approach.

The research questions addressed in this study provided a rich field of inquiry, the breadth of which stretches beyond the span of this study. To illustrate some of the further possible routes of study, I chose to organise them around the two meta themes emerging from my research questions:

- The visual dynamics
- The dynamics and content

---

[34] See page 104 here

The Internet can be seen as catering for two overarching perceptions, which I have outlined in the following table

Information Superhighway	Cyber Society
The Internet viewed as a super database	The internet facilitating the emergence of virtual society/ies
Facilitating access to people; groups; organisations for retrieving existing information- people perceived as sources of information	Facilitating access to people; groups; organisations for observing people driven processes/ interactions where information is created and shared
People; groups; organisations perceived as entities where information is stored	People; groups; organisations perceived as networks generating, constructing and relying mutual understandings
Studies of the internet in this perception tends to investigate its content (Web Content mining – as seen in Kosala 2000)	Studies of the internet in this perception tends to investigate its structure to identify links and relations leading to networks and social structures (Web Structure mining as seen in Kosala2000)

Similarly, emerging patterns in the online discussion forums observed in this study can be seen to underpin the participants' perceptions of the use of the internet, either as a place for extracting and disseminating information or as a social sphere for exchanging, and debating topics and ideas.

The notion of disseminating information versus exchanging and debating can be related to teaching/ learning approaches, some of which are seen as teacher centred and others as learner centred. The teacher centred approach perceives teachers as sources of information, and learners as passive recipients of information. On the other hand, the learner centred approach perceives the teachers as a facilitator of knowledge construction(Tapscott, 2005). The emerging patterns exhibited in Chapter Four of this study suggested a link between cyber classroom dynamics, and teaching /learning approaches, suggesting that the 'Orbitors' model implies teachers centred learning situations whereas the 'Chainies' could imply socio constructivist collaborative learning. However, these are preliminary observations, and further study is needed in order to ascertain these possible implications.

FURTHER STUDIES RELATING TO THE INTERRELATION OF DYNAMICS
AND CONTENT

At the time of writing this study, the EC approach is not yet automated and the application was manually administered, making it a very labour intensive and time consuming process, leaving very little time for further pursuing the dynamics>content link, however, some preliminary indications were identified, and are outlined below. Further investigations of these briefly observed notions could contribute to our future understanding of the occurrences in online discussion forums.

Patterns and their Content The novelty of the EC lies in its ability to illustrate the link between dynamics and content, as exhibited in the findings where the complex chains pattern showed high ratios of discussions around course related issues. However, this link was only briefly addressed, and further investigation of the link may reveal issues such as:

- Which patterns were formed around specific content areas
- Which patterns were most prevalent around informal and more social and emotional interactions

- Whether patterns were affected by different situations, like for example, the introduction of a new concept, or when people's zone of comfort was contested, or power struggles within the group occurred, or when people collaborated for fulfilling a task, or would there be different forms of networks for achieving different tasks as suggested by Nardi Whittaker, & Schwarz, (2000).

Content and Roles The principle of interchangability between participant and their message prompted possible links between content and roles. Enabling to relate content conveyed by a certain author to their role or position within the network, may be in turn pursued for identifying how roles affect content conveyed.

Good Message = Generating Debate The EC approach enables identifying 'pivot EC' representing a cluster of messages spawning new directions in the discussion thread's conversation. Investigating the messages comprising these 'pivot EC' would enable identifying the features of 'a good message'. Because of the interchangeability of messages and their authors this would also enable identifying individuals who are 'contributors of good messages'.

Patterns and Teaching Approaches further research into the interpretation of the visual patterns obtained by the application of the EC is needed. In this study I suggested a possible interpretation of the Chainies as representing a collaborative mode of teaching and learning. However, investigation of the content of the interactions may reveal that all the Chainies represent are sequences of Questions and Answers rather than active collaboration and social construction of knowledge.

Visualising Supra Individual Processes The study recognises the reciprocal link between individual learning and social interactions, and suggests an alternative method of observing this link using the Garfinkel's Documentary Method of Interpretation (DMI), as a choice mechanism constructing a socio thematic network. However, further investigation of this notion within social learning theories is needed.

Notions and Realisations Emerging from the Study

Freezing Conversations Contributing to online discussions is a bit like thawing a conversation, responding and re- freezing it for further contributions.

The Constructivist Fleeting Sense of Reality and Knowledge Is reality out there if we construct it from artefacts found in our surroundings?
If reality is constructed of existing things, then is constructivism another form of objectivism?
But, if all existing things are the creation of our interpretations of the world, then are the artefacts out there or are they in our minds?
Not all artefacts we use in our construction of reality are creations of our own minds but rather of those of other human beings. Therefore, reality is out there is it not? And

whose reality is it when we construct it from artefacts created by minds other than our own?

All I can say is that in this work I have attempted to tackle this fleeting feature of the notion of reality and the notion of knowledge but to no avail. My only contribution in this study is the suggestion of looking at frozen bits of reality or knowledge for revisiting them, reconstructing, and reinterpreting them. Reality for me is made of constant chains of freezing and thawing ideas that when frozen become entities that can be captured by ones self or others, and thawed for further investigation and meaning making.

Following Progression Online Following any progression in online a-synchronous discussion forums is similar to linking between dots on a paper, and by drawing lines between them to complete the picture of *'who talked to whom and about what'*. Losing the temporal framework in online a-synchronous discussion threads, does not mean the conversation is unorganised, or not progressing in terms of a process occurring. In off line contexts we tend to frame progress in terms of elapsing time between beginning and end or from one phase to the next. In the online context conversations seem to progress along content and contexts created by messages and their linked responses. Movement or progression can be observed in the different dynamics these generate detectable through the visual representations provided in this study by the EC approach.

The Notion of Roles
1) Roles are determined by dynamics: Dynamics position a message (interchangeable with its author/ actor), and position determine centrality – hence determine 'Role'
2) Dynamics are determined by the DMI: The pattern or the nature of response perceived as required from interpreting messages in the thread. In other words, the application of the DMI by the participants generates the dynamics.

Work Concepts Unfolded Three levels of interchangeability feature throughout the work:
- Actor > artefact – an actor is interchangeable with the message
- Actor > role – an actor's role is interchangeable depending on it position in the network (which is represented by the different messages the actor contributes)

- Actor > Structure – an actor's actions construct the structure, and the structure affects the actor's actions

Process Occurring in Work Discussion threads visualised as networks of 'Roles' populated by actors who are represented by messages, which supply the materials (content and contexts) supporting the 'on the fly' construction of knowledge achieved by the application of the DMI by actors.

Two Levels of DMI Application

1) Participants choosing and applying themes, topics and notion through their own context
2) Participants acting according to the pattern or model they think is expected of them

The End

The study shows a way of analysing online discussion forums in a manner which looks at visualising sequences of mental processes expressed through the choices participants exert throughout their activities in the Online Learning Discussion Forums (LDF) I have observed. To corroborate these choices I utilised the automatic recording and coding mechanism of the server running the discussion forums. This combination of mental processes with network server codes is a manifestation of the essence of this study in which agent- here presented by the mental processes, and structure- here represented by the network codes, are complementing each other rather than creating conflicting or constraining situations. This conceptualisation is projected throughout the study on three levels:

Research Methodology showing a research model in which Ethnomethodology (EM), (the study of methods of social action), is correlated with structural analysis

Social Theory following the Structuration school of thought represented by Bourdieu and Giddens(Parker, 2000)   showing that people construct their environment and meanings; they construct the structures whether they be mental or social

E-Learning Context online discussion forums manifest the actions of individual learning as they operate in a social network which is not the sum of specific individuals, but rather a structure constructed by their practices. Hence observation of learning in online discussion forums should be carried out with the understanding of network and the practices it represents rather than the sum of their individual contributions (messages). Having said that, the network approach acknowledges the importance of the individual allowing for the study of the evolvement of meaning-making processes unfolding the mental processes experienced and expressed by individuals, enabling the trailing of their sequence of thought as they contribute to the construction of the network.

In studying social constructivist collaborative learning environments, the important task is to understand the relation between the individual and the social. This study suggests an analytic approach for investigating this relationship. However, this is merely a preliminary study in which the EC approach was introduced. Small samples and excursions were explored for testing out the new approach, merely opening the way for future studies.

A Request to Future Users

I would like to suggest that the graphic patterns emerging from the analysis of the EC approach would not be perceived in anyway as representing a reality, but rather as abstract illustration of it, hence they can be used as indicator, implying a reality not as presenting a situation, but rather representing it.

The EC approach was developed as an analytic framework, not as ready to apply generic templates, hence careful analysis of the findings it offers is needed in each and every context it may be used.

7. REFERENCES

Adams, B. N., & Sydie, R. A. (2001). *Sociological Theory*. Thousand Oaks: Pine forge press.

Allen, R. E. (1990). *"The Concise Oxford Dictionary of Current English* (eight edition ed.). Oxford: Clarendon Press.

Alt, B. (2000, August 23 2000). "The Variety of Online Discussion Media". Retrieved 28.8.03, 2003, from http://epdigest.com/articles/community/20000823

Anderson, T. (2001). Assessing Teaching Presence in a computer conferencing context. *Journal of Asynchronous Learning (JALN)*, *5*(2).

Anderson, T. (2003). Modes of Interaction in Distance Education: Recent development and Research Questions. In M. G. Moore & W. G. Anderson (Eds.), *Handbook of Distance Education* (pp. 129-147). NJ: Lawrence Erlbaum Associates publishers.

Anderson, T., & Kanuka, H. (1997). Online Forums: New platforms for Professional Development and Group collaboration. *JCMC, 3*(3).

Anderson, T., & Kanuka, H. (2002). *e-Research: Methods, Strategies, and Issues*. Boston: allyn and Bacon.

Andrew, M. D. (1996). *From the Efficient factory to the Diverse Community: The paradigm shift in the nature of teaching in the public school*. Paper presented at the Annual Roland and Charlotte Kimball Faculty Fellowship 1996 Award, university of New Hampshire.

APAONLINE. (2003, 2003). Electronic References. Retrieved August 2004, 2004, from www.apastyle.org/elecsource.html

Aviv, R., Erlich, Z., Ravid, G., & Geva, A. (2003). Network Analysis of Knowledge Construction in Asynchronous Learning Networks. *Journal of Asynchronous Learning (JALN), 7*(3).

Bandura, A. (1989). Human Agency in social cognitive theory. *American Psychologist, 44*(9), 1175-1184.

Barab, S., & Schatz, S. (2001). *Using Activity Theory to Conceptualize Online Community and Using Online Community to Conceptualize Activity Theory*. Paper presented at the American Educational Research Association, Seattle, WA.

Beniam, D. (1995). "Constructivism as an Educational Philosophy- (A thumbnail Sketch). Retrieved 11/3/99, 1999, from http://asu.alasu.edu/academic/COE/construc.htm

Benson, D., & Hughes, J. A. (1983). *The Perspective of Ethnomethodology*. London: Longman.

Bereiter, C. (1999). *Education and Mind in the Knowledge Age*. CSILE.

Berelson, B. (1952). *Content Analysis in Communication Research*. Glencoe: Free Press.

Berkowitz, S. D. (1982). *An Introduction to Structural Analysis -The Network Approach to Social Research*. Toronto: Butterwroths.

Berkowitz, S. D. (1988). Afterward: Toward a Formal Structural Sociology. In B. Wellman & S. D. Berkowitz (Eds.), *"Social Structures - A network Approach* (Vol. 2). New York: Cambridge University Press.

Bertin, J. (1981). *Graphics and graphic information-processing* (W. Berg, J. & P. Scott., Trans.). Berlin: de Gruyter.

Blake, C. T., & Rapanotti, L. (2001, March 2001). *Mapping Interactions in a Computer Conferencing Environment*. Paper presented at the Euro CSCL, Maastericht.

Blatchford, P., Kutnick, P., Baines, E., & Galton, M. (2003). Toward a social pedagogy of classroom group
work. *International Journal of Educational Researcher, 39*, 153-172.

Bliss, J., Askew, M., & Macrea, S. (1996). Effective Teaching and Learning: scaffolding revisited. *Oxford review of Education, 22*(1), 37-61.

Bohnsack, R. (2002). *The Documentary Method- Exemplified by the Interpretation of Group Discussions.* Paper presented at the Women in European Universities, Munster.

Bohr, N. (1987(1958)). *Unity of Knowledge. In the Philosophical Writings of Neils Bohr: Volume 2- Essays 1932-1957 on Atomic physics and Human Knowledge.* Woodbridge, CT: Ox Bow Press.

Bonk, C. J., & Cunningham, D. J. (1998). Searching for Learner-Centred, Constructivist, and Sociocultural Components of Collaborative Educational Learning Tools. In C. J. Bonk & K. S. King (Eds.), *Electronic collaborators: Learner-centred Technologies for literacy apprenticeship and discourse* (pp. 25-50 chapter 22). N.J.: Erlbaum.

Borgatti, S. P., & Cross, R. (2003). "A relational view of information seeking and learning in social networks". Retrieved June 2003, 2003

Borgatti, S. P., & Everett, M. G. (1996). Network Analysis of 2-Mode Data. Retrieved 22.1.03, 2003, from www.analytictech.com/borgatti/2mode.htm

Borgatti, S. P., Everett, M. G., & Freeman, L. C. (2002). UCINET 6 for Windows Software for Social Network Analysis. (Version 6.26). Harvard: Analytic Technologies.

Bourdieu, P. (1977). *Outline of a Theory of practice.* Cambridge: Cambridge University press.

Bourdieu, P. (1980/1990). *The Logic of Practice* (R. Nice, Trans.). Stanford: Standford University Press.

Bourdieu, P. (1985). *Interview with C.Mahar,.*Unpublished manuscript, Palmerston North.

Bourdieu, P. (1989). *La nobless d'Etat. Grands sorps et Grandes ecoles.* Paris: Editions de Minuit.

Bourdieu, P., & Wacquant, L. J. D. (1992). *An Invitation to Reflexive Sociology.* Chicago: University of Chicago Press.

Bullen, M. (1999). Participation and critical thinikgn in online universtiy distance education. *Journal of Distance Education, 13*(2), 1-32.

Burbules, N. C. (1993). *Dialogue in Teaching - Theory and Practice* (1 ed.). New York: Teachers College Press.

Burnett, G. (2000). Information exchange in virtual communities: A typology. *Information Research,, 5*(4).

Chan, C. K., Lam I. C.K., & van Aalst, J. (2003, 21-25 April 2003). *social constructivist Assessment, Knowledge Building Discourse, and conceptual understanding.* Paper presented at the Annual Meeting of the American Educational Research Association, Chicago.

Chibelushi, C., Sharp, B., & Salter, A. (2004, 13 April.). *A Text Mining Approach to Tracking Elements of Decision Making: a pilot study.* Paper presented at the 1st International Workshop on Natural Language Understanding and Cognitive Science (NLUCS2004) collocated with ICEIS 2004., Porto, Portugal.

Chirnside, D. (2002). Online Support for courses at the Christchurch College of Education using StudentNet, a 'Learning management system' what is possible with Studentnet, why bother with StudentNet, and where might we go. Retrieved 18.8.02, 2002, from http://staffnet.cce.ac.nz/spaces/space.php?space_key=13

Cohen, I. J. (2000). Theories of Action and Praxis. In B. S. Turner (Ed.), *The Blackwell Companion to Social Theory* (2nd ed., pp. 73 -112). Oxford: Blackwell Publishers Ltd.

Cohen, L., & Manion, L. (1994). *Research Methods in Education* (Fourth edition ed.). London: Routledge.

Collins, B., & Moonen, J. (2001). *Flexible learning in a digital world.* London: Kogan Page.

Collins, M., & Berge, Z. L. (2001). Resources for moderators and facilitators of online discussion. Retrieved 15.3.04, 2004, from http://www.emoderators.com/moderators.shtml

Collins, R. (1981). Micro Translation as a theory-building strategy. In K. Knorr-Cetina & A. V. Cicourel (Eds.), *Advances in Social Theory and Methodology.* London: Routledge.

Collis, B. (1996). *Tele-learning in a digital world. The future of distance learning.* UK: International Thompson Computer Press.

Collison, G., Elbaum, B., Haavind, S., & Tinker, R. (2000). *Facilitating Online Learning: Effective Strategies for Moderators.* Madison: Atwood Publishing.

Coser, L. A. (1977). *Masters of Sociological Thought: Ideas in Historical and Social Contexts* (Second ed.). New York: Harcourt Brace Jovanovich, Inc.

Coulon, A. (1995). *Ethnomethodology* (Vol. 36). London: Sage Publications.

Cox, G., Hall, M., Loopuyt, M., & Carr, T. (2002, October 2002). *Analysing student interaction and collaboration online using communicative action theory and exchange structure analysis.* Paper presented at the Multi Media Group Colloquium, South Africa.

Creese, E. (2003). Group dynamics and learning in an Organisation Behaviour virtual learning community: the case of six virtual peer-learning teams. *ultiBASE publication., Nov03.*

Cross, R., Parker, A., & Borgatti, S. P. (2002). A Bird's-eye view: Using social network analysis to improve knowledge creation and sharing. Retrieved 8.4.03, 2003, from www-3.ibm.com/services/learning/solutions/ideas/whiepapers/ibvsna.pdf

Daradoumis, T., Marques, J. M., Guitert, M., Gimenez, F., & Segret, R. (2001, 1-5 April 2001). *Enabling Novel Methodologies to Promote Virtual Collaborative Study and Learning in Distance Education.* Paper presented at the 20th World Conference on Open Learning and Distance Education (The Future of Learning - Learning for the Future: Shaping the Transition). Dusseldorf, Germany.

DatabaseJournal. (2003). Interactive Online SQL Training. Retrieved 28.8.03, 2003, from http://sqlcourse.com

Davydov, V. V. (1999). The content and unsolved problems of activity theory. In Y. Engestrom, R. Miettinen & R.-L. Punamaki (Eds.), *Perspectives on activity theory.* Cambridge: The Press Syndicate of the University of Cambridge.

de Laat, M. (2002). *Network and content analysis in an online community discourse.* Paper presented at the Networked Learning Conference (NLC, University of Sheffield.

De Nooy, W. (2003). Fields and Networks: correspondence analysis and social network analysis in the framework of field theory. *Poetics, 31*(5-6).

Degenne, A., & Forse, M. (1999). *Introducing Social Networks.* London: Sage Publications.

Di Eugenio, B. (2001). Natural-Language processing for computer-supported instruction. *Intelligence-new visions of AI in practice, 12*(4), 22-32.

Diani, M. (2000). Simmel to Rokkan and Beyond: towards a Network Theory of (New) Social Movements. *European Journal of Social Theory, 3*(4), 387-406.

Dillenbourg, P. (1999). What do you mean by collaborative learning? In P. Dillenbourg (Ed.), *"Collaborative Learning: Cognitive and Computational approaches"* (pp. 1-19). Oxford: Elsevier.

Dillenbourg, P., Baker, M., Blaye, A., & O'malley, C. (1996). The evolution of research on collaborative learning. In E. Spada & P. Reiman (Eds.), *Learning in Humans and Machine: Towards an interdisciplinary learning science* (pp. 189-211). oxford: Elsevier.

Dobson, M., LeBlanc, D., & Buroyne, D. (2004). Transforming Tensions in Learning Technology Design: Operationalising Activity Theory. *Canadian Journal of Learning and Technology, 30*(1), online.

Donahue, M. J. I. (1997). An Introduction to Chaos Theory and Fractal Geometry. 2004, from http://www.duke.edu/~mjd/chaos/chaosp.html

Duffy, T. M., & D.J., C. (1996). constructivism: Implications for the design and delivery of instruction. In D. Jonassen (Ed.), *Handbook of research on educational communications and technology* (pp. 170-198). NY: Scholastic.

Durkheim, E. (1938). *"The Rules of Sociological Method"* (S. a. M. Solovay, J.H., Trans. eighth ed.): The Free press of Glencoe.

Durkheim, E. (1952). *Suicide: a study in sociology* (A. Spalding & G. Simpson, Trans.).
London: Routledge.

Durkheim, E. (1953). *Sociology and Philosophy.* NY: The Free Press.

Dysthe, O. (2002). The Learning Potential of a Web-Mediated Discussion in a University
Course. *Studies in Higher Education, 27*(3), 339-352.

Edwards, C. (2002, 26-28 March 2002). *Discourses on Collaborative networked learning.* Paper
presented at the Network Learning 2002, Sheffield UK.

Elwell, F. W. (1996). The sociology of Max Weber. Retrieved 9.10.04, 2004, from
http://www.faculty.rsu.edu/%7Efelwell/Theorists/Weber/Whome.htm

Elwell, F. W. (1999). *Industrializing America: Understanding Contemporary Society through Classical
Sociological Analysis.* West Port: Praeger.

Emirbayer, M. (1997). Manifesto of a relational sociology. *American Journal of Sociology, 103*,
281-317.

Engeström, Y. (1987). *Learning by expanding.* Helsinki:: Orienta-konsultit.

Engstrom, Y. (1999). Activity theory and individual and social transformation. In Y.
Engestrom, R. Miettinen & R.-L. Punamaki (Eds.), *Perspectives on activity theory* (pp.
19-39). Cambridge: Cambridge University Press.

Everton, S. F. (2002, August 2002). "A Guide for the Visually Perplexed: Visually
Representing Social Networks. Retrieved 17.12.02, 2002, from
http://vlado.fmf.uni-lj.si/pub/networks/pajek/apply.htm

Ferdig, R. E., Roehler, L. R., & Pearson, D. P. (2002). *Building Electronic Discussion Forums to
Scaffold Pre-Service teacher Learning: Online Conversations in the Reading Classroom Explorer.*
Ann Arbor: CIERA- centre for the Improvement of Early Reading Achievement -
University of Michigan.

Fernback, J. (1997). "The individaul within the Collective: Virtual Ideology and the
Realisation of Collective Principle. In S. Jones (Ed.), *Virtual Culture- Identity and
Communication in Cybersociety* (pp. 36-55). London: Sage Publications.

Freeman, L. C., & White, D. R. (1993). "Using Galois Lattices to represent network data.
"Sociological methodology, 23, 127-147.

Freire, P. (1970). *Pedagogy of the oppressed.* NY: Seabury.

Gadamer, H. G. (1975). *Truth and Method.* N.Y.: Seabury Press,.

Garfinkel, H. (1959). *Parson's Primer. Unpublished manuscript of Garfinkel's course. Sociology 251 :
Topics in the problem of social order.*Unpublished manuscript, LA.

Garfinkel, H. (1967). *Studies in Ethnomethodology.* New Jersey: Prentice-Hall, Inc.

Garfinkel, H. (2002). *Ethnomethodology's Programme- Working out Durkheim's Aphorism.*
Lanham: Rowman and Littlefiled Publishers, inc.

Garrison, R. (2000). Theoretical Challenges for distance education in the 21st centruy:a
shift from structural to transactional issues. *International Review of Researchin Open and
Distance Learning, 1*(1), 1-17.

Garton, L., Haythornthwaite, C., & Wellman, B. (1999). Studying Online Social Networks.
In S. Jones (Ed.), *Doing Internet Research: Critical Issues and Methods for Examining the
Net* (pp. 75-107). Thousand Oaks: Sage Publications.

Ghosh, G. (n.d.). e-Learning : Rhetoric vs Reality. Retrieved 10.1.05, 2005, from
http://www.humanlinks.com/manres/articles/e_learning.htm

Gibbs, G., & Simpson, C. (2002). *How assessment influences student learning-A conceptual overview*
(report No. SSRG42/2002): Student Support Research Group (SSRG) at the Open
University UK.

Giddens, A. (1976). *New Rules of Sociological Method.* London: Hutchinson.

Giddens, A. (1979). *Central problems in Social Theory: Action, Structure, and Contradiction in Social
Analysis.* Berkeley: The Macmillan Press Ltd.

Giddens, A. (1984). *The Constitution of Society: Outline of the Theory of Structuration.* Berkeley: University of California Press.

Gilfillan, I. (2002). "Introduction to Relational Databases". Retrieved 28.8.03, 2003, from www.databasejournal.com/sqletc/article.php/1469521

Gingrich, P. (2003). Theories of praxis. Retrieved 20.11.04, 2004, from http://uregina.ca/~gingrich/319j2203.htm

Goodwin, C., & Duranti, A. (1992). Rethinking context: An introduction. In A. Duranti & C. Goodwin (Eds.), *Rethinking context: Language as an interactive phenomenon* (pp. 1-42). Cambridge: Cambridge University Press.

Graham , M., & Scarborough, H. (1999). Computer Mediated Communication and collaborative learning in an undergraduate distance education environment. *Australian journal of Educational Technology, 15*(1), 20-46.

Granovetter, M. S. (1973). "The Strength of Weak Ties". *American Journal of Sociology, 78*(6), 1360-1380.

Gubrium, J. F., & Holstein, J. A. (1997). *The New Language of Qualitative Method.* NY: Oxford University Press.

Guitert, M., Daradoumis, A., Gimenez, F., & Marqus, J. M. (1999, June 20-24, 1999.). *Towards A Model that Supports Cooperative Work in a Virtual Campus.* Paper presented at the 19th World Conference on Open Learning and Distance Education., Vienna, Austria.

Gunawardena, C. N., Lowe, C. A., & Amderson, T. (1997). Analysis of a global online debate and the development of an interaction analysis model for examining social construction of knowledge in computer conferencing. *Journal of Educational Computing Research, 17*(4), 397-431.

Gunawardena, C. N., & Stock McIsaac, M. (2004). DISTANCE EDUCATION. In D. Jonassen (Ed.), *Handbook of Research on Educational Communications and Technology* (2nd ed., pp. 355-395). Mahwah, N.J.: Lawrence Erlbaum Associates Publishers.

Gunawardena, C. N., Wilson, N. A. C., Lopez-Islas, P. L., Ramirez-Angel, N., & Megchun-Alpizar, R. M. (2001). A cross cultural study of gropu process and development in onlnie conferences. *Distnace Education, 22*(1), 85-121.

Gurwitsch, A. (1966). The Last Work of Edmund Husserl. In *Studies in Phenomenology and Psychology* (pp. 399-447). Evanston: Northwestern University Press.

Habermas, J. (1984). *The theory of communicative action- Reason and the rationalisation of society* (Vol. Vol 1). Boston, MA: Beacon Press.

Hanneman, R. A. (online). "Introduction to Social Network Methods". Retrieved 31.12.02, 2002, from http://wizard.ucr.edu/~rhannema/SOC157/TEXT/TextIndex.html

Harasim, L. M. (1990a). Online Education: An Environment for collaboration and intellectual Amplification. In L. M. Harasim (Ed.), *Online Education: Perspectives on a new Environment* (pp. 39-64). NY: Praeger.

Harasim, L. M. (Ed.). (1990b). *Online Education- Perspectives on a New Environment.* NY: Praeger.

Hare, A. P., Borgatta, E. F., & Bales, R. F. (Eds.). (1966). *"Small Groups-Studies in Social interaction"* (revised edition ed.). New York: ALFRED. A.Knopf.

Harker, R., Mahar, C., & Wilkes, C. (Eds.). (1990). *An Introduction to the Work of Pierre Bourdieu.* NY: St. Martin's Press.

Hatch, E. (1973). *Theories of Man and Culture.* NY: Columbia University Press.

Hauben, M. (n.d.). History of ARPANET- Behind the Net : The untold history of the ARPANET or THE "Open" history of the ARAPNET/Internet. Retrieved 26.12.03, 2003, from http://www.dei.isep.ipp.pt/docs/arpa.html

Have, P. T. (2004). Ethnomethodology. In C. Seale, G. Gombo, Gubrium J. F. & D. Silverman (Eds.), *Qaulitative Research Practice* (pp. 151-164). London: Sage Publications.

Haythornthwaite, C. (2002). Building Social Networks via Computer Networks: Creating and Sustaining Distributed Learning Communities. In K. A. Renninger & W. Shumar (Eds.), *Building Virtual Communities: Learning and Change in Cyberspace* (pp. 159-191). Cambridge: Cambridge University Press.

Henri, F. (1992). Computer conferencing and content analysis. In A. R. Kaye (Ed.), *collaborative learning through computer conferencing: The Najaden papers* (pp. 117-136). Berlin: Springer-Verlag.

Herring, S. (1999). Interactional Coherence in CMC. *Journal of Computer mediated Communication, 4*(4).

Herring, S. (2004). Computer Mediated Discourse Analysis: An Approach to Researching Online Behaviour. In S. Barab, R. Kling & J. H. Gray (Eds.), *Designing for Virtual Communities in the Service of Learning*. Cambridge: Cambridge University Press.

Holmberg, B. (1986). A Discipline of Distance Education. *Journal of Distance Education, 1*(1).

Holmberg, B. (1989). *Theory and practice of Distance Dducation*. London: Routledge.

Holmberg, B. (1991). Testable theory based on discourse and empathy. *Open Learning, 6*(2), 44-46.

Holzschlag, M. E. (2001). Freedom in Structure. 2004, from http://www.webtechniques.com/archives/2001/07/desi/

Hung, D., Chen, D. T., & Tan, S. C. (2003). A Social -Constructivst Adaptation of Case-Based Reasoning: Integrating GBS with CSCL. *Educational Technology, 43*(2), 30-35.

Hung, W. L. D., & Chen, D.-T. V. (2002). Learning within the Context of Communities of Practices: A RE-Conceptualisation of Tools, Rules and Roles of the Activity - System. *Education Media International (EMI), 39*(3/4), 247-255.

Ioannides, Y. (2003). Topologies of Social Interactions. *ECON papers - department of Economics Tufts University*.

Issroff, K., & Scanlon, E. (2002). Using technology in higher education: An activity theory perspective. *Journal of Computer Assisted Learning, 18*,(1), 77-83.

Jeong, A. C. (2003). The Sequential Analysis of Group Interaction and Critical Thinking in Online Threaded Discussions. *The American Journal of Distance Education, 17*(1), 25-43.

Jonassen, D. (1994, April 1994). Thinking Technology: Toward a Constructivist design Model. *Educational Technology, 34*, 34-37.

Jonassen, D., Davidson, M., Collins, M., Campbell, J., & Bannan Haag, B. (1995). Constructivism and Computer -Mediated Communication in Distance Education. *The American Journal of Distance Education, 9*(2), 7-26.

Jonassen, D. H. (1991). Evaluating constructivistic learning. *Educational Technology, 28*(11), 13-16.

Jones, C. (1998). Evaluating a collaborative online learning environment. *Active Learning, 9*, 31-35.

Jones, S. (Ed.). (1999). *"Doing Internet Research- Critical issues and Methods for Examining the Net"*. London: Sage Publications.

Kanuka, H., & Anderson, T. (1998). Online Social Interchange, Discord, and Knowledge Construction. *Journal of Distance Education, 13*(1).

Kanuka, H., & Anderson, T. (1999). Using Constructivism in Technology-Mediated Learning: Constructing Order out of the Chaos in the Literature. *Radical Pedagogy, 1*(2).

Kemery, E. R. (2000). Developing on-line collaboration. In A. Aggarwal (Ed.), *Web-based learning and teaching technologies: Opportunites and challenges* (pp. pp 227-245). USA: IDEA group publishing.

Kendall, L. (1999). "Recontextualising "Cyberspace"- Methodological Considerations for On-line Research". In S. Jones (Ed.), *"Doing Internet Research- Critical Issues and Methods for Examining the Net"*. London: Sage Publications.

Klamma, R., Rohde, M., & Stahl, G. (Eds.). (2005). *Community-Based Learning: Explorations into Theoretical Groundings, Empirical Findings and Computer Support*. Los Angeles: SIG Group.

Klamma, R., & Spaniol, M. (2005). Supporting Communication and Knowledge Creation in Digitally Networked Communities in the Humanities. In R. Klamma, M. Rohde & G. Stahl (Eds.), *Community Based Learning: Exploring into Theoretical Groundings Empirical Findings and Computer Support* (pp. 58-64). Los Angeles: SIG Bulletin.

Kneser, C., Pilkington, R., & Treasure-Jones, T. (2001). The Tutor's Role: An investigation of the power of Exchange Structure Analysis to identify different roles in CMC seminars. *International Journal of Artificial Intelligence in Education, 12*, 63-84.

Koschmann, T., Stahl, G., & Zemel, A. (in press). the Video Analyst's Manifesto (or Implications of Garfinkel's Policies for Studying Practice within Design -based Research). In R. Goldman, B. Barron, S. Derry & R. Pea (Eds.), *Video Research in the learning sciences*. Mahwah N.J.: LEA.

Lai, K.-W. (Ed.). (2001). *"E-Learning- teaching and Professional Development with the Internet"*. Dunedin: University of Otago Press.

Lally, V., & de Laat, M. (2002). *Deciphering Individual Learning Processes in Virtual Professional Development*. Paper presented at the Networked Learning Conference (NLC), University of Sheffield.

Laurillard, D. (1993). *Rethinking university teaching : a framework for the effective use of educational technology*. NY: Routledge.

Lave, J., & Wenger, E. (1991). *"Situated Learning Legitimate peripheral participation"*. NY: Cambridge University Press.

Levin, J. A., Haesun, K., & Riel, M. M. (1990). Analysing Instructional Interactions on Electronic message Networks. In L. M. Harasim & M. Turoff (Eds.), *Online Education: Perspectives on a New Environment* (pp. 185-215). NY: Praeger.

Licklider, J. C. (1968). The Computer as a Communication Device. *Science and Technology, April*.

Lipponen, L. (2002). *Exploring foundations for computer-supported collaborative learning*. Paper presented at the CSCL 2002, Boulder Colorado.

Lueg, C., & Fisher, D. (2003). *From Usenet to CoWebs*. London: Springer.

Lynch, M. (1993). *Scientific practice and ordinary action: Ethnomethodology and social studies of science*. Cambridge: Cambridge University Press.

MacLeod, S. (2002, 2002). Durkheim's Functionalism and Agency. Retrieved 9.10.04, 2004, from http://scottmacleod.com/2001Oct26Durkheim.htm

Marra, R. M., Moore, J. L., & Klimczak, A. K. (2004). Content Analysis of Online Discussion Forums: A comparative Analysis of Protocols. *Educational Technology Research and Development, 52*(2), 23-40.

Mason, R. (1991). Analysing Computer Conference Interactions. *Computer in Adult Education and Training, 2*(3), 161-173.

Mason, R. (1992). Evaluation methodologies for computer conferencing applications. In A. R. Kaye (Ed.), *Collaborative learning through computer conferencing* (pp. 105-116). London: Springer-Verlag.

Mason, R., & Kaye, T. (1990). Toward a New Paradigm for Distance Education. In L. M. Harasim & M. Turoff (Eds.), *Online Education: Perspectives on a New Environment* (pp. 15-39). NY: PRAEGER.

Mayring, P. (2000). Qualitative Content Analysis. *Forum Qualitative Social research, 1*(2).

McCollum, A., Calder, J., Ashby, A., Thorpe, M.,, & Morgan, A. (1995). *Quality and effectiveness in vocational education,.* Paper presented at the One World Many Voices, proceedings of the 17th World Conference for Distance Education,, Birmingham,.

McGregor, J. (2004). Space, Power and the Classroom. *Forum: for promoting 3-19 comprehensive education, 46*(1), 13-18.

McLuhan, M., & Fiore, Q. (1967). *The Medium is the Message.* London: Allen Lane, Penguin Press.

Meyer, K. A. (2004). Evaluating Online Discussion: Four Different Frames of Analysis. *JALN Journal of Asynchronous Learning Networks, 8*(2), 101-114.

Miller, G. A. (n.d.). WordNet- a lexical database for the English language. Retrieved 20.3.05, 2005, from http://wordnet.princeton.edu/

Monroe, B. (2003). *Fostering Critical Engagement in Online Discussion: Te Washington State University Study* (newsletter). Washington: Washington Center for improving the Quality of Undergraduate Education.

Mooney, M., M., & Singer, B. (1988). Causality in the Social sciences. *Socilogical Methodology, 18*(1988), 347-409.

Moore, M. G., & Anderson, W. G. (Eds.). (2003). *Handbook of Distance Education.* NJ: Lawrence Erlbaum Associates Publishers.

Morrison, D. (2003). Using Activity Theory to Design Constructivist Online Learning Environments for Higher Order Thinking:A Retrospective Analysis. *Canadian Journal of Learning and Technology, 29*(3), N/A.

Moser, H. (2000). Thick description and abduction: Paradigm change in social research. In H. Moser (Ed.), *New ways of the educational Research (in German).* Zurich: Psetalozzinum Publishing House.

Murakami, A., Nagao, K., & Takeda, K. (2001, 30th November 2001). *Discussion Mining: Knowledge Discovery from Online Discussion Records.* Paper presented at the 1st NLP and XML Workshop, Tokyo.

Nadel, S. F. (1957). *The Theory of Social Structure.* London: Cohen and West Ltd.

Nardi, B. A. (1996). Activity Theory and Human-Computer Interaction. In B. A. Nardi (Ed.), *Context and Consciousness: Activity Theory and Human -Computer Interaction* (pp. 7-17). Cambridge, MA: The MIT Press.

Nardi, B. A., Whittaker, S., & Schwarz, H. (2000). It's Not What you Know, It's who you know: Work in the Information Age. *First Monday, 5*(5).

Norrick, N. R. (2001). *"Discourse Analysis- Lecture Script".*Unpublished manuscript, Saarlandes.

Orleans, M. (2000). Phenomenology. In E. F. Borgatta (Ed.), *Encyclopaedia of Sociology* (2nd ed., Vol. 3, pp. 2099-21077). New York: Macmillan Reference USA.

Packer, M. J. (2000). An interpretive methodology applied to existential psychotherapy. *Methods: A Journal For Human Science., annual edition*(2000).

Palincsar, A. S. (1986). Reciprocal teaching. In *Reciprocal teaching.* Oak Brook, IL:: North Central Regional Educational Laboratory.

Palloff, R. M., & Pratt , K. (1999). *"Building Learning Communities in Cyberspace- Effective strategies for the online classroom"* (First ed.). San Francisco, California: Jossey-Bass Inc Publishers.

Parker, J. (2000). *Structuration.* Buckingham: Open University Press.

Parsons, T. (1968a). Emile Durkheim,. In D. L. Sills & R. K. Merton (Eds.), *International Encyclopaedia of Social Sciences.* NY: Macmillan.

Parsons, T. (1968b). *The structure of Social Action: a study in Social Theory with special reference to a group of recent European writers* (2nd ed. Vol. 2). New York: The Free Press.

Parsons, T., . Shils.E., Naegele, K., & Pitts, J. (Eds.). (1961). *Theories of society : foundations of modern sociological theory*. NY: Free Press of Glenco.

Piaget, J. (1997). Development and Learning. In M. Gauvain & M. Cole (Eds.), *Readings on the development of children* (pp. 19-28). New York: Freeman.

Plato. (1986). *FIVE DIALOGUES: Euthyphro; The Apology; Crito; Meno; Phaedo* (G. M. A. Grube, Trans.). Indianapolis: Hackett Publishing Co.

Poole, D. M. (2000). Student Participation in a Discussion oriented Online Course: A Case Study. *Journal of Research on Technology in Education, 33*(2), 162-177.

Poore, S. (2000). Ethnomethodology. from http://www.hewett.norfolk.sch.uk/curric/soc/ethno/intro.htm

Porter, D. (n.d.). Distance Learning Information. Retrieved march 2004, 2004, from http://www.cdlponline.org/dlinfo/cdlp1/distance/

Potter, W., & Levine-Donnerstein, D. (1999). Rethinking validitiy and reliability in content analysis. *Journal of Applied Communication Research, 27*(3), 258-284.

Preece, J. (2000). *"Online Communities- Designing Usability, Supporting Sociability"*. New York: John Wiley and Sons Ltd.

Prideaux, G. D. (1997). Notes on a Discourse Analysis of Selected Zündelsite Materials. Retrieved January 2005, 2005, from http://www.nizkor.org/hweb/people/p/prideaux-gary/

Pulkkinen, J. (2003). *The Paradigms of E-Education*. Unpublished Academic Dissertation, University of Oulu, Olulu.

Radcliffe-Brown, A. R. (1940[2002]). On Social Structure. In J. Scott (Ed.), *Social Networks: Critical Concepts in Sociology* (Vol. 1, pp. 25-39). London: Routledge.

Radcliffe-Brown, A. R. (1965(1952)). *Structure and Function in Primitive Society*. New York: Free Press.

Ramsden, P. (Ed.). (1988). *Improving learning : new perspectives*. London: Kogan Page.

Ratner, C. (1999). Three Approaches to Cultural Psychology: A Critique. *Cultural Dynamics, 11*, 7-31.

Ravenscroft, A., & Matheson, M. P. (2002). Developing adn evaluating dialogue games for collaborative e-learning. *Journal of Computer Assisted Learning, 18*(1), 93-10.

Rheingold, H. (1998). The Virtual Community-Homesteading on the Electronic Frontier. e version. Retrieved 18.3.02, 2002, from www.rheingold.com/vc/book

Richardson, V. (Ed.). (1997). *"Constructivist Teacher Education: Building New Understandings"*. London: The Flamer Press.

Ritzer, G. (2000). *Sociological Theory* (5th ed.). NY: McGraw Hill Higher Education.

Ritzer, G. (2002). *Contemporary Sociological Theory and Its Classical Roots: The Basics*. Maryland: McGraw-Hill.

Ritzer, G., & Goodman, D. J. (2004). *Sociological Theory* (6th ed.). NY: McGraw- Hill Higher Education.

Roberts, T. S. (Ed.). (2004). *Online Collaborative Learning: Theory and Practice*. Hershey: Information Science Publishing.

Rogers, E. M., & Bhowmik, D. K. (1971). "Homophily-Heterophily relational concepts for communication research2. *Public Opinion Quarterly, 34*(4), 523-538.

Rogers, Y. (2004). Distributed Cognition and Communication. In K. Brown (Ed.), *The Encyclopedia of Language and Linguistics* (2nd ed.). Cambridge: University of Cambridge.

Rogoff, B. (1995). Sociocultural activity on three planes. In J. V. Wertsch, P. del Rio & A. Alvarez (Eds.), *Sociocultural Studies of mind* (pp. 139-164). NY: Cambridge University Press.

Romiszowski, A., & Mason, R. (2004). Computer -Mediated Communication. In D. Jonassen (Ed.), *Handbook of research on educational communications and technology* (2nd ed.). Mahwah, N.J.: Lawrence Erlbaum.

Ronteltap, F., & Eurelings, A. (2002). Activity and Interaction of Students in an electronic learning environment for problem-based learning. *Distance Education, 23*(1), 11-22.

Rorty, R. (1979). *Philosophy and the Mirror of Nature.* Princeton: Princeton University Press.

Rose, J. (1999). Towards a structurational theory of IS, theory development and case study illustrations. In Pries-Heje (Ed.), *proceedings of the 7th European Conference on Information Systems.* Copenhagen: Copenhagen Business School.

Rosenberg, M. J. (2001). *E-Learning: Strategies for Delivering Knowledge in the Digital Age.* New York: McGraw-Hill.

Rourke, L., & Anderson, T. (2004). *Validity in Quantitative Content Analysis.*Unpublished manuscript.

Rourke, L., Anderson, T., Garrison, R., & Archer, W. (2001). Methodological Issues in the Content Analysis of Computer Conference Transcripts. *International Journal of Artificial Intelligence in Education, 12*(1), 8-22.

Rowntree, D. (1997). *Making Materials-Based Learning Work.* London: Kogan Page.

Royal Anthropological Institute of Great Britain and Ireland. (1951). *Notes and Queries on Anthropology* (6th edition. ed.). London: Routledge and K. Paul.

Sack, W. (2000). Conversation Map: an Interface for Very-Large-Scale Conversations. *Journal of Management Information Systems, 17*(3), 73-92.

Sacks, H., Schegloff, E. A., & Jefferson, G. (1974). A simplest systematics for the organisation of Turn-Taking for Conversation. *Language, 50*(4(1)), 696-735.

Salmon, G. (2000). *E-Moderating: The Key to Teaching and Learning Online.* London: Kogan Page.

Sanders, D. W., & Morrison-Sjetlar, A. (2001). Students attitudes toward Web-enhanced instruction in an introductory biology course. *Journal of Research on Computing in Education, 33*(3), 251-262.

Scott, J. (2000). *"Social Network Analysis- a handbook* (second ed.). London: Sage publications.

Sherry, L. (1996). Issues in Distance Learning. *International Journal of Educational Telecommunications, 1*(4), 337-365.

Sherry, L. (2000). The Nature and Purpose of Online Conversations:

A Brief Synthesis of Current Research. *International Journal of Educational Telecommunications., 6*(1), 19-52.

Shimojima, A., Skoiso, H., Swerts, M., & Katagiri, Y. (1998). *An Informational Analysis of Echonic Responses in Dialogue.* Paper presented at the The Twentieth Annual Conference of the Cognitive Science Society.

Simmel, G. (1950). Quantitative Aspects of the Group. In K. H. Wolf (Ed.), *The Sociology of Georg Simmel.* Glancoe: The Free Press.

Simmel, G. (1955(1922)). *The Web of Group Affiliation* (R. Bendix, Trans.). Glenco Illinois: The Free Press.

Simoff, S. J. (1999, Dec 12-15). *Monitoring and Evaluation in Collaborative Learning Environments.* Paper presented at the Computer Sup[port for Collaborative Learning CSCL, Paolo Alto.

Simpson, R., & Galbo, J. (1986). Interacting and Learning: Theorising on the art of Teaching. *Interchange, 17*(4), 37-51.

Singer Gordon, R. (2000, January/February 2000). "Online Discussion Forums - Finding community , commentary, and (hopefully) answers". *Link-Up, 17,* 12-15.

Stahl, G. (2003). *Can shared knowledge exceed the sum of its parts?* Paper presented at the International Conference on Communities and Technologies (C&T), Amsterdam.

Stahl, G. (2005). Mediation of Group Cognition. In R. Klamma, M. Rohde & G. Stahl (Eds.), *Community -Based Learning: Explorations into Theoretical Groundings, Empirical Findings and Computer Support* (pp. 13-18). Los Angeles: SIG Group.

Stephenson, K., & Zelen, M. (1989). Rethinking Centrality: Method and Examples. *Social Networks, 1989*(11), 1-37.

Stubbs, M. (1983). *Discourse Analysis: The Sociolinguistic Analysis of Natural Language*. Oxford: Basil Blackwell.

Tapscott, D. (1998). *Growing up digital : The rise of the net generation*. New York: McGraw-Hill.

Tapscott, D. (2005). The Net Generation and the School. Retrieved May 10th, 2005, from www.mff.org/edtech/article.taf

Tharp, R. G., & Gallimore, R. (1991). A theory of teaching as assisted performance. In P. Light, S. Sheldon & M. Woodhead (Eds.), *Learning to Think* (pp. 42-62). London: Routledge in association with The Open University.

Thomas, M.-. (2002). *Student participation in Online discussion: The implications of learning activities and discourse development on assessment*. Paper presented at the Evaluation and Assessment 2002.

Thomsen, S. R., Straubhaar, J. D., & Bolyard, D. M. (1998). Ethnomethodology and the study of online communities: exploring the cyber streets. *Information Research, 4*(1).

Tidwell, L. C., & Walther, J. B. (2002). Computer-Mediated communication efffects on disclosure, impressions, and interpersonal evaluations:Getting to know one another a bit at a time. *Human Communication Research, 28*(3), 317-348.

Tornow, J. (1997). *Link/age: Composing in the on-line classroom*. Logan UT: Utah State University Press.

Treleaven, L. (2004). Anew Taxonomy for Evaluating Studies of Online Collaborative Learning. In T. S. Roberts (Ed.), *Online Collaborative Learning: Theory and Practice* (pp. 160-181). Hershey: Information Science publishing.

Turkle, S. (1995). *Life on the Screen: Identity in the Age of the Internet*. New York:: Simon and Schuster.

Udehn, L. (2002). The Changing face of Methodological Individualism. *Annual Review of Sociology, 28*, 479-507.

Van Ments, M. (1990). *"Active Talk: The Effective Use of Discussion in Learning"*. London: Kogan Page Ltd.

Villalba, C., & Romiszowski, A. j. (1999). *AulaNet and other Web-based learning environments: a comparative study in an International context*. Paper presented at the 1999 ABED International conference, Rio de Janeiro.

Voiskunsky, A. (1997). Telelogue Conversations. *Journal of Computer Mediated Communication, 2*.

Von Glaserfeld, E. (1989). Constructivism in Education. In T. Husen, Postlethwaite, T.N. (Ed.), *International Encyclopedia of Education:Suplementary Vol.1. Research and Studies*. Oxford: Pergamon.

Vygotsky, L. (1978). *Mind in Society: The Development of Higher Psychological Processes*. Cambridge Massachusetts: Harvard University Press.

Wagner, E. D. (1994). In Support of a Functional Definition of Interaction. *American Journal of Distance Education, 8*(2), 6-26.

Wang, Y. (2000). Web Mining and Knowledge Discovery of Usage Patterns. Retrieved 7.10.03, 2003, from http://citeseer.nj.nec.com/cache/papers/cs/22023/http:zSzzSzdb.uwaterloo.cazS z~tozsuzSzcourseszSzcs748tzSzsurveyszSzwang.pdf/wang00web.pdf

Warschauer. (1997). Computer-Mediated Collaborative learning: Theory and Practice. *Modern Language Journal, 81*(3), 470-481.

Wasserman, S., & Faust, K. (1994). *Social Network Analysis: Methods and Applications* (Vol. 8). NY: Cambridge University Press.

Weiss, R., & Morrison, G. (1998, February 18-22, 1998). *Evaluation of a graduate seminar conducted by listserve*. Paper presented at the National Convention of the Association for Educational Communications and Technology (AECT), St. Louis, MO.

Wellman, B. (2003). The Three Ages of Internet Studies: Ten, Five, and Zero Years ago. Retrieved 30.9.03, 2003, from www.chass.utoronto.ca/`wellman/publications/index.html

Wellman, B., & Berkowitz, S. D. (Eds.). (1988). *Social Structures: a network approach* (Vol. 2). NY: Cambridge University Press.

Wellman, B., & Gulia, M. (1999). NET SURFERS DON'T RIDE ALONE: VIRTUAL COMMUNITIES AS COMMUNITIES. In P. Kollock & M. A. Smith (Eds.), *Communities in Cyberspace*. London: Routledge.

Wellman, B., & Haythornthwaite, C. (2002). *The Internet in Everyday Life*. Oxford: Blackwell Pubishing Company.

Wertsch, J. V. (1991). *"Voices of the Mind- A Sociocultural Approach to Mediated Action"*. Cambridge MA: Harvard University Press.

Wetherell, M., Taylor, S., & Yates, S. J. (2001). *"Discourse as Data: A Guide for Analysis"*. Milton Keynes: Sage Publications Ltd.

White, N. (2004, 2004). Glossary of Online Interaction. *Full Circle Associates* Retrieved March, 2005, from http://www.fullcirc.com/community/interactionterms.htm

Wilson, T. P. (1974). Normative and Interpretative Paradigms in Sociology. In J. D. Douglas (Ed.), *Understanding Everyday life*. London: Routledge & Kegan Paul.

Zaiane, O. R., & Luo, J. (2001, August 6-8, 2001.). *Towards Evaluating Learners' Behaviour in a Web-Based Distance Learning Environment*. Paper presented at the International Conference on Advanced Learning Technologies, Madison, WI.

Zajac, R. J., & Hartup, W. W. (1997). Friends as coworkers: Research review and classroom implications. *The Elementary Schools Journal, 98*(1), 3-13.

Zeitlyn, D. (1990). Professor Garfinkel Visits the Soothsayers Ethnomethodology and Mambila Divination. *MAN (N.S.), 25*(4), 654-666.

Zemliansky, P. (n.d.). *"Buidling Online communities: Why Use Discussion Forums in the Writing Class"*.Unpublished manuscript.

8. APPENDICES

Appendix 1

Elaine 13624-13624
Subject: Discussion thread about portfolios or crit ped
Posted by: Elaine on *05-10-02* at 12:33   Hot Tip

Subject: Discussion thread - Assessing and Evaluating adult
Posted by: Jan on *05-10-02* at 12:33   Comment
Portfolio - change of Focus
I started my portfolio in April and my topic was on teaching professional practice
and professional studies to teacher trainees. It was cruising along. I felt I was
meeting the course requirements but it was not particularly challenging.
Then...about a month ago I was majorly challenged by a very angry distance
student about the way that I had marked his assignment. At the time i sought
opinions from colleagues and other students, etc etc. Then i realised I was
actually applying Brookfield's lenses and that this would fit the portfolio brief,
and the incident has really challenged my practice and my thinking! Hence my
change of focus. Does anyone know of any recent research about evaluating
and assessing adult students' work?
Jan

13624-13639
Subject: Discussion thread - Assessing and Evaluating adult
Posted by: Jan on *05-10-02* at 12:33   Comment

Portfolio - change of Focus

I started my portfolio in April and my topic was on teaching professional

practice and professional studies to teacher trainees. It was cruising along. I

felt I was meeting the course requirements but it was not particularly

challenging.

Then...about a month ago I was majorly challenged by a very angry distance

student about the way that I had marked his assignment. At the time i sought

opinions from colleagues and other students, etc etc. Then i realised I was

actually applying Brookfield's lenses and that this would fit the portfolio brief,

and the incident has really challenged my practice and my thinking! Hence my

change of focus. Does anyone know of any recent research about evaluating

and assessing adult students' work?

Jan

Subject: On autobiography mainly
Posted by: Elaine on *06-10-02* at 12:33
Comment

Hi, Jan - great topic - I think it will be a very valuable one because it relates

directly to your own practice.

You obviously have a handle on three of Brookfield's lenses - literature -

students - peers ... your autobiography could be another. For example you

might like to write (or think - or talk with a buddy who will challenge you) in some depth about a bad experience you yourself might have had in relation to 'receiving feedback as an adult' - and perhaps apply Smyth's model to it). I mention this because I am aware that some people seem to have interpreted autobiography much more narrowly than others - and of course, I do not know how you are thinking about it. Some people are seeing it as (a) keeping a journal and others as (b) thinking about critical incidents. Both of these are thinking tools - and I guess are forms of autobiography - but there are also other kinds of analysis that help to recall how experiences from the past might have influenced your current, strongly held assumptions (eg Brookfield's 3 types) - power relationships - hegemony - etc.

You are asking about literature - and that is important - people may have suggestions - in addition - have you tried Masterfile? Dave Clemens at the library?

I suspect another question related to the theory or the literature is to do with the position you yourself hold in relation to your position as a teacher and the status and nature of the learner - and the student's understanding of the teaching learning process - and whether there is a philosophical mismatch. If one of you is working from behaviourist perspective and the other from a constructivist position (either way) then there is liable to be a misunderstanding. Similarly if one of you is operating in a hierarchical way and the other strongly believes in a more horizontal model of colleagueship then there are likely to be misunderstandings. Or if one of you sees the world in terms that are strongly realist and believes there are right and wrong answers - and the other is more fluid and sees that our world is understood in terms of its social construction then there can be dispute. In each case I think the problem arises because people are talking past each other's assumptions. This is one of the key things I believe about the value of critical reflective practice - if one is aware of ones assumptions then two things can happen (1) one is able to be more analytical in situations of discord and (2) one is actually able to view the world from different perspectives and therefore be better able to make choices (rather than be pushed around by habits). I link all this to pragmatism (see the Cherry holmes reading).

Enough - I hope others are able to comment on assessment within adult education. Others perhaps have similar experiences. I know I dealt with a complaint earlier this year where a student argued that I had treated her unfairly (not in this course). I have written about it within my thesis because there is an issue here about sensitivity to student concerns - the actual issue is now resolved and I am leaving it for a term or so (so that she no longer sees me as her 'teacher') before going back and asking if she will talk with me about how the misunderstanding arose - I want to try to understand it better from her perspective.

Have a good term, Jan. Thanks for the submission.

Elaine

Subject adult marking
Posted by : Anthea on *12-10-02* at 12:33   Comment

about a month ago I was

>majorly challenged by a very

>angry distance student about the

>way that I had marked his

>assignment. At the time i

>sought opinions from colleagues

>and other students, etc, etc.

It is great to see that you did this type of reflection (automatically without having to consciously think about it).

I have heard many stories about the way lecturers mark work. Some are seen as critical and picky and others complain that some are too easy!

I personally would think that marking adults work would be more difficult than children's work because children just accept (usually having to)what they get (sometimes not happily). Whereas I would imagine adults would scrutinize (as I do) their marking and where they went wrong and we (most of the times) compare our results with other adults! I think it is good to let your markers know how you feel as they may not aware of the effect of their comments (some markers being far too critical). I want to know where I went wrong and what I can do next time so the same mistake is not repeated! Not made to feel useless!

Gee...I hope my children do not feel this way with my marking. In future with my children I think I would like to discuss assessment with them. Why should they just accept what I have said without expressing their feelings. It might not make a difference but at least they are heard!

13624-14117 EC
Subject: adult marking
Posted by: Anthea on *12-10-02* at 12:33
Comment

about a month ago I was

>majorly challenged by a very

>angry distance student about the

>way that I had marked his

>assignment. At the time i

>sought opinions from colleagues

>and other students, etc, etc.

It is great to see that you did this type of reflection (automatically without having to consciously think about it).

I have heard many stories about the way lecturers mark work. Some are seen as critical and picky and others complain that some are too easy!

I personally would think that marking adults work would be more difficult than children's work because children just accept (usually having to)what they get (sometimes not happily). Whereas I would imagine adults would scrutinize (as I do) their marking and where they went wrong and we (most of the times) compare our results with other adults! I think it is good to let your markers know how you feel as they may not aware of the effect of their comments (some markers being far too critical). I want to know where I went wrong and what I can do next time so the same mistake is not repeated! Not made to feel useless!

Gee...I hope my children do not feel this way with my marking. In future with my children I think I would like to discuss assessment with them. Why should they just accept what I have said without expressing their feelings. It might not make a difference but at least they are heard!

Subject: adult marking
Posted by: Jan on *13-10-02* at 12:33
Comment

Thank you for your comments Elaine and Anthea, which are helpful.

I have become aware that there are issues of power in here!! Doing the learning assignment made me aware that although I held some humanist ideas I am certainly not constructivist. In the subject area that I was marking I do see myself as something of an 'expert' from my many years of successful primary teaching.

This critical incident challenged me, and also discussing with colleagues and reading some of the current ideas in adult teaching and learning I am perhaps operating in a mode that was more appropriate 10 years ago.

However I do still have ideas about standards and that some of the work that I mark indicates to me that these students don't meet a standard and I wouldn't want them teaching my child! I'm not sure how resolvable this is! I am enjoying reading more about adult education in the broad sense which I had never come across before.

Jan

13624-14155
Subject : adult marking
Posted by : Jan on *13-10-02* at 12:33
Comment

Thank you for your comments Elaine and Anthea, which are helpful.

I have become aware that there are issues of power in here!! Doing the learning assignment made me aware that although I held some humanist ideas I am certainly not constructivist. In the subject area that I was marking I do see myself as something of an 'expert' from my many years of successful primary teaching.

This critical incident challenged me, and also discussing with colleagues and reading some of the current ideas in adult teaching and learning I am perhaps operating in a mode that was more appropriate 10 years ago.

However I do still have ideas about standards and that some of the work that I mark indicates to me that these students don't meet a standard and I wouldn't want them teaching my child! I'm not sure how resolvable this is! I am enjoying reading more about adult education in the broad sense which I had never come across before.

Jan

Subject : Minimum standards
Posted by : Elaine on *14-10-02* at 12:33
Agree

HI, Jan

>However I do still have ideas

>about standards and that some of

>the work that I mark indicates

>to me that these students don't

>meet a standard and I wouldn't

>want them teaching my child!

I agree wholeheartedly - I guess the question to me is about how we can get the standards of these students raised so that they become self questioning and self-motivated learners who want to critique their own work before they submit it - or who need constructive feedback on how to improve it once they have submitted it.

The assessment within MTchLn is geared to address exactly this point about minimum standards - if you don't get a pass of better you get a resubmit - end of story - no apology - but you also get some supportive guidance about how to do better. People tend to find that they get advice from me - even if they are producing work at distinction level - that is because I see it as a responsibility to challenge everyone.

Not always popular - but usually most people appreciate it - in the long run (or so they tell me .... b u t is this a blind spot - who knows - I'll wait for the next critical incident and wonder again then ... - or perhaps I could try to seek feedback through the student lens - as per Brookfield - or other models ...)

Cheers and happy hunting

E

Visualising Social Networks- the EC approach

This process involves the following software packs:

MS EXCEL

MS ACCESS

UCINET version 6 (including NETDRAW)

1. Access the spreadsheets produced by StudentNet for each Forum/Group,
2. Rename each of the original files and named it after its component
3. Import the EXCEL file into ACCESS using: FILE >get external>import.
4. Create a CROSS TAB query in ACCESS using :
   "First Name" only!! in the first stage;

   Thread key, in the second stage;

   "Post key" count in the third stage;

5. In ACCESS under TOOLS > office link> analyse with EXCEL
6. In EXCEL, clean out any empty rows and columns
7. Import the EXCEL CROSS TAB file into UCINET using:
   Spreadsheet > import

8. Under TRANSFORM in UCINET go to BIPARTITE save as bipartite, using the name of the Forum or Group. Also save it as a TXT file as this will show the actual matrix generated by the UCINET.
9. NETDRAW - under FILE go to OPEN, choose the bipartite file using OPEN> UCINET DATA SET>NETWORK
10. Manually drag the Post+ Parent nodes, adjoining them with the relevant post key to create the ECTP35PT
11. under PROPERTIES edit node shapes and colour, make 'arrows' invisible
12. FILE > SAVE DIAGRAM AS > JPEG
13. if needed Copy JPEG file to 'paint' convert to 'gif' file

sources :

'justifying the visual categories continue.doc'.

diary entry 24.12.02

---

[35] this manual arrangement however did not disturb the actual matrix used for mathematical measurements i.e. centrality

The progression of the term Boundaries

Neuman (1997) comments that interpretive researchers are seen by their critical counterparts as passive and amoral. Conversely critical researchers rock the boat by "intentionally raising and identifying more problems than the ruling elites in politics and administration are able to accommodate, much less to solve....The critical researcher asks embarrassing questions, exposes hypocrisy, and investigates conditions in order to encourage dramatic grass-roots action." Hmmmm ....yes that sounds like lob-in-a-grenade-and-watch-'em-scramble Maurice! And then we have I-like-my-job-and-want-to-keep-it-Chicken-Jennifer

Maurice120171208712017
Response Flames and grenades - battle metaphors
Hi Jenny et Elaine >*The critical researcher asks embarrassing* >*questions, exposes hypocrisy,* >*and investigates conditions in* >*order to encourage dramatic* >*grass-roots action."* >*Hmmmm ....yes that sounds like* >*lob-in-a-grenade-and-watch-'em-scramble Maurice!* Well, what can I say?! ... "I'm a nice person really" (... in keeping with the aphorism: "it's better to love yourself than be starved of affection") ... How much of this is social conditioning of roles? >*Okay, I'm having a laugh at that -* >*I think your heat shields are very strong, Maurice.* That's really interesting, Elaine - because that was part of what I was trying to learn through this whole RP boundaries thing ... but there's a big difference between heat shields up close and having people and issues at a distance by keeping them across the other side of the moat until you feel ready to let down the drawbridge - which is what various people have been advising me for years ... Mind you, that all depends on whether one occupies a castle or lives a more Bedouin existence. Yesterday I asked some colleagues about how they see my boundaries ... and one who's known me fairly well for 17 years snorted affectionately and said: "You don't have any", while another who's only worked with me for 4 years said something to the effect that that's my problem - getting too involved in everything and not taking enough time out to smell the daisies ... and a third said that I'm always in the firing line because of the job I do and the expectations and frustrations of staff when they try to use computers ... and then another said that I keep my personal self well protected behind my boundaries. Such a range of views to reflect on ... with elements of "truth" in every one of them! ... and I undertook the boundaries issue **because** I am constantly processing (CPU rarely idle) and I was a bit concerned because my older brother recently had a heart attack - life's too wonderful to not ride on towards the sunset, yet at the same time it's too short to stay uninvolved, so I thought I'd be brave (for me!) and put some thoughts out here in StudentNet. I'm relieved! ... This must be progress! ... I'm learning something significant here - particularly about not being too precious about my ideas/thoughts/words. (Jenny's trying to get me to co-author a submission with her - actually, I need to rephrase that - she's already **persuaded** me to agree to work with her on that ... and I didn't say NO??!! (what happened to my boundaries!!!??) - and she pointed out that once you write something it's out there and anyone can pull it to bits ...) Thanks, Jenny, I obviously needed that challenge and you are giving me the opportunity! I guess I think it's also probably hard for us to comment critically about each other's work, because we are ever more closely members of this learning community supporting each other - how does that work for you, Elaine? ... are you able to be easily dispassionate about your marking? ... didn't you spend

some time with ERO? What tricks did you learn from that role? Enough for today! :-) Maurice03 Sep 2002 12:25

Debbie120171213812087
Comment: This must be progress!
Hi Maurice, it's great to hear you "opening up" (as they say in support group circles) and feeling the benefit of talking about your boundaries on Studentnet. It certainly was interesting to hear the different response you received as you asked your colleagues how they view you and your boundaries. I think being aware of our boundaries is hugely important. I didn't read the message from Elaine to you but I found it very interesting her to read her comment regarding you having good heat shields (or something to that effect). I guess it's up to us if we see boundaries as walls that protect us, or bridges that connect us with our fellow peers and colleagues. I feel 'boundaries' is closely linked with my focus of supporting colleagues, and what I find is that the more I am aware of how much I am prepared to extend my own boundaries with my colleagues the more collaborative work we are all doing together. In fact I almost feel a focus change coming on again, just simply to - collaboration. This reflective process is an interesting journey, is it not? Cheers, Debbie.03 Sep 2002 22:12

Maurice120171216712138
Response: well - it's movement anyway!
Hi Debbie >*It certainly was* >*interesting to hear the* >*different response you received* >*as you asked your colleagues how* >*they view you and your boundaries.* ... I asked another one today and she (who's only known and worked with me for probably 8-10 years) told me my boundaries are fluid ... [=last-minute input for my RP final submission!!] >*and by the way I think being aware* >*of our boundaries is hugely important.* Well, Debbie, then I'd like to ask you *how* you maintain your boundaries/bridges or what analogy you might use to describe your situation. I'm mindful of a famous poem titled "Mending Wall" by Robert Frost ... which begins with: *"Something there is which doesn't love a wall"* and ends: *"Good fences make good neighbors."* I just found it again on a Frost fan's website >*I guess it's up to us if we see* >*boundaries as walls that protect* >*us, or bridges that connect us* >*with our fellow peers and colleagues.* ... a bridge is usually a span between areas clearly separated by a river or whatever ... and to me that's a different though related topic, because I'm constantly building and repairing bridges >*I feel 'boundaries'* >*is closely linked* [there's that bridge again!] *with my focus* >*of supporting colleagues, and* >*what I find is that the more I* >*am aware of how much I am* >*prepared to* **extend** *my own boundaries* ... so are they extensible enough to comment here - or how does the medium influence this decision? ... >*... with my colleagues* >*the more collaborative work we* >*are all doing together.* How would you then rate us working together as a StudentNet community compared to the face-to-face interactions at work, in terms of how well and how deeply we collaborate? Or is this sort of question at the boundary of your comfort-zone? >*This reflective process is an interesting journey, is it not?* Obviously! ... or we wouldn't be spending time involved in these "conversations"! regards :-) Maurice PS: thanks for the response!04 Sep 2002 13:02

Debbie120171219812167
Comment good fences make good neighbours
Hi Maurice, I enjoyed the poem (in a farmy sort of way), and I would like to take you up on a few of the questions you posed to me. I guess firstly I think we (being the ironists that we are)are seeing the metaphor of the "bridge" from slightly different perspectives (please let me know if This isn't so). See I'm a visual person and what I see when I talk about walls and bridges in connection with boundaries is I see that I can build thick walls around - me much like a castle and let nobody in or I can draw down the draw "bridge" and allow my

boundaries to connect with and let people in. Interesting question - how does the medium of student allow for extending boundaries. I guess because I liken it to two (or three) people having a conversation together - only it's up the front of the classroom where everyone else can listen (there's the visual person in me again), I tend to have a problem with fully extending my boundaries in this medium. I guess the flip side to it (and I've been giving this one a bit of thought lately) is that we have to display good listening skills i.e.: there's no talking while the other person is talking - this allows me the time to say what I want to say and how I want to say it. Obviously I also can't read your eyes to read your response, your body language to read if you are getting fidgety etc... As for deep collaboration, I feel this medium seems to fall short encouraging deep collaborative working relationships with each other as peers and colleagues. I think about the classroom scenario again and think that general classroom discussion is represented well in this medium, but the one-to-one conversations which quite often create a lot of meaning for some people are not really happening. As you can see it has not pushed my boundaries of my comfort zone at all to talk about boundaries, communication etc... I welcome good honest communication. Cheers, Debbie.04 Sep 2002 21:19

Maurice120171227312198
Response: deep collaboration
Hi again Debbie >.. *or I can draw down the draw "bridge"* >*and allow my boundaries to* >*connect with and let people in.* Understand now! >*StudenNet ... I tend to have a problem with fully* >*extending my boundaries in this medium.* As I read it, what you're saying is not that the technology itself is an impediment to communication, but the fact that it's asynchronous (not happening at the same time) and lacking in the visual cues of normal small group conversations. Yet I see many students texting and using the chat rooms - so I am wondering why it's hard for us to go for >*... deep collaboration, I* >*feel this medium seems to fall* >*short encouraging deep* >*collaborative working* >*relationships with each other as* >*peers and colleagues.* >*... the one-to-one conversations* >*which quite often create a lot of* >*meaning for some people are not* >*really happening.* ... and you're saying that's because we have others "listening in" on our conversations, so we monitor more carefully what we write and take fewer chances?? I know it's easier for me to engage in face-to-face conversation because I can react and change tone, direction, retract or whatever depending on the feedback cues I'm reading, but here on StudentNet it's not like that. Does this mean that e-mail is preferable as a medium for the deep and meaningful over these forums? ... or that it is simply a reflection of the ways people react in meetings, where there is seldom an even distribution of involvement? mmm Keep musing! :-) Maurice PS: will you suggest where we can all meet on Wednesday 2nd?05 Sep 2002 16:49

Debbie120171238112273
Comment: deep collaboration
Hi Maurice, I thought it was really interesting to receive the survey from Bridget O'Reagan regarding the effectiveness of Studentnet at the same time that we are discussing it on-line. I guess I haven't really given the individual e-mail suggestion a try simply because I didn't feel the need to say something that I couldn't say within the forums. I guess the challenge is to understand how this form of communication can work in a collaborative manner. For the most part I think it does. Just keeping up a dialogue with someone and extended my train of thought within that dialogue, helps me to reflect, think more critically and pose some questions to continue the collaboration. Our process of collaboration at present at my centre is based around our new assessment practices. We have moved from a system of "fitting the child into the curriculum" (i.e.: a curriculum strand) to noticing meaningful experiences for the child, this then enables us to recognise how "our curriculum is fitting into the child" and we respond with ideas that will extend that child or group of children

further. My assumptions were that as we move into practicing more of a social constructivist program the emphasis would move away from "the individual" in favour of "the group", but what I think we are finding is that it actually allows more one-on-one time for the individual - within the social setting. So what I see is that the benefits of collaboration are not only for the group as a whole, but that within this the individual has room to grow at their own pace. If Helen is reading this, what was the name of that place that we met Maurice and Jenny at? Would that be suitable again? Is it an evening meal we were planning Maurice, or lunch time? Thanks for your replies, it's great to keep up the discussion. Cheers, Debbie.06 Sep 2002 21:43

Maurice120171241112381
Response: deep collaboration
Hi Debbie don't you think it's interesting the way we often preface our submissions with the personal greeting: *Hi somebody*? ... which perhaps makes the whole process more personal even though we are effectively writing to the whole group ... anyway, >... *really interesting to receive >the survey from Bridget O'Regan >regarding the effectiveness of >Studentnet at the same time that >we are discussing it on-line.* Yes, quite fortuitous really, as I think we're likely to be able to give more useful feedback as a result, which will hopefully lead to further improvements ... >... *Just keeping up a dialogue with >someone ... helps me to reflect, think more >critically and pose some >questions to continue the collaboration.* Essentially it's the **dialogue** that's the critical component ... and StudentNet allows us to individually choose what times it best suits us to say something. That's what you mean, isn't it? >*So what I see is that the >benefits of collaboration are >not only for the group as a >whole, but that within this the >individual has room to grow at >their own pace.* I find it easy to agree with that ... >*Is it an evening meal we were >planning Maurice, or lunch time ?*I had thought of an evening meal, because I have no idea of when the lunchtimes would be ... and an evening would give us more time to discuss life, the universe, and 811 ... regards :-) Maurice08 Sep 2002 11:30

Helen20171244512381
Comment meeting place
>*If Helen is reading this, what >was the name of that place that >we met Maurice and Jenny at? >Would that be suitable again? > >Is it an evening meal we were >planning Maurice, or lunch >time?*
The Bohemian and yes it could be! 08 Sep 2002 21:52

Debbie120171250012445
Comment meeting place
To Helen, Maurice and all, Thanks Helen for replying to my message, so I'm wondering if that could be the place we want to meet. Shall we say 6.30 (is that too early) at the Bohemian on Weds the 2nd of October? It seemed a nice quiet place, hopefully we should be able to hear ourselves think! I'll put the invite out in Comspace. You know the saying be careful for what you dream for, you just might get it! Well anyway, tonight at our committee meeting they passed the motion that they would fund all remaining funds that Kathy and I can't find for our trip to Reggio Emillia in April - isn't that amazing! Cheers, Debbie. 09 Sep 2002 22:02 Jennifer120171251712500CommentHooray"Luck = opportunity meets preparation!" Excellent to hear Debbie that you and Kathy are well supported. Deserved. Cheers Jenny10 Sep 2002 13:28

Maurice120171252612500
Agree meeting place
Hi all >*Shall we say 6.30 (is >that too early) at the Bohemian >on Weds the 2nd of October?* That sounds great! ... I'll look forward to seeing you all ... >*they would fund all remaining funds >that*

Kathy and I can't find for >our trip to Reggio Emillia in >April - isn't that amazing! That's just truly amazing! Awesome ... I'd really like to more about it all - even if we're no longer doing courses together .. :-) Maurice > >Cheers, Debbie. >10 Sep 2002 16:43 Debbie120171258312526Comment other forms of reflective writing Hi to Maurice and Jenny, Thanks for your congrats regarding getting the funding for Italy, haven't really processed that info as it is too far ahead in my thinking but think it is wonderful! On receiving my feedback from my critical reflection assignment I've had some points of interest raised to which I want to put out to you. Elaine talked about other forms of reflective writing for me to consider, however I'm feeling a little bit vague so would like some feedback. I would like your thoughts on what you see autobiographical writing to be. Another form of reflective writing she talked about was synthesising ideas from a number of sources - this I have trouble with as well. Maurice and I have been discussing how we can use collaboration on Studentnet effectively, which got me to thinking I'll open these queries for feedback, and decided that I am not going to feel ridiculous in the process. An interesting quote from Brookfield is "because of the fear of looking stupid, much critical reflection begins with solitary analysis". Looking forward to your responses. Cheers, Debbie.11 Sep 2002 17:06

Jennifer120171261212583
Comment Metaphorical writing
Thanks for sharing your learning with us Debbie. (I am working on my ability to critique.) In terms of writing...I used a survival advice memo to attempt assumption hunting. It is written hypothetically to a person taking your job. The memo reveals aspects of teaching that are most crucial to you and assumptions that are most influential. "To the teacher taking my job......" Also Deshler (cited in Brookfield I think) wrote about metaphorical writing. The following is from the net and I have no URL as I was aiming to merely to play with the idea. Hope it is helpful Debbie. EXPANDING KNOWLEDGE BY METAPHORICAL THINKING AIM Use metaphorical thinking to reflect on how personal, cultural, and organizational socialization informs how we make meaning. Metaphorical thinking allows us to reflect and critique assumptions that influence our decisions, feelings, thoughts and actions (Deshler in Mezirow and Associates, 1990, Page 296). STEP ONE Select an experience from your personal, cultural or organizational domain. In this exercise you may select your experience with The (CCE) or some other aspect of your practice with continuous improvement. STEP TWO Create a metaphor that reflects your experience. In writing, we explore the world of the metaphor. What values are reflected in the world of the metaphor, what do authorities say about this world, what does it mean? What does our culture say? What does our society say about the world of the metaphor? What beliefs do we hold about this world? What assumptions are embedded in the world of the metaphor? STEP THREE Compare this to your experience, values, and beliefs about your experience. Share your exploration with your partner. STEP FOUR Now, create a different metaphor that better expresses your meanings about your experience. In writing, as before, explore the world of this metaphor. CONCLUSION What has changed in the way you make meaning of your experience as a result of metaphorical exploration? What assumptions got challenged? How does this change any action you might make in the future? CONCLUSION Share your thoughts with your partner. This exercise was adapted from David Deshler's article, "Metaphor Analysis: Exorcizing Social Ghosts" in Jack Mezirow Jossey-Bass, San Francisco, 1990. 11 Sep 2002 19:52

Maurice120171281612583
Response other forms of reflective writing

Hi Debbie >*Maurice and I have been* >*discussing how we can use* >*collaboration on Studentnet* >*effectively, which got me to* >*thinking I'll open these queries* >*for feedback, and decided that I* >*am not going to feel ridiculous* >*in the process.* well ... I was thinking how very cohesive all your comments were ... >*Looking forward to your responses.* Sorry, but that will have to all wait for a while till I see you in person ... because I'm now off for a week before the Christchurch course - out of touch in a glide-time holiday while someone else covers my classes. ... Luxury, eh! till then :-) Maurice14 Sep 2002 20:07

Debbie120171271112612
Comment: Metaphorical writing
Hi Jenny, Thanks for sharing the idea of metaphorical writing with me. What a great way of critically reflecting. I can really relate to the use of metaphors and have used some interesting ones during the course of this paper (many inspired by our friend Elaine). I see the possibilities that could come out of this process would be allowing me the chance to take things a little more slowly and see things from other perspectives. I liken this to something Brookfield said (when he talks about critical reflection) "...turning logic on it's head, reversing images, looking at situations sideways and making imaginative leaps". Thanks Jenny. Cheers, Debbie.

Categorisation of discussion topics:
Course related ECs
Ex 1 - Module 9-10 one thread13328- parent 13377 (category 3b)

**Criterion: Comments about course related issues, readings tasks, and ideas +
Sharing personal work experience**

Jennifer133281337713371QuestionShould culture
Hi Jennifer, An interesting comment on the *"one size fits all teacher stereotype"* that we should
be doing the job in a prescribed way. It must be very unsettling for new teachers who are
torn between *the should* pressure and their professional judgement. I wonder where this
perception of one way the right way comes from? Is it teacher education or the school
system? What guilt do we carry for what we feel we should be doing? I experience guilt
over the fact that I do not write behavioural objectives as I was taught to in my training.
(Occasionally I do when in unfamiliar territory) Has anyone else experienced guilt for not
doing what is perceived by others to be the **right thing**?
  **Criteria: Sharing personal work experience + personal views, opinions, linking
ones circumstances to other educators, and theories**

Merian133281338613377CommentShould culture
Hi Jenny >that we should be doing the job in a prescribed way. When I was working as
Principal in two teacher school I experienced difficulty with the teacher in planning. She
was of the mind that there was only one way to plan-hers which involved very detailed
planning straight from the curriculum, a very narrow focus on what was being taught. She
was adamant that ERO liked it that way and that she was not going to change because that
was right. It was frustrating for me because I had never taught within the bounds of such
constraints. In my experience there are many teachers like this who plan for hours with the
most wonderful objectives, and learning outcomes. The curriculum is put before the
student because with all the planning of the units little is followed up on the achievements
or non achievement of these outcomes and the next unit is planned independent of the
other. The content becomes the most important thing rather than the skills. This all
harkens back to some of the points that Ray was making in his discussion about the
curriculum. I used to be hung up on doing the right thing until I realised that I was
supposed to be taking students on from where they were at and that I had to think outside
the square to do it. I felt that as long as I was keeping within the curriculum bounds I could
do it. I think that the "right way" idea has come from the fear of ERO and how they have
commented and how it has been interpreted. Also teachers come back from courses with
the idea that the ideas that they have learnt are the "right way". The introduction and hype
of the new curriculum documents have also made people look for the right way to do
things and of course having them come so quickly pushed teachers into planning their
"brains out". No one told us to throw out the old ways of doing things which were not all
bad-just different. People like to hang on to successful ways of doing things and if they are
leaders then it becomes the "right way". I remember one school where all the junior room
had to be arranged exactly the same way and the planning all had to be done exactly the
same way. It killed all innovation and creativity but it was "the right way" for that senior
teacher and what's more no one opposed it! Have any of you experienced being in a school
like this? I am rambling -its one of my soapbox topics! Cheers, Merian

EX2- Module5-8 13618 – 14157 (category 4a)

Criteria: Comments about course related issues, readings tasks, and ideas.
Hi Anthea A colleague has sent me some readings re my current issue, one of which relates to yours. This is on the idea that a 'critical incident' can 'push' a teacher into the next phase of their career. From their research they came up with several stages. I don't agree with the idea of hierarchical stages although they define a career as a series of personal changes rather than an hierarchical sequence. The first phase was characterised by 'reality shock', survival, learning the school culture, establishing an identity and reputation in the school etc. etc. It seemed to make sense to me! Jan

Anthea 136181446614157Comment Phases of starting fresh
The >first phase was characterised by >'reality shock', survival, >learning the school >culture, establishing an identity >and reputation in the school >etc. etc. It seemed to make >sense to me! Most definitely, The first words to my mouth " That is so true". I did a teaching audit from Brookfield and found that I reflected on "survival techniques" that I had learnt in my first year of teaching. This has made me more aware of how I reflect on my learning. I have begun to look at my personal development and not just certain "skills" I may have learnt along the way! Looking at the phases of beginning teaching is interesting, because I will have to go through them again when I start teaching again next year. (After a year off and being a mum at the same time, those aspects of beginning to teach will definitely apply! - but at least I will be aware of them!) Anthea

EX 3 - Module 9-10 group 2+3 -13966-13966 (category 2)

Criteria: Instructions for tasks, course work, use of the technology involved in the course +Housekeeping messages

Hi, everyone. Please register here and let us all know when you plan to post your question onto the group 2 sharing area below. Also - could you give us all an idea of when you are likely to be able to loggon and comment on each others' questions. Taking part in this conversation is an important part of the final section of this work. Thanks Elaine. 09 Oct 2002 23:24

Criteria : task related + Housekeeping messages

Paul 139661413613966QuestionGreetings, all
Hello Elaine! Correct my assumptions if necessary. We lead this substantive discussion and advice (Gift!)to next year's cohort in lieu of the literature review set by Ian? This being the case I will post a theme in the next day or two, or next week if not. This also presumes my draft Reflective Practice assignment is OK.

Socio emotional EC samples

EX 1: Comspace thread 1695- parent 1695 (category 3a)

Criteria- sharing personal issues, situations, circumstances, Expression of feelings,

Maurice 169516950SuggestionMODULE 2 Interesting bio synopses .

Hi all I've just spent a little while browsing through the member profiles ... very interesting - thanks all! ... felt mine was far too brief after reading a couple of the others ... but guess what I found when I went to read Elaine's and Ian's!! ... (anyway, that's probably enough stirring for one day!) ... with the day off tomorrow from the PPTA strike I may well get started on my thinking about the first assignment ... I got my first posting of library books in the mail today ... so better get started on them too! :-) Maurice28 Feb 2002 16:58

Criteria - Thanking members, Expressions of support, and inclusion

Elaine 69517581695Formal TaskWoops –
I leap to fix the gap! Join me, others? Thanks, Maurice - I take the hint. Would others please follow? If you have not submitted a bio please do so - and check out who else in on the course while you are up there in the MEMBERS area. Elaine

Ex2 – Module 5-8 thread13618- parent14115 (category 4a)

Criterion: sharing personal issues, situations, circumstances
Anthea 136181411513618Answer
I should be able to have it done by these dates
Hi, Sorry I have taken a while to log onto the Studentnet no excuse really - actually just really tired. I will get my draft in by either the 13 or the 14th of this month. It is really rough though!

Criterion: Thanking members + Expressions of support, and inclusion

Elaine136181424514115WaffleThanks
Thanks, Anthea - lovely that you are back again - thanks for your inputs. Elaine

EX 3 – workshop insights and questions thread 3889 parent 3889 (category 2)

Criterion: Humour

Anne 388938943889QuestionSocial Constructionism
Who are you? Are you a personality or a character? Do you exist when you are alone? 09 Apr 2002 15:40 Chris

Criterion: Humour

Chris 388939023894CommentSocial Constructionism Anne –
is this part of the enculturation process about living in Bluff? Just wondering! Chris

Mix excerpts

Ex- 1 Afternoon Thread – 607- parent 1837 (category 4a)[36]

Criterion - task

Chris 6071837607Formal TaskCrit reflection opposes blaming

Kia ora to my team mates - wherever you are! Apologies for being late, but here goes - then it's your turn! The sentence tat I have chosen from Brookfield is right at the beginning. 'Without a critically reflective stance toward what we do, we tend to accept the blame for problems that are not of our own making.' I find this very powerful, because in the teaching profession it does seem to be so easy to put ourselves down, especially with the pressures from media, parents and wider society. All this rather than to acknowledge from time to time, that we had a real success with 'Paul', who as a special needs student was unable to write more than a sentence, but after six months in your room with 10 minutes individual writing help daily, can now complete 2/3 of a page on his own. And he's proud of it! After a tearful meeting during lunchtime last Friday with a stressed colleague, this reading has even more meaning for me. Ka kite Chris

Criterion- Sharing personal circumstances

Paul 60718901837GreetingGreetings – more later

Greetings Chris I'm later to this course than you. I'm testing my ICT skills. A huge learning curve! Will respond in a more academic way once I've got my head round the technology. Regards Paul (another special student!)

Criterion - Expressing personal opinion

Paul 60723621837AgreeSeeking continuous improvement

I agree Chris. I would also say that we need to be realistic about our own 'craft'. I believe we should always be seeking continuous improvement. Regards Paul11 Mar 2002 16:28 Carol 60725811837AgreeWe do good work Tenakoe Chris, I think my statement of Brookfields links in with the everyday realities of what you say about the moments of each day that remind us that we are doing a really good job and a very worthwhile job. Cheers

Ex2- breakfast thread 211- parent 761 (category 4a)

Criteria – task + expressing personal views, opinions referring only to ones' self

Meryl 211761211Formal Task Hegemony / acceptance

---

[36] **The context of the excerpts in ex 1 – a task where people are asked to:**

(1) Please read the Brookfield article (RP 2) and select one sentence from it. The sentence should be one that struck a chord with you when you read it. Maybe it shocked you, or surprised you, or you thought "that's a new way of looking at it", or maybe it just rang true and you thought "I wish I'd said that", or .... (2) Quote the sentence to the group and tell them REALLY SUCCINCTLY why this sentence impacted on you. Really succinctly might be just one sentence. (3) Tell a story about yourself that builds on instruction (2) above. Remember that the idea is that you four should get to know each other (in the context of reflective practice).

Hi Breakfast Group 1 "The dark irony and cruelty of hegemony is that teachers take pride in acting on the very assumptions that work to enslave them." (Brookfield, p15) This insightful statement can apply on many levels. Teaching is a complex process and to understand the 'forces' that shape our lives and those we teach, rather than dutifully doing what's expected, is a refreshing thought. Perhaps this statement impacted on me because I "get on and do the task" spending time and effort doing so, without being able to articulate why it is important. Often I have "stirrings" of questions, but fail to see possibilities beyond the task at hand, and think (assume) this is the right thing to do. Acceptance rather than conscious selection is the norm. How much of what I am/do, is from wearing "blinkers"? These were some of my thoughts from this passage.

Criteria- expressing personal views, opinions referring only to ones' self

Rosie   211913761OpinionSmall group task 1Hi Meryl,

That hegemony got me really thinking last year when I was first introduced to this idea of critical reflection. I now ask Why and So What? and am attempting to guide my students on a similar path. Do we teach to change the world? Look forward to the next comment. Rosie

Ex 3- Breakfast thread 211- parent 1446 (category 4a)

Criteria: sharing personal issues, situations, circumstances + expressing personal views, opinions referring only to ones' self
Merian   2111446211ResponseThe circle
Hi everyone! I am late responding but work load has prevented me from doing it sooner. The sentence that made me really think is found in the one under the section The Circle. "But for the students who are shy, self conscious about their different skin colour, physical appearance, or form of dress, unused to intellectual discourse, intimidated by disciplinary jargon and the culture of academe, or embarrassed by their lack of education, the circle can be a painful and humiliating experience." I suddenly realised what I was doing to my English class of students who have severe learning needs in literacy and who have a shallow depth of oral language. My idea was to have their attention but I have been more successful since I have stopped that practise. It is so important to consider all the implications of doing something differently, it may suit the teacher but what about the students-specially 14 yr old boys!

Criteria : Sharing personal work experience (part of the reflective activity required in the course)+ sharing personal views, opinions, linking ones circumstances to other educators, and theories

Rosie   21115421446Agree
Looking over shoulders I liked the circle idea too Merian and applied it to my students (adults) last year until I read Brookfield. The other one I have discussed with my students is trying to be involved and 'supportive ' in learning tasks as I look over their shoulders at their work. I hated it when tutors did it to me so it was a reminder of looking at myself through the student's eyes when they said how much it stopped them concentrating!

Examples of sort order in the three modes of representation available in the LMS observed
Note: these representing options are the prevalent ones in most LMS

Screen dumps	Save/Print	Spreadsheet
13146-0	13146-0	13146-0
13149-13146	13149-13146	13149-13146
13357-13149	13357-13149	13257-13146
13932-13149	13932-13149	13344-13146
13257-13146	13257-13146	13932-13149
13271-13257	13271-13257	13357-13149
13298-13271	13298-13271	13271-13257
13311-13298	13311-13298	13325-13257
13318-13311	13318-13311	13298-13271
13324-13318	13324-13318	13311-13298
13327-13318	13327-13318	13318-13311
13325-13257	13325-13257	13324-13318
13344-13146	13344-13146	13327-13318
13346-13344	13346-13344	13346-13344
13380-13346	13380-13346	13380-13346
13390-13380	13390-13380	13390-13380
13399-13390	13399-13390	13391-13380
13400-13399	13400-13399	13401-13380
13391-13380	13391-13380	13399-13390
13401-13380	13401-13380	13400-13399
13405-13401	13405-13401	13405-13401
13409-13405	13409-13405	13409-13405
13682-13409	13682-13409	13682-13409

Screen dumps	Save/Print	Spreadsheet
14140-0	14140-0	14140-0
144221-14140	14221-14140	144221-14140
14514-144221	14514-14221	14367-14140
14367-14140	14367-14140	15406-14140
14520-14367	14520-14367	14514-14221
14606-14520	14606-14520	14520-14367
14672-14520	144672-14520	14606-14520
14767-14672	14767-14672	14672-14520
15406-14140	15406-14140	14767-14672

www.ingramcontent.com/pod-product-compliance
Lightning Source LLC
La Vergne TN
LVHW022302060326
832902LV00020B/3226